Sign Language Interpreting

Related Titles of Interest

SIGN LANGUAGE INTERPRETING

Exploring Its Art and Science

David A. Stewart
Michigan State University

Jerome D. Schein
Professor Emeritus, New York University

Brenda E. Cartwright
Lansing Community College

Allyn and Bacon
Boston • London • Toronto • Sydney • Tokyo • Singapore

We offer this book to the twenty-first-century stakeholders who will build, tend, and use the bridges over the communication gaps between those who communicate in sign language and those who do not. In keeping with our philosophy, we have worked to develop a text that will serve deaf people, nondeaf people, interpreters, and the general public. All of them share, to some degree, in the consequences of this vital enterprise.

Executive editor: Stephen D. Dragin
Series editorial assistant: Elizabeth McGuire
Manufacturing buyer: David Suspanic

Library of Congress Cataloging-in-Publication Data

Stewart, David Alan
    Sign language interpreting : exploring its art and science / David
A. Stewart, Jerome D. Schein, Brenda E. Cartwright
        p.   cm.
    Includes bibliographical references and index.
    ISBN 0-205-27540-0
    1. American Sign Language.   2. Speech.   3. Language and culture.
4. Psycholinguistics.   5. Sociolinguistics.   I. Schein, Jerome
Daniel.   II. Cartwright, Brenda E.   III. Title.
HV2474.S68   1998
362.4'283—dc21   97-38135
                                                                  CIP

Printed in the United States of America
10 9 8 7 6 5 4 3   02 01 00 99

CONTENTS

PREFACE

A gulf of silence separates deaf people from those who try to communicate orally with them. Deaf people cannot hear conversational speech and most nondeaf people speak, thus creating an impasse when they meet. The gulf between them is widened because people who lost their hearing early in life or who were born deaf communicate in sign language, and most nondeaf people do not know sign language. To bridge the ensuing gap, sign language interpreters intervene; signing what is spoken and speaking what is signed. Simple as that solution may sound, the theory and practice of sign language interpreting involve complex communication processes requiring skilled professionals to execute optimally.

The recent emergence of sign language interpreting as a profession, more clearly than any other single event, signifies the vast change in the public's attitudes toward people who are deaf. At least in part, the growth of interpreting services over the past three decades reflects the willingness of North American societies to include in all of their activities people who depend on signed communication. Practitioners and entrepreneurs—educators, psychologists, rehabilitators, storekeepers, doctors, politicians, lawyers, theatrical producers, and more—have discovered the value of interpreted communication, whether to serve their clients better or to attract customers. Equally important, deaf people themselves have come to expect, even to demand, the inclusion sign language interpreting affords them.

We recognize the revolution that has taken place and that continues to evolve in the lives of deaf people. Changes in policies and practices affecting deaf people have been recent and revolutionary, as will be documented in the chapters that follow. Although we give particular attention to interpreting in the United States and Canada, we realize that conditions for deaf people are shifting all over the world. We report some of those developments in the pages that follow, although we do not pretend to have written a comprehensive world view of sign language interpreting.

Our aims in writing this book are manifold:

- To record the extent of the changes in sign language interpreting
- To predict its future directions
- To provide a textbook for those who have an interest in this new profession
- To direct researchers to areas that merit their attention
- To educate all of the stakeholders about its theory and practice

Note that we do not address this book only to sign language interpreters. Nor do we focus entirely on deaf people. No, sign language interpreting always involves three, and sometimes four, groups of people: those who know and use sign, those who do not, and those who interpret. The fourth group consists of those who administer and finance interpreting programs.

That we are interested in educating deaf people about interpreting and interpreters may seem surprising to some. Many deaf people, however, never have had the opportunity to study this subject in any depth. We regret that curricula in schools and classes that include deaf students seldom contain units on interpreting. How else can deaf students learn how to make effective use of interpreters? Where will they discover the limits of what interpreters can provide? Who will teach them about their rights and about interpreters' appropriate expectations? Answers to these questions and many more related to interpreting issues should be taught in schools, not left to deaf people to learn from experience. After all, deaf people will encounter interpreters throughout their adult lives. Moreover, most deaf people have nondeaf parents who have no experience with or knowledge of interpreters; therefore, the task of educating deaf people about interpreters lies with the schools.

We also believe strongly that nondeaf persons who frequently encounter deaf people and agencies that contract for interpreting services should receive instruction about what they can and cannot reasonably expect and about how to improve the quality of the process.

The fourth interested group consists of the public, represented by agencies that underwrite interpreting, legislators, program administrators, and others whose facilities and services accommodate deaf people. This fourth group not only pays interpreters when appropriate, but also subsidizes programs that prepare interpreters—a vital aspect of sign language interpreting, since such educational programs did not exist forty years ago.

To these four groups, then, we offer this book. If it succeeds, it will provide them with valuable insights. It will also serve as a guide to further excursions into the arcane subjects that are relevant to sign language interpreting: the cultures of deaf and nondeaf people, economics, the process of interpretation, linguistics, physiology, psychology, sociology, and even politics—all have a bearing on the interactions that take place when a sign language interpreter intervenes in the communication process.

The book begins with a brief history of interpreting and goes on to describe several models of interpreting, factors involved in interpreting, and settings for interpreting, as well as the ethics of interpreting as a profession. A chapter-by-chapter preview of the contents appears on pages 9–11 of Chapter 1.

Interpreting will develop optimally if representatives of *all* those who have an interest in it seek agreement about how best to manage the interpreting process. Collectively, all concerned parties should contribute to shaping policies and procedures. We are aware that as our knowledge of sign language interpreting grows, our current beliefs about the processes of interpreting and the models we use to depict these processes may be affected. Thus, we attempt to present fully the problems, the issues, and the options in this field to the extent they are known today. Bolstered by the available information, a rational discourse can lead to the development of professional interpreting in ways that will satisfy the majority of participants.

Obviously, no one book will do justice to all of these topics. We hope that what we have written provides a basis from which readers can determine their interests and needs in this area. If they are not satisfied with what is written about any aspect, the book points toward other texts, institutions, and experts who can fulfill their demands for knowledge (provided the knowledge they seek is available). When adequate information has not been garnered, this book indicates avenues that researchers can traverse in the never-ending search for more knowledge.

ABOUT THE AUTHORS

David A. Stewart is professor and director of the Deaf Education Program at Michigan State University, where he uses sign language interpreters in the courses he teaches and the meetings he attends. Deaf since birth, he is fluent in English and ASL. He has conducted research on the culture of Deaf people and on the use of signing in the education of deaf children.

Jerome D. Schein is professor emeritus of sensory rehabilitation, New York University, and adjunct professor of education, University of Alberta. For almost four decades, he has taught and researched in the field of deafness, including conducting several studies of sign language interpreting and directing the National Interpreter Training Consortium.

Brenda E. Cartwright is the director of the Interpreter Education Program at Lansing Community College. Born to deaf parents, she is a fluent ASL/English bilingual. She holds a Comprehensive Skills Certification (CSC), Certificate of Interpretation (CI), and Certificate of Transliteration (CT) from the Registry of Interpreters for the Deaf. She has been recognized for her work as an outstanding interpreter educator in the Midwest and as a skilled interpreter by the Deaf Citizens of Michigan.

1

INTRODUCTION

The principal task of an interpreter is to help one person understand what another person is saying. The situation that immediately comes to mind is one in which an interpreter uses sign language so that a deaf person can understand what a nondeaf person is saying. But because the nondeaf person likely does not know how to sign, we expand the role of the interpreter to include voicing what the deaf person is signing for the benefit of the nondeaf person.

Although this example is illustrative of most interpreting situations, it is not the complete picture. Interpreting is not a simple voice-to-sign or sign-to-voice task. Good interpreting involves a command of two languages and an understanding of the cultures associated with those languages. Interpreters must have an awareness of the background that people bring to their communications, such as whether or not they are teachers, law enforcement officers, retail salespersons, or members of other professions and trades. To plan accurate interpretations, interpreters must have a practical understanding of the content that is being conveyed from one language or code to another. To avoid misinterpretations, they must have a sense of the speaker's emotions. There are many more factors involved in the task of interpreting. Effectively analyzing and integrating responses to these factors is the goal of those who undertake interpreting as their profession.

It is impossible to describe the "typical" interpreter. Interpreters come from many walks of life and bring to their field a diversity equal to that of the situations in which they find themselves. This diversity helps the field mediate communication between people.

Let us introduce you to three sign language interpreters, Ruth, Debbie, and Frank. They represent different reasons for becoming interpreters, different preparations for their positions, and different types of practice.

- Ruth's mother and father are deaf. They communicate with extended family members by lipreading, gesture, homemade signs, and written notes. With Ruth, however, they signed American Sign Language (ASL) from the day she was first held in her mother's arms, even though she has normal hearing and speech. With that background interpreting came naturally to her. Today, Ruth has a thriving private practice interpreting in a large metropolitan area.
- Debbie's parents are not deaf, but when she was growing up she had neighbors who were deaf. They often asked her to babysit, and she learned fingerspelling and some signs from them. When she was looking for a job after graduating from high school, Debbie saw an advertisement for a teacher's aide who could work with deaf students. She applied for the position and was hired by the school with the understanding that her role would eventually be switched to that of an interpreter. Upon accepting the job, she enrolled in an interpreter-preparation program in a nearby community college. Now in her third year as an interpreter and aide, Debbie has started taking courses toward a university degree in elementary education. She plans to become a teacher of deaf students.
- Frank never saw anyone sign until one Sunday when his church was visited by a "signing choir," a group of young people who rendered hymns in ASL. He was fascinated by the beauty and power of their presentation. Then and there he decided to learn ASL. Without giving any further thought to how he would make use of that knowledge, he grasped every opportunity to study sign language that came his way. He was encouraged by a sign teacher to enroll in a two-year interpreting program at his local community college. Now he interprets full-time for a rehabilitation agency.

Ruth, Debbie, and Frank are a composite example of interpreters. Elements of these sketches occur in many interpreter biographies, although the real stories have details that make them unique. These three brief accounts illustrate various paths people follow to an interpreting career. How their diverse backgrounds have shaped their professional lives will be examined in the pages that follow. At this point, however, we only want you to recognize that professional interpreters have significantly different antecedents and motivations and pursue their careers in a variety of settings.

OUR PHILOSOPHY

Although we have begun this book by introducing three interpreters, and we will be considering many others, we hasten to say that this book does not see interpreting solely from the interpreter's point of view. Interpreting is a *social process* whose outcomes depend on all of the participants, not on the interpreter alone. The effectiveness of interpreting is also determined by the other participants—both those who are deaf and those who can hear. They play crucial roles in the clarity of communication that is the essence of interpreting. That is what we mean by describing interpreting as a social process.

In the preface we spoke about a communication gap between normally hearing and deaf people. This *gap* has three referents, not one. First is the obvious communication gap between those who cannot hear and those who do not sign. Second is a gap between general impressions of what interpreting means and what it is really like, between what naive persons expect interpreters to do and what they actually can do. The third gap is between an unsystematic, largely anecdotal knowledge of interpreting and a scientific account of the process.

Interpreting for deaf people has become a profession relatively recently. For that reason, many questions arise about it that do not usually arise about older professions:

- What are the qualifications of sign language interpreters?
- How do you define a *qualified* interpreter?
- Where and how do interpreters prepare for their profession?
- What conditions affect their services, and how do they manage those conditions?
- What factors distinguish sign language interpreting from other types of interpreting? How are they similar?
- Where do interpreters work? By whom are they employed?
- Are there rules of conduct that govern their professional behavior?
- How are interpreters compensated? By whom?

In addressing these and other questions we will aim to be descriptive, not prescriptive. Lest we be accused of intellectual cowardice, we present as many opposing views as we can, without choosing among them, in order to be consistent with our view of interpreting as a social enterprise. The answers to the questions just posed and to many others often involve policies as well as facts; they frequently depend on preferences as well as on theoretical considerations. That is why we avoid insistence on any one solution to the problems that interpreting poses. We believe the stakeholders should develop answers by consensus. To do so, however, they need to be aware of the problems and possible solutions.

The Stakeholders

We avoid saying "interpreting for deaf people" because deaf people rightly point out that interpreters would not be needed if those with whom they communicate knew sign. The interpreter serves the needs of both those who cannot hear but know sign and those who do not know sign, whether or not they can hear. That means that there are three groups of stakeholders in decisions about interpreting: the sign language interpreters, the deaf participants, and the nondeaf participants.

There is a fourth category of stakeholders: those who engage interpreters. Schools, rehabilitation services, government agencies, and other segments of the general public all have a stake in the interpreting process, whether directly, as employers, or indirectly, as taxpayers (see Figure 1-1). The public interest, too, should be considered in policymaking that affects sign language interpreting.

The Interpreter's Role

We reject a purely *mechanistic* view of interpreters. As we hope to clarify in Chapter 3, what the interpreter does is influenced on the one hand by the initiator of a message, and on the other hand by the receiver of the message. If the initial message is unclear, the interpreter does not bear the sole burden for clarifying it. If the persons to whom a message is directed lack the abilities or education to comprehend that message, the interpreter alone cannot overcome their deficits. Interpreting is the result of actions of the three or more parties involved. Hence, we do not regard interpreters as "bridges." True, their *function* is to span the gulf between parties who do not share a common language, but in carrying out that function, interpreters contribute actively to the communication process. Both their strengths and their weaknesses affect the human interaction called interpreting. They have complex, demanding roles in every phase of the interpreting process, but all of the participants enhance or debilitate it by their actions and by their inherent limitations.

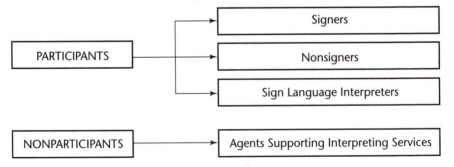

FIGURE 1-1   The Four Primary Stakeholders Associated with a Sign Language Interpreting Situation

TERMINOLOGY

In our writing, we aim to be *clear* but not simple, *comprehensive* but not complex, *deep* but not exhaustive. We believe that too much damage has been done to the study of deaf people and Deaf culture by the careless use of language. Many terms we use can be defined in two or more ways—ways that contradict each other. As an example, there is some confusion in the field with the use of the terms *deaf* and *Deaf*. The first is generally taken to refer to any person who has a hearing loss severe enough to hinder communication through the use of speech and hearing. The capitalized *Deaf* denotes cultural and linguistic elements pertinent to the Deaf community. Thus, a Deaf person might be someone who has some degree of hearing loss, identifies with the Deaf community, and uses ASL as a primary means of communication. Some authors, however, now use *Deaf* to refer to any person with a hearing loss who uses signing to any degree—a confusing use of the term that muddles the intended orthographic distinction.

We will try to use key terms in a precise fashion that conveys the usual meanings given them by professionals. That is why we define terms that are so often used that they may not seem to need explicit definitions. And that is why we risk our readers' annoyance by introducing terminology throughout the book along with explicit definitions in the main text. Precision in the use of words is the hallmark of professionals. For interpreters, correct use of language is the very essence of their profession.

SOME PROFESSIONAL ISSUES

Many issues that are fundamental to interpreting need to be addressed, because leaving them unstated does far more harm than exposing them to broad scrutiny and open discussion. It is important to have agreements within the profession and to have understandings with those served by the profession. Here we present some issues that give a foretaste of what is to follow. As we investigate specific aspects and technical matters in the following chapters, we hope that readers will be stimulated to raise their own questions and seek their own answers. Those that follow may help to start that process.

Profession or Trade?

Dictionaries provide us with definitions that sometimes conflict or, at least, are ambiguous. Consider two definitions of *profession* from two authoritative sources:

- *Profession:* The occupation which one professes to be skilled in and to follow. (a). A vocation in which a professed knowledge of some department

of learning is used in its application to the affairs of others, or in the practice of an art founded upon it. Applied spec. to the three learned professions of divinity, law, and medicine; also to the military profession. (b). In a wider sense: Any calling or occupation by which a person habitually earns his living. (*The Shorter Oxford English Dictionary*, 1973, Oxford University Press, p. 1680)
- *Profession:* (1) a vocation requiring knowledge of some department of learning or science; *the profession of teaching.* (2) any vocation or business. (*The Random House Dictionary of the English Language*, 1983, p. 1148)

On the basis of these two definitions, most people would agree that interpreting *is* a profession. True, it is not one of the learned professions, but that does not mean that it does not require expertise and knowledge of a very high order, nor does not being one of the learned professions demean the interpreting profession.

The semantic distinction between a *profession* and a *trade* bears on two issues vital to interpreters: compensation and control. Should interpreters be paid like tradespeople, like persons whose occupations require less education and do not require that they abide by a code of ethical behavior? Or should interpreters be compared to attorneys, clerics, and physicians and be paid accordingly? Second, are interpreters mere hourly employees, with little say in how they do their work? Or are they professionals who should be accorded wide latitude in determining how and under what conditions they conduct their assignments?

Deciding how to characterize an interpreter does not answer these questions, but it can frame the discussions differently. As professionals, interpreters would seem to be entitled to pay consistent with their education, experience, and skills, not on scales set for teacher aides and clerical workers. With respect to control of their practices, it would seem that interpreters' decisions about their employment conditions would deserve the same weight that is given to other professionals in the performance of their duties.

Social Relations Between Interpreters and Deaf People

As president of the National Association of the Deaf, Robert Sanderson presented his views of interpreters at the Ball State conference in 1964 (see box titled "The Value of Interpreting"). For Sanderson, interpreters were his friends, people he could call on for the *favor* of interpreting. Ironically, Ball State, along with subsequent events, changed that attitude—probably irrevocably. Not that deaf people may not regard interpreters in a friendly fashion, just as they might regard their physicians or attorneys, but fundamentally they now see interpreters as professionals who render them paid services, not favors.

The Value of Interpreting

Speaking at the first national workshop on interpreting in the United States, the president of the National Association of the Deaf closed his remarks with these words:

> Without interpreters, our world would be much narrower than it is. These wonderful people, understanding, dedicated, are our bridges and our gates to the world of sound, our escape from silence. Through their ears we communicate with the hearing. Through their hearts we feel the ties of brotherhood even through the invisible wall of silence that sets us apart.
>
> We know that we impose upon them, often too much; and that we abuse their friendship and stretch their tolerance. Yet I know that they realize their satisfaction in knowing that they serve their fellowman. I can think of no higher satisfaction, no higher calling; I can think of no other group of people who are held in higher esteem than that in which we deaf people hold our friends, the interpreters. (Sanderson, 1964, p. 34)

Given the history of interpreting services for deaf people, it should be no surprise that some deaf persons oppose the purchase of interpreting services. That attitude may be generational, with only older deaf adults among the few resenting having to pay for what they used to get free of charge. When they were young, their schoolteachers and parents interpreted for them. As young adults, they encountered interpreters in church who signed as a religious duty. In none of these instances did anyone pay for the interpreting, nor did those who performed those services usually complain. As exemplified by one interpreter years ago, "We are all the time assisting our deaf brothers and sisters. Our gifts are ours to use in His service, and to His glory" (MacKenzie, 1964, p. 54).

Younger deaf people schooled in integrated classes have experienced interpreters as paid members of school staffs. As deaf adults they usually recognize the advantages of a professional service as opposed to the unregulated, undependable favors of amateurs—no matter if they are friends or relatives and no matter how talented they may be as signers. In turn, most interpreters do not see themselves as superior beings ministering to inferior deaf people. Like members of any other profession, interpreters regard deaf people as equals and expect pay for the services they render.

The issue of compensation aside, however, other questions remain. For example, how should Interpreters relate to deaf people outside of interpreting assignments? Because Deaf communities in most areas are small, it is difficult for interpreters to maintain impartiality—that is, to mingle with the very same people for whom they interpret yet not to let that interfere with their relationship. Interpreters often find that when they attend social events they are called on—or feel obligated—to interpret without any prior agreement to do so. This on-the-spot interpreting assignment, even when it is brief and done free of charge, reduces the interpreters' enjoyment of the entertainment and denies them opportunities to relax and interact socially and informally with others.

But the fact remains that some deaf people and interpreters do socialize with one another. Indeed, some deaf people regard interpreters who stay aloof from social contacts as being "standoffish" and disdainful of deaf people. "They are only interested in using us to make a living" is something more than one interpreter has heard. Other deaf people resent interpreters who *do* take part in social interactions with deaf people. They see the presence of interpreters socially as an intrusion. The severity of the intrusion may be worsened by the perception of an interpreter's access to the social life of deaf people as due to the interpreter's knowing sign language rather than to a sincere desire for lasting social contact. Today, many deaf people believe, as a practical matter, that interpreters should mingle socially with them to broaden their knowledge and understanding of Deaf culture and to learn colloquial signs. In other words, there is an educational motive to the social interactions of interpreters and deaf people that might ultimately benefit both. It is an issue that merits exchanges of opinions between deaf people and interpreters.

How Effective Is Interpreting?

Do interpreted messages carry the same information load as those in which speakers sign for themselves? How effective is mediated or facilitated communication in education, rhetoric, psychotherapy, and interpersonal exchanges? Although answers to these questions are crucial to assessing the value of interpreters, they are not readily available. The context and the participants in an interpreting situation play roles in determining the effectiveness of interpreting. Accuracy of the interpreted message, too, is an insufficient measure of effectiveness. An accurately interpreted message has little value if a deaf person does not have access to the code in which it was presented. For instance, an interpreted message that contains the fingerspelling of several technical terms is worthless if an ASL-dominant deaf person receiving the message lacks the English vocabulary necessary to understand the fingerspelled words. Similarly, a message interpreted into ASL is of little value if the deaf person does not have the language skills needed to understand ASL.

Still, we need to ask what would be the consequences of finding that interpreted communication was not as effective as direct communication? Would interpreting be abandoned? To the last, we would respond, Certainly not! Then why question the effectiveness of interpreting? Why not assume it is fine and leave it at that? Because if it is less effective than directly signed communication, then researchers should investigate the reasons for this. This is true for all situations involving interpreters, but perhaps especially true for interpreting in school settings, where there is much variation in the language, education, and signing ability of deaf students. Teasing out the interpreting factors that reduce or enhance effectiveness would then direct efforts to improve interpreting services—a goal that all stakeholders could enthusiastically support.

Progress begins with questioning the status quo.

ORGANIZATION OF THE BOOK

Here we offer a chapter-by-chapter preview of the contents that follow.

Chapter 2. From Favor to Profession: The History of Interpreting

Sign language interpreting may be old, but the interpreting *profession* is of recent origin. This chapter outlines the history of interpreting and of the interpreting profession. In doing so, it also considers some philosophical points underlying the practice of interpreting.

Chapter 3. Models of Interpreting

To clarify what we mean by interpreting and set the stage for the remainder of the book, we devote this chapter to advancing our conception and reviewing other interpreting models, each of which views interpreting from a somewhat different stance: interactive, interpretive, communicative, and sociolinguistic. Doing so enables us to (1) delineate factors that influence interpreting, (2) suggest ways to prepare interpreters so they can improve their services, and (3) propose fruitful directions for much-needed research.

Chapter 4. Physical Factors

Interpreting is influenced by environmental conditions: positioning vis-à-vis initiators and receivers, ambient noise, lighting, other potential visual distractions. Interpreters are also affected by mental fatigue and by the strain signing places on their hands, wrist, and arms. The discussion of these factors considers how to recognize and deal with these factors.

Chapter 5. Psychological Factors

More than language is involved in interpreting. The psychological component of "more" is considered in this section of the book, especially with respect to the relationships between participants. The interpreting process itself arouses psychological questions, especially those relating to cognition. Interpreters must contend with psychological stresses, some like those that arise in any work and some that are specific to interpreting.

Chapter 6. Varieties of Interpreting

This chapter examines some special interpreting assignments—health-related, legal, theatrical, and so on. Each setting brings with it specific problems for interpreters, and they have devised strategies and tactics for managing the problems in these varied situations.

Chapter 7. Language and Culture

It may overstate the obvious to say it, but the interpreter's stock in trade is language. In this chapter, language is discussed strictly from the standpoint of interpreting. The languages from which and into which one interprets affect the process—a point this chapter will clarify.

Chapter 8. The Business of Interpreting

This section of the book attempts a broad description of the participants. Of course, almost anyone might be involved in an interpreted communication at one time or another, but the focus here is on typical participants: both deaf and nondeaf. Then the chapter takes up such economic questions as those addressing supply and demand, cost–benefit analyses, interpreter compensation, and who is responsible for paying interpreters.

Chapter 9. Ethics

Fundamental to any profession are its ethical principles: its standards of practice and codes of behavior. From their founding, interpreter organizations in the United States and Canada have endorsed sets of ethical principles. These have changed over time. The changes are delineated, and the principles now adopted by interpreters in those two countries are discussed.

Chapter 10. Educational Interpreting

Educational interpreting gets a special chapter because it is the single largest source of interpreter assignments. Like the other settings, the classroom raises issues that are unique to it.

Chapter 11. The Future

The book closes with a look to the future of interpreting for deaf people. This concluding chapter summarizes trends, advances hopes, and offers guesses at the developments that lie ahead. Above all, the final chapter reinforces a major theme of this book: *interpreting is an evolving process.* Many of its critical issues are in flux; some have had little attention directed toward their recognition and resolution, and others will change as a result of continued debates among those concerned.

Each chapter is designed to stimulate discussion among students of interpreting as well as to encourage a greater appreciation of the complex issues embedded in the field of interpreting.

Attached to the main body of this book are three appendixes. Appendix A provides a current listing of all certifications offered by the Registry of Interpreters for the Deaf. Appendix B contains forty ethically challenging scenarios to be used to stimulate discussions about how interpreters might behave in certain situations. Real incidents that have happened to interpreters provide an opportunity for readers to reflect on the dilemmas that can arise during the course of interpreting. Appendix C contains examples of real-life experiences of interpreters, many of which an interpreter could not be prepared for in advance. Though brief, they provide an opportunity for readers to reflect on the intricacies that can arise during the course of interpreting. Finally, the book contains nine profiles of interpreters and deaf people who relate their thoughts on various aspects of interpreting.

2

FROM FAVOR TO PROFESSION: THE HISTORY OF INTERPRETING

WHEN AND WHERE DID INTERPRETING ORIGINATE?

The use of interpreters probably dates from first encounters between three persons, only one of whom shared a common system of communication with the other two. The one who knew both parties' languages became the de facto *interpreter*. Such informal use of mediated or facilitated communication very likely goes back to the earliest social interactions between different linguistic groups, but the literature does not help us identify the first interpreters nor the precise dates of their services.

The famous Rosetta Stone was engraved around 300 B.C. and found in the town of Rosetta, Egypt, in 1799. It made the deciphering of hieroglyphics possible because it contained the same message written in Egyptian hieroglyphics, Egyptian demotic, and Greek capital letters. The Rosetta Stone provides tangible evidence that bilingual persons performed the important functions of enabling people with different languages to communicate with each other. But the fact that the stone's three versions of two languages are written—literally carved in stone—suggests that it was probably not among the earliest examples of interpreting, since writing came fairly late in human development (DeFrancis, 1989).

What we can infer from our knowledge of people and the multiplicity of languages is that interpreters have played significant roles in human communication for a long time—although we do not know precisely how long. As for where interpreting was first practiced, the most credible answer must be: wherever people from diverse linguistic backgrounds met.

THE PROFESSIONALIZATION OF INTERPRETING

Because we are concerned with *professional* interpreting, we ask when inter-preting became a profession. Persons who were paid to interpret appear in the writings of Pliny, in the first century A.D. The Roman legionnaires needed bilingual persons to negotiate with the nations they conquered. Doubtless other conquerors made similar arrangements but did not employ as assidu-ous an amanuensis as Pliny. Similarly, explorers of lands populated by peo-ple whose languages they did not know certainly included interpreters among their personnel, whether the interpreters were recruited onsite or brought along from the onset of the journeys.

Translators who made writings in foreign languages available to those who could not read the originals are credited with providing the foundations of Western civilization. One historian dates their professionalization from the 1800s:

> Western Europe owes its civilization to translators. From the Roman Empire to the Common Market, international commerce and admin-istration has been made possible by translation; the first Christian translators were the four Evangelists who recorded in Greek what Christ and his disciples had said in Aramaic; and it is only since the early nineteenth century that scientists have ceded to professional translators the responsibilities of turning essential books into the lan-guage of their fellow countrymen. (Kelly, 1979, p.1)

Viewed from that historical vantage point, the advent of sign language inter-preting as a profession is not so far behind as one might at first believe. In-terpreters have now become an integral part of the major international organizations, like the League of Nations and its successor, the United Na-tions (Seleskovitch, 1978). The United Nations now employs several hundred full-time and part-time interpreters to accommodate the numerous languages spoken by its members. International sign language interpreters also have be-come part of the international scene at meetings of the World Federation of the Deaf.

INTERPRETING WITH DEAF PARTICIPANTS

Although sign language interpreting is ancient, the interpreting *profession* is relatively new. It began as an effort to create greater access for deaf people when interacting with those who were not deaf and did not sign. It did not evolve because legal, medical, and other social institutions decided to reach out and communicate better with their deaf clients, but because deaf people and their advocates demanded equal access to public facilities. To acknowledge this history, we will use the term *nondeaf* rather than *hearing* to describe participants in interpreted situations who do not sign.

Preprofessional History

The predecessors of today's interpreters are those anonymous individuals—especially friends and family—who have interpreted for deaf people over the past millennium. Very little has been written about who they were and what they did. Nonetheless, it is important to record our debt to these pioneers, lest we falsely imply that sign language interpreting only began in the 1960s.

Although most interpreters now take courses to prepare themselves for their demanding profession, before 1964 no school in the United States or Canada offered such preparation. Today, almost every state in the United States and many provinces in Canada have programs preparing interpreters at the college level, and laws in both countries assure deaf people of a right to interpreters in a wide variety of settings, including the law courts and public schools.

The Birth of Professional Interpreting in the United States

Professional interpreting for deaf people in the United States has a well-documented, though brief, history. Its birthdate is June 14–17, 1964. That is when Ball State Teachers College, in Muncie, Indiana, hosted the Workshop on Interpreting for the Deaf. The workshop was sponsored by the Vocational Rehabilitation Agency of the then Department of Health, Education and Welfare (Smith, 1964). The chair of the Ball State conference, who was the superintendent of a school for deaf students, reviewed the earlier history of interpreting for deaf people from an educational point of view. In his opening address, he noted that no national meeting had ever addressed this topic:

> Efforts to educate the deaf in this country date back a century and a half. The first permanent school for the deaf in America was established in Hartford, Connecticut, in 1817 . . . . In this long history of the education and of the socio-economic progress of the deaf, accomplishment in a variety of educational settings and by use of many and diverse methods of instruction, there has been no national conference called to consider and to identify the occasions and situations in which deaf persons need the assistance of interpreters to discharge properly their responsibilities or to exercise their privileges as citizens. (McClure, 1964, p. vi)

The date of the Ball State conference coincided with the revolutionary spirit of the time: in that same year, for example, Martin Luther King received the Nobel Peace Prize. Just as King and others fought for the rights of African Americans to have full access to all things entitled to them as citizens, the Ball State meeting announced to the world that deaf people had the right to full access to communication.

Given the historical importance of the Ball State meeting, it is of interest to know what transpired on the journey to that milestone. Certainly, interpreting occurred in situations outside of classrooms and with deaf persons who were not students. What was interpreting like before Ball State? The literature is largely silent on that topic. Kanda (1987) writes, "Until the 1960s, deaf people relied on skilled amateurs, often children of deaf adults" (p. 91). Some famous interpreters of the nineteenth century were Thomas Hopkins Gallaudet, who interpreted for Laurent Clerc, considered the first deaf person to have formally taught deaf children in the United States, and Alexander Graham Bell, who signed on occasions for deaf adults despite his vociferous objections to the use of sign language (Bruce, 1973).

While not addressing the history of interpreting for deaf people per se, one author gave a vivid account of what interpreting was like prior to 1964. Answering the questions about interpreter backgrounds at that time, the then executive director of the National Association of the Deaf (NAD), Frederick C. Schreiber, said:

> Presently, we have two basic sources on which we draw for interpreting when needed. These are our children and the educators of the deaf who are familiar with the language of signs. Neither of the two, however, has a full concept of the function of an interpreter, and as a consequence, the full value and benefit of a competent interpreter is yet to be appreciated. In addition, the demand on the schools for interpreting services has grown to alarming proportions. While it is realized that school people are truly interested and have made great sacrifices to be of service, there is such a thing as beating a willing horse to death, and that is not too far in the offing in this case, since nothing has been done to alleviate the situation or to seek new interpreters to help carry the load. It must be remembered, also, that in most cases, interpreting is done voluntarily, and there is and never has been much percentage in looking a gift horse in the mouth. So long as the services of interpreters are obtained on a voluntary basis, there is little hope for the establishment of standards of competency that must be made before we can hope to get away from the minimum levels on which we now rest, and little hope for the creation of an effective recruitment program unless such standards are set. (Schreiber, 1964, pp. 35–36)

Echoing Schreiber's "gift horse" characterization of interpreters was another NAD executive's view of interpreters as "friends" (see the box on "The Value of Interpreting" in the preceding chapter). Because at that time the majority of interpreting was done as a favor, imposing standards on interpreters made little sense: How could one ask for credentials from someone who was proffering a gift? So the change from friendly gift to professional service introduced a significant advance in communication for deaf people.

INTERPRETER ORGANIZATIONS

Participants at the Ball State meeting voted to establish a national body of professional interpreters (Quigley & Youngs, 1965). Before 1964 there was no organization representing interpreters who served deaf people in the United States, and no formal recognition of such service as a profession. The same lack of recognition appears to have prevailed in Canada, Great Britain, and the rest of the world.

National Registry of Interpreters for the Deaf

The new U.S. organization established at the Ball State conference originally had the somewhat florid title, National Registry of Professional Interpreters and Translators for the Deaf (Williams, 1964). That name was soon shortened to National Registry of Interpreters for the Deaf or, simply, Registry of Interpreters for the Deaf (RID; see the boxed list of RID presidents). Important to the functioning of the new organization was a federal grant from the U.S. Vocational Rehabilitation Agency (later the Rehabilitation Services Administration) that funded the Ball State conference and then provided funds enabling RID to hire a director and clerical support, and to rent space to house its activities.

Odd as it may seem now, the *professional organization* preceded the *profession*. At RID's inception, there were no formal education programs for interpreters, no code of ethics, no formal recognition by government agencies, and very few full-time practitioners—fewer than 300 in the entire United States (Schein & Stewart, 1995). In 1964, one became an interpreter by interpreting! At the Ball State conference, the executive director of the National Association of the Deaf listed the qualifications of sign-language interpreters at that time:

At present we have at least four minimum requirements with regard to interpreters. These are: they must be able to hear; they must be able to sign; they must be willing; and they must be available. (Schreiber, 1981, p. 50)

Many of RID's first members were not even interpreters. Some were deaf people who joined to show their support for the concept of an interpreting profession; some were education and rehabilitation personnel who joined to stay in touch with this new activity; and some were persons who could sign fluently but who were not available as interpreters because they held full-time employment positions or were deaf. The founding of the RID, then, did not so much bring together many interpreters spread across the nation as it encouraged and guided the development of interpreting as a profession.

Before RID, sign language interpreting was largely done as a *favor*. RID changed that. It raised interpreting from an informal activity to a professional service by establishing a code of ethics, providing a forum for interpreter interactions, publishing newsletters and other printed materials, and setting the precedent for payment for its members' services. The boldness of RID's move and its foresight are captured in the following statement:

> That surprising move—establishing a professional organization before there was a profession—proved to be an inspired one. The RID, by its very existence, allayed questions that might have proved embarrassing and, worse, that might have impeded the growth of the interpreting movement. State officials, knowing little about deafness

---

Presidents of the Registry of Interpreters for the Deaf

The following people have had the role of president of the Registry of Interpreters for the Deaf (RID) since its inception in 1964:

Kenneth Huff	1964–1968
Ralph Neesam	1968–1972
Carl Kirchner	1972–1978
James Stangarone	1978–1980
Judie Husted	1980–1983
Dennis Cokely	1983–1987
Anna Witter-Merithew	1987–1989
Jan Kanda	1989–1991
Janet Bailey	1991–1995
Daniel Burch	1995–

and less about interpreting, were easily convinced that everything was in order, simply because there was a *registry* of interpreters. They did not inquire whether the persons listed were qualified or where they had obtained their training. (Does one ask such questions of the bar association or the medical society?) Furthermore, since RID existed, there must have been a well-established demand for the service, or else why have such an organization! (Schein, 1984, p. 112)

The creation of RID was also significant in that it gave the Deaf community an ally in its long-standing fight for recognition as a unique cultural entity in society buoyed by its own language, American Sign Language (ASL).

Association of Visual Language Interpreters of Canada (AVLIC)

Almost from the founding of RID, some interpreters from Canada joined it, and some continue to belong to this day. That arrangement, however, posed problems for Canadians seeking certification, because the examination made no allowances for differences between U.S. and Canadian customs and colloquialisms, while expecting Canadian applicants to be familiar with U.S. geography and politics (Russell & Malcolm, 1992). In 1979, Canadian interpreters founded the Association of Visual Language Interpreters of Canada (AVLIC). AVLIC's constitution and by-laws were ratified in 1980.

In addition to the national organization, AVLIC, Canada has several provincial affiliates of AVLIC, a number of local groups, and a few chapters of RID—as examples, the Alberta Chapter of RID, the Ontario Association of Sign Language Interpreters, and the Saskatchewan Association of Visual Language Interpreters. Although it has developed independently from any other interpreting association, AVLIC maintains cordial relations with its professional neighbor, RID.

AVLIC conducts the Canadian Evaluation System (CES) for certifying interpreters. Fundamental to CES and to AVLIC's relations with the Canadian Deaf community is the consumer representation on the CES board and in its examination procedures. Participation of Deaf people at every step in the evaluation process, from development of the test items to scoring candidates' performances, fosters the Deaf community's respect for interpreter certification. This close cooperation with the Deaf community has enabled AVLIC to withstand complaints by failed candidates that CES standards are too high:

> [CES] must meet the needs of the Deaf community and we believe that lowering the standard would hinder AVLIC in achieving the

goal of ensuring that quality interpretation is provided across Canada. (Russell & Malcolm, 1992, p. 26)

Interpreter Organizations in Other Countries

Although sign language interpreting occurs around the world, its development as a profession is virtually nonexistent in many countries. As an example, prior to 1977, most interpreting for deaf Britons fell to welfare officers and social workers, who were required to demonstrate their spoken-language-to-sign-language and sign-language-to-spoken-language interpreting skills as prerequisites for employment in positions in which they worked with deaf clients (Llewellyn-Jones, 1981). That this arrangement was unsatisfactory was made clear by the government's action in 1977. But precisely who was dissatisfied—the government, the British Deaf Association, or both—and why remain unclear. The fact is that the British government acknowledged the importance and shortage of interpreters in 1977 when it gave financial support to the British Deaf Association's Communication Skills Project. The project included funds designated for the establishment of an interpreter registry, the British RID, and assigned to it responsibilities to set standards for the education of interpreters and procedures for their evaluation. As in Canada and the United States, the trend in Great Britain is towards increased and improved examination procedures in order to achieve higher quality interpreting.

In recent years, other countries have followed suit in establishing professional organizations of interpreters. As this trend continues, it would be helpful to know what stimulates a country to make this move. Deaf people socializing with people from other countries likely talk about the services they enjoy or lack back home. Countries lacking in the area of essential services available to deaf people pick up valuable information from more fortunate countries. Moreover, we can expect the expansion of interpreter organizations around the world to be assisted with the increase in the number of people who have access to the Internet. The Internet will more quickly disseminate information about interpreting and allow people from different countries to participate in on-line conversations where people can provide logistical and moral support.

Another major factor spurring the establishment of interpreter organizations is the travel of large numbers of deaf people to international conferences such as those sponsored by the World Federation of the Deaf and various sporting events. When a country desires to host an international event that many Deaf people will attend, they must accommodate the communication demands imposed by the many different sign languages of the participants. At the very least, the host must be prepared to make the proceedings of a conference or the announcements of a sporting event accessible to its own citizens.

If an organization for interpreters is not available, then such arrangements by the hosting nation become problematic.

SOCIAL AND LEGAL MILESTONES

Establishing interpreting as a profession helped to advance social services for deaf people. Seen as a favor, interpreting could easily be denied, limiting deaf people's access to governmental and voluntary social services. The founding of RID led legislators to view interpreting as deaf people's *right*. Only ten years after Ball State, federal law laid the grounds for deaf people to demand interpreters in situations in which they previously had had to make their own arrangements for effective communication or do without.

Profile: Pamela Brodie

Pamela Brodie is the interpreter/coordinator of special projects for the superintendent at the Ohio School for the Deaf. She has an associate degree in interpreting and a master's degree in social agency. She holds a Comprehensive Skills Certificate from the Registry of Interpreters for the Deaf (RID) and is a practicum supervisor for interpreting students. She has held various positions with the national governing body of the RID and its Ohio chapter.

As a freelance interpreter, she has worked in a variety of settings and is concerned about the relationship of participants in the interpreting process. She senses tension between the interpreting profession and members of the Deaf community and feels that both groups must work toward a better understanding of the interpreting process. In the following passage, Pamela reflects on this relationship which illustrates that sign language interpreting is still in the early stages of its development as both interpreters and deaf people are struggling to define their relationship with one another.

> Relationships established with Deaf people we interpret for have a direct bearing on the degree of success we experience in our work. We (Deaf people and interpreters) do not talk to each other about the process of interpreting. We don't discuss what it means to provide or receive interpreting services and we certainly don't discuss the outcome of an interpreting event. This lack of communication has resulted in what has been labeled by some the "Cold War" between Deaf people and interpreters.

Profile: Pamela Brodie   *Continued*

As my own interpreting career progressed, I found that I was not satisfied with the results of my work. I handled problems and conflicts that arose for me on the job as did people who were my models—I sought out other interpreters for advice on how to resolve the problem. Colleagues were always helpful, but there were many times when there seemed to be no solution. I often felt I was at loggerheads with the people I interpreted for.

That is the paradigm under which most of us still function: We perform an interpreting assignment, it goes well or poorly as the case may be, and both parties leave the assignment with individual perspectives as to what happened. Both parties will in turn repeat the same mistakes in other interpreting events even though they work with different people. The interpreting process and its success is reduced to a gamble.

I will never forget the day I sat down with the Deaf person I had just interpreted for and asked if we could talk about what had happened. Both of us were uncomfortable talking about our perceptions, and we both had some pretty negative opinions about each other and what had happened. In the process of sharing, we came to realize that we were working against each other—not approaching the process in a cooperative fashion. Techniques I used to moderate conversation were felt to be oppressive; I, in turn, had felt badly used and deliberately set up to fail. We had to resolve our differences if we were to be effective together. That event changed my approach to interpreting. Each event became an opportunity to learn from someone new, to share ideas and improve our chances of success.

How can others begin this process of reflecting upon one's work as an interpreter? Start by choosing someone with whom you feel a certain level of comfort. Choose a moment that is not emotionally charged, and keep it simple. Ask about one specific part of your work in the interpretation and reciprocate by giving an idea about how they can help improve the interpretation. Make a suggestion that will help them monitor your performance.

Establishing a successful interpreting relationship does not happen overnight. It takes many interactions like the one above to develop trust. Each relationship that you build furthers understanding of the interpreting process and affords us the special link with Deaf people which makes us more effective.

Communication Access by Law

In the United States, the Rehabilitation Services Administration (RSA; also previously known as the Office of Vocational Rehabilitation and the Vocational Rehabilitation Administration) has led federal agencies in focusing the government's concern about communication with deaf people. Indeed, prior to 1960, it was the only federal agency that had a subdivision devoted to deaf services. That branch was headed by Boyce Williams, himself deaf from early in his teens. Not surprisingly, then, the Vocational Rehabilitation Act Amendments of 1965 (P.L. 89-333) authorized affiliated state rehabilitation agencies to employ interpreters for deaf clients, as needed—a giant step ahead of other government agencies.

A decade after Ball State, the U.S. Congress mandated interpreting for deaf people in additional settings by passing the Rehabilitation Act Amendments of 1973. The law contained Title V, justifiably referred to as the "Bill of Rights for the Handicapped." Section 504 of that title consists of a single sentence:

> No otherwise qualified handicapped individual in the United States . . . shall, solely by reason of handicap, be excluded from the participation in, be denied the benefit of, or be subjected to discrimination under any program or activity receiving Federal financial assistance.

Section 504's power is out of all proportion to its brevity. By leaving undefined key terms like *participation,* the section gives wide latitude to administrators and the courts in determining how to implement its provisions.

Paradoxically, although vagueness in terminology can broaden a law's scope, it can also weaken a law by leaving its interpretation to individual administrators and the courts. Mandating services is only as effective as the willingness of citizens to obey and of the government to enforce the mandate. In practice, Section 504 has been broadly construed to cover activities far beyond rehabilitation. And since so many state and local programs involve some federal money, the impact on deaf persons' daily living has been substantial.

The 1973 law's principles have been carried forward and expanded in the Americans with Disabilities Act (ADA), passed in 1990. The ADA stipulates that all businesses with fifteen or more employees must make reasonable accommodations to persons with disabilities. For deaf persons, that usually means the provision of qualified interpreters. The law does not make clear two key terms: *qualified* and *reasonable accommodation.* With respect to qualifications, the law stressed that interpreters "interpret effectively, accurately and impartially" (Kincaid, 1995, p. 1) but says nothing about how these qualities are to be measured. Should RID certification be required? Would graduation from an approved interpreter education program suffice? How about the approval of the deaf participant as a measure of qualification? That is, can deaf persons use interpreters whom others might judge to have only minimal skills?

More nebulous is the meaning of *reasonable accommodation*. Does ADA give carte blanche to deaf people to use interpreters whenever they choose? No, the law does not apply to churches. State and federal government services must comply, but how they do so—what is "reasonable"— is open to interpretation. An example of a type of accommodation that can be made is illustrated by a movie shown at the Mount St. Helen's National Park. The movie is captioned with text that transcribes all of the spoken parts of the movie inserted onto the screen. By allowing people to read the text, an accommodation has been made for those people who cannot hear or understand the spoken parts of the movie. In addition, assistive listening devices are available for hard-of-hearing patrons who wish to listen to the movie's dialogue, but if a deaf person is unable to read English and desires a sign language interpreter, the park is obligated to provide one. Confusing? Consider further examples, sometimes seeming to conflict with one another:

- In a retail store, a notepad may be considered a reasonable accommodation when dealing with deaf customers. When deaf people apply for jobs, however, they may request an interpreter during the hiring process. Once they are hired, a notepad, computer screen, or other means of communication might be deemed reasonable for day-to-day communication.
- Hospitals and medical service providers must provide interpreters for routine visits, as well as for surgery, childbirth, and other serious procedures. They must make their facilities free of communication barriers for deaf and hard-of-hearing people by providing text telephones, assistive listening devices, and closed-captioned decoders; interpreters are not the only reasonable accommodation. ADA even extends the rights to deaf people who are caring for a normally hearing patient. In an actual case, a deaf man asked for a sign language interpreter so he could discuss with the surgeon his father's proposed operation. The hospital agreed to hire an interpreter after a state agency argued that ADA gave the deaf man the right to an interpreter.

The full meaning of ADA, however, will not be known until after extensive judicial reviews, because the law can be construed in different ways. As one critic has written,

The new law [ADA] is so complicated and unclear that the only way managers [of businesses] can know exactly what it requires of them is to be told by a judge, [and many employers will ignore the law, because] it would be simpler and cheaper in the long run to wait and see if anyone sued. (Janofsky, 1993, p. A12)

Whether or not that dire prediction is realized remains to be seen. But even if many employers and caregivers do violate ADA, they will not completely dim the great advance that has been made by society's recognition and the government's codification of deaf people's right to communication that is meaningful to them.

Interpreting in the Courts

Very clear and highly relevant to interpreters is the Bilingual, Hearing and Speech Impaired Court Interpreter Act, passed by the U.S. Congress in 1977. This law requires that a federal court must appoint—and pay for—interpreting for a deaf person in any criminal or civil action initiated by the federal government. The law provides that the director of the Administrative Office of the U.S. courts shall determine the qualifications of persons wishing to serve as interpreters. Each federal district is required to maintain a list of interpreters who meet federal standards. In passing this law, the Congress also requires the director to consult with organizations concerned with deaf people, and specifically mentions RID and NAD.

Commenting on this act, the head of the National Center on Law and the Deaf says, "One shortcoming of this law is that it does not provide for an interpreter for a deaf person who is challenging a denial of federal rights. Only criminal and civil cases initiated by the U.S. Government require appointment of interpreters" (DuBow, 1979, p. 94). Despite this flaw, the law establishes a valuable precedent for deaf people. Further discussion of legal interpreting will be found in Chapter 6, "Varieties of Interpreting."

Educational Interpreting

For a long time a majority of deaf students received their education in residential and day schools especially designed for their benefit, and educational interpreting played a minor role in their lives. However, the Education of All Handicapped Children Act (P.L. 94-142), passed by the U.S. Congress in 1975, changed that situation by requiring that all children with disabilities, including those who are deaf, be educated in "the least restrictive environment." Educational administrators tended to interpret that phrase to mean that students should, to the extent feasible, be placed in regular classrooms. For deaf students, that arrangement was feasible only with the use of interpreters. The result has been an enormous increase in the demands for, and in the employment of, interpreters. A subsequent amendment to this legislation in 1990, the Individuals with Disabilities Education Act (IDEA), P.L. 101-476, reaffirmed the earlier act, thus sustaining the demand for interpreters in education.

Because educational interpreting has become so important, Chapter 10 has been devoted entirely to it.

Interpreter Certification and Licensing

A logical development in any profession is the formal recognition given it by government through certification and licensing. In this regard, interpreting has moved with surprising speed, considering that its professional life dates only from 1964. The fact that RID conducted its first certification examinations in 1972 constitutes rapid progress indeed. By 1992, RID had estimated its certification roster to be about 3,070 interpreters. Appendix A lists RID certifications.

In the United States, some states conduct their own certification programs, though they usually accept RID certification. Only South Dakota, at this writing, issues interpreting *licenses*, and it has enacted strict laws governing interpreter practices. Other states may follow in time.

In Canada, AVLIC's efforts for national certification of interpreters continues with government support. A separate program conducted by Canada's secretary of state qualifies interpreters to serve that federal office. Attaining the secretary of state's approval signifies exceptional qualifications and entitles those so designated to a higher-than-average pay scale (over CDN$600 per day) and excellent working conditions, such as frequent rest periods when two or more interpreters are working together.

While professions often advance certification and licensing as means of assuring quality services to the public, partakers of those services seldom realize that these credentials specify only *minimum* competencies. An interpreter who barely passes a certification examination receives the same certificate as one who attains the highest grades. RID has reduced that spread by issuing certificates indicating minimum competency at various levels and in different interpreting specialties. In addition, the RID publishes a monthly newsletter called *RID Views* that contains, among other things, information about their National Testing System, dates and locations for written and performance examinations throughout the United States, and discussions of interpreter certification.

Additionally, certificates restrict only how professionals can present their qualifications, not the interpreting assignments that they can accept. Interpreters who only have an RID Certificate of Transliteration, for example, cannot claim that organization's Reverse or Comprehensive Skills qualifications, but they can, nevertheless, accept an assignment requiring reverse interpreting. Licenses, on the other hand, restrict practice. In South Dakota, interpreters who are not licensed cannot interpret, regardless of their abilities or of how they advertise their qualifications. Some critics of licensing regard it as a means of protecting practitioners, not consumers, by limiting competition. Whatever the present sentiments may be, the trend toward certification seems inexorable. As for licensure, its future remains a question mark.

PREPARATION OF INTERPRETERS

The history of interpreting cannot be complete without considering the education of interpreters. The first formal programs in North America were offered by California State University at Northridge in 1965 and by the National Technical Institute for the Deaf in 1966. Both institutions, however, prepared interpreters only for their own deaf students, although a few interpreters who were prepared in these programs eventually left to serve other constituencies. Programs to prepare interpreters to practice in the community were started in 1969 at St. Paul Technical-Vocational Institute (now St. Paul Community College) and New York University. From those slender beginnings, interpreter preparation grew to 56 college-level programs in 1989 and to over 100 programs today. Of course, the precise number of programs will fluctuate from year to year, as some withdraw and others join the efforts to prepare interpreters, but the rapid, sizable response of educational institutions to satisfy demands for qualified interpreters, their recognition of the interpreter shortage and their willingness to invest in relieving it, deserves commendation. How did their involvement come about?

National Interpreter Training Consortium (NITC)

In the United States, the most significant development in interpreter preparation was the advent of the National Interpreter Training Consortium (NITC). The Rehabilitation Act Amendments of 1973 stimulated the demand for interpreters. In 1974, however, RID had only 500 members, many of whom were unavailable for duty because they held full-time administrative positions or were themselves deaf. The tiny number of interpreters relative to a deaf population estimated at over 250,000 people (Schein & Delk, 1974) meant that deaf rehabilitation clients would go unserved because few agencies had counselors able to sign fluently. The NITC provided an answer.

The NITC was made up of six universities and colleges that had initiated interpreter preparation: Arizona University, California State University at Northridge, Gallaudet University, New York University, St. Paul Community College, and the University of Tennessee. Each was assigned a region of the United States in which to prepare interpreters and to cooperate with other universities and colleges willing to establish programs. NITC took a three-pronged approach to overcoming the interpreter shortage:

- Brief workshops to upgrade the skills of those already in the field
- Intensive three-month courses for those without previous interpreting experience
- Programs to prepare interpreter educators

In addition, NITC members worked together to generate curricula and cooperated with RID to develop its certification examination. All of this activity was funded with annual grants of $300,000 from the Rehabilitation Services Administration.

How well did the NITC succeed in meeting its objectives? The following briefly summarizes the results:

> By 1980 . . . RID had certified over 3,000 interpreters. Many more awaited certifying examinations. The number of interpreter trainers increased from virtually none to a little over one hundred. The original six NITC members had, for company, 45 programs throughout the United States, though not one in each state as had been hoped. Ignoring all the other benefits of NITC . . . the 2,500 additional interpreters cost the taxpayers an average of about $333 each. Less than the cost of many hearing aids. (Schein, 1984, p. 114)

These results should be evaluated in light of the conditions that existed in 1974. Today it would be ludicrous to consider a three-month program to prepare new interpreters, but such recruiting and educating appeared very different at that time in view of the thin ranks of interpreters. In 1980 the U.S. Congress authorized the annual funding of nineteen programs to continue interpreter preparation. That legislation remains in effect. Perhaps educators and interested citizens might want to preserve the memory of the NITC to serve as a model for the next time a similar personnel shortage arises.

Canadian Interpreter Preparation Programs

In Canada, formal programs for interpreter preparation began in 1973 or 1982, depending on how such preparation is defined. Vancouver Community College offered sign-language classes in 1973, and many of those who took these classes became interpreters; until 1986, however, it did not offer specific courses on interpreting. Red River Community College offered an interpreter curriculum in 1982, most widely accepted as the year for the inception of interpreter preparation at a higher-education level in Canada. By 1994, Canada had nine programs. This increase in educational facilities for interpreters reflects changes in the awareness of interpreting's importance to deaf people (see Taylor, 1988, and Schein, Mallory, & Carver, 1990, for further details).

The fact that Canadian institutions of higher education did not prepare interpreters before 1973 does not mean deaf people in Canada did not have professional interpreters available to them. Interpreters and consumer groups organized workshops on specific topics at which interpreters could upgrade their knowledge and skills. Furthermore, even though the United States was not much further ahead in preparing professional interpreters, it opened its educational facilities to Canadian interpreters.

While most of the Canadian programs are one academic year in length, at least one has moved to a two-year curriculum, and there are discussions of extending programming to a full four-year bachelor's degree. Educational costs aside, one factor inhibiting the move toward more extensive preparation is that the present programs do not meet the needs for interpreters. Between 1983 and 1990, 276 interpreter students graduated from the eight college programs. At that graduation rate, however, the number of new interpreters will fall at or below replacement for those who leave the profession each year. Deaf people in Canada, then, cannot expect to have the interpreter shortage relieved in the near term—a discouraging prospect.

INTERPRETING IN OTHER COUNTRIES

Provision of interpreters is now so commonly accepted in the U.S. and Canada that it may surprise some readers that, for example, *there is not a single interpreter-preparation program in all of Central and South America!* That situation is certain to change in the very near future, as deaf people are becoming increasingly aware of how inadequately prepared interpreters limit their ability to interact with the larger social and commercial worlds and to gain a greater measure of control over their own destinies.

Even more surprising, many countries not only lack programs to prepare interpreters, but actually *deny* interpreting to the majority of their deaf citizens. For example, until recently, Thailand generally opposed signing and specifically refused interpreting to deaf people. This prejudice against sign language extends to the hearing children of deaf couples. As Wrigley recounts:

> Most hearing educators [of deaf Thai children] know only the public world of the schoolchild. To them, the simple level of sign language required merely to gain control and maintain obedience within the classroom . . . confirms their belief and "knowledge" that sign language is a simplistic form of communication, a mere subset of a language by which a lesser-born form of human is indulged or "provided for." . . . Today we are witnessing the first generation of hearing children of Deaf Thais who are learning the sign language of their parents. In the past, Deaf Thais were rarely allowed to marry . . . . How-

ever, hearing children who actually grow up with active and direct relations with their deaf parents in Thailand are almost exclusively those in poorer, working-class circumstances. (Wrigley, 1996, p. 136)

Wrigley goes on to point out how the lower economic status of bilingual children will impact upon them should they wish to become interpreters. He notes that a hearing child with deaf parents "had signing skills good enough to pass as a Deaf person," but because she had limited formal schooling she could not "produce the vocabulary nuances of educated Thais. And, of course, she had no familiarity with the class-bound formalities of elite rhetorical practices" (Wrigley, 1996, p. 137).

On a positive note, the relationship of hosting international events and interpreting was apparent when New Zealand held the 1989 World Games for the Deaf in Christchurch (see Stewart, 1991, for a thorough discussion of the role of sports in the lives of deaf people). Jennifer Brain, a Deaf officer of the New Zealand Association of the Deaf, commented on the sudden prominence given to interpreters during and after the Games. She noted that prior to the Games deaf people had great difficulty in obtaining interpreting services, as there were only two full-time interpreters in New Zealand and a prevailing attitude among hearing people that "interpreters would take away deaf people's independence." But the Games demonstrated to "hearing people in positions of power . . . that the availability of interpreters actually improves [the] quality of life for many deaf individuals" (Brain, 1990, p. 46). Within just a few years after the Games, an interpreter education program was established in New Zealand. This is a significant event given that, until recently, deaf people had no right to an interpreter in New Zealand courts. Along with highlighting the important role that interpreters play in the lives of deaf people, the Games contributed recognition to New Zealand Sign Language as the primary language of New Zealand Deaf community.

While North Americans can look down on attitudes and practices toward deaf people in some foreign countries, they should look up to Sweden, where the government has provided free interpreting services to deaf people since 1969, and where schools for Swedish deaf students, since 1983, have taught Swedish Sign Language along with a written form of spoken Swedish (Wallin, 1994). Other government provisions make Sweden an exemplar for nations that wish to provide deaf people with a level playing field.

NURTURING THE INTERPRETING PROFESSION

Our look at the history of interpreting accentuates the relatively short life span of interpreting as a profession when compared to such well-established professions as teaching, law, and medicine. The field of interpreting will continue to evolve as we learn more about the characteristics and effects of interpreted communication among different groups of participants. Present categories of interpreting and certification procedures may change to reflect this growing body of knowledge, but the fundamental premise of interpreting between two or more parties in an interaction will remain. As we will discuss at length in Chapter 11, advancing the profession will be greatly accelerated by obtaining research answers to many still unsolved questions and by arriving at consensus on many unresolved policy issues.

Those are two of the lessons that history offers to us.

3

MODELS OF INTERPRETING

What are the effects on transmitting information and feelings through a human filter—the interpreter? How does interpreting alter the communication process? Questions like these lie at the base of interchanges between persons who depend on third parties to inform their communications. Few would argue that interpreting modifies communication. But to what extent and in what directions these modifications occur remain open to question and invite study.

Sign language interpreting appears deceptively simple. To a naive person, the interpreter simply signs what another person has spoken, and vice versa. The misconception is that saying something in signs is easy once a person knows how to sign. An experienced interpreter knows that this is far from the truth. At the very least there are three steps that all interpreters must take in the act of interpreting. They must (1) understand the meaning of the message expressed in the original language; (2) be able to encode the meaning in the target language, and (3) be able to express the message in the target language so that the original meaning remains intact. To this last step we can add the conditions that not only is the message accurately coded in the target language, but also that the emotions with which the message was originally expressed are conveyed and that the target language is expressed in such a way that the intended audience understands it. This three-step process is the basis for our Cognitive Model of Interpreting, shown in Figure 3-1.

THE COGNITIVE MODEL OF INTERPRETING

The Cognitive Model of Interpreting is similar to the Pedagogical Model of the Interpreting Process proposed by Colonomos (1992) but simplifies further the processes involved in interpreting. The first step of the model assumes that

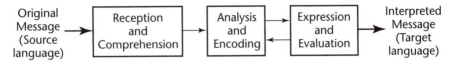

FIGURE 3-1   A Cognitive Model of Interpreting

the interpreter understands the language in which the source message is presented. Once comprehension of the message occurs, the interpreter then analyzes the message to determine how the meaning will be encoded in the target language. Although the processes of analyzing and encoding are theoretically separate, we have not chosen to separate them in our model. We view the interpreter as more than just a tool for switching communication from one language to another. Interpreters' personalities and intuitions affect how a message is interpreted (Robinson, 1991). We expect that their knowledge of the topic under discussion, their feelings within the context of the interpreting situation, and their experience all will influence what interpreters hear or see in a message, which in turn affects how the message is eventually expressed.

This last step, the expression of a message, includes evaluation, because interpreters are susceptible to visual feedback cues from the participants as well as to their own feelings about how accurate their interpretation (signed or spoken) may be. At times, the accuracy of a message might not be fully determined until the message is actually expressed. A nod of a participant's head or a participant's puzzled look is an example of feedback to the interpreters. This feedback, positive or otherwise, then influences the analyzing and encoding processes as interpreters attempt to make adjustments to enhance the accuracy of an interpreted message as well as the comprehension of the message once delivered.

The Cognitive Model of Interpreting does not address the full range of interactive aspects of interpreting. The model, for example, does not account for the effects on interpreting that stem from the other participants in an interpreting situation, nor does it account for the effects of the environment. These other components of interpreting are presented later in this chapter when we discuss our Interactive Model of Interpreting.

The benefit of beginning with an uncomplicated model is that it enables us to examine the elementary constitution of the interpreting process. That is, what is it that interpreters understand about the original message? What do they think the message will look like when it is transmitted in a target language? How do they go about doing the actual transmission, either in signs or in speech?

Indeed, the three steps depicted in the model are the foundations on which most interpreter education programs are based (Colonomos, 1992).

These programs seek to strengthen a student's understanding of the grammar of American Sign Language and English and to expand their vocabulary in both of these languages. The programs help students map one language onto the other language, by showing them how linguistic tools associated with each language can be used to retain the meaning of a message while changing the form in which it is expressed. Finally, the programs provide opportunities for students to practice to ensure that their performance in the target language is an accurate interpretation of the original message.

MODELS VERSUS THEORIES

There are several models of sign language interpreting. They range from ignoring to emphasizing the significance of participants' cultural backgrounds; from regarding interpreters as helpers to considering them machines or conduits; from assigning a role to the environment to according it no place at all; from focusing mainly on the deaf person's or the interpreter's contributions to recognizing that all participants influence the communication process. That interpreting models differ is unremarkable, since professionals often disagree about aspects of their work. What makes examination of various perspectives worthwhile is that the models often lead to differences in educating interpreters and in how interpreters practice their profession.

In this chapter we use *model* rather than *theory* when discussing conceptions of sign language interpreting. A model is a hypothetical representation of a process or object; it serves to display, verbally or graphically, an event, object, or series of events. Students of physics are familiar with the notion of an atom, for example, which is a model that helps physicists to conceptualize elements they cannot observe directly.

We avoid the term *theory* because it implies a more formal set of systematic principles and hypotheses. In contrasting theories and models, Twain (1975) notes:

> Construction of adequate theory is a profoundly difficult but essential task . . . . Scientific theory, of course, differs in logic, in construction, and in the extent to which it is testable and tested from the more casual theorizing on which action is based, but theory and conceptualization are not foreign to practice . . . . In recent years, models have often been used as alternatives to theories. *Model* has much the same meaning as it does in ordinary language . . . . (pp. 40–41)

Theorization is not, in our opinion, justified by the current state of the interpreting art. Views presented so far, including our own, lack the rigor, fruitfulness, and testability to warrant being called *theories*. In what follows, then, we examine sign language interpreting as a complex psychological process that can be variously *modeled*. All of the models that we will describe offer variations of and additions to the basic elements of interpreting shown in the Cognitive Model of Interpreting. Their elaboration helps us to delve deeper into the processes that have an impact on effective interpreting. We first consider our Interactive Model of Interpreting and then contrast it with four models that have contributed to the current development of thinking about sign language interpreting.

THE INTERACTIVE MODEL OF INTERPRETING

We term our approach an *interactive model* because it encompasses the contributions not only of all the participants, but also of the environment—physical and psychological—in which the participants interact. Our approach groups the components that affect interpreting into the following categories:

- *Participants:* The three or more people interacting in an interpreted discourse.
    - —*Initiator:* The person who expresses something by speech or sign. Also referred to as the *source*.
    - —*Receiver:* The individual or group who receives the message. Also called the *target*.
    - —*Interpreter:* The individual who perceives the message, briefly stores it in memory, selects an appropriate way of expressing it in a second language or another form of communication, and then expresses it. Though stated in the singular, interpreting may involve more than one interpreter, as in the case of *relay* interpreting, in which the expression by the first interpreter is interpreted by a second interpreter in another language or modality.
- *Message*: That which is being expressed by the initiator, both verbally and nonverbally.
- *Environment*: The physical and psychological context in which an interpreted discourse occurs. We subsume the social context of an interpreted discourse under the psychological context.
- *Interactions*: While the model displays each of the preceding categories singly, the effects on the interpreting process of any one of them depend on the others.

Thus, for the Interactive Model, interpreting is a concatenation of the interaction of many factors, not solely the activities of the interpreter; and the action of the participants is dependent on the action of the other participants or, in some cases, the lack of action. As an example, we can expect interpreters to change the sign code in which they are interpreting if the deaf participant shows no indication of understanding the interpreted messages.

The main components of the Interactive Model are illustrated in Figure 3-2, with the interaction components signified by arrows. Descriptions of the components follow. In the chapters that follow, discussion of the model's elements will be expanded, appearing and reappearing in connection with various topics. Here, we introduce each factor with only sufficient detail to enable the reader to grasp the model and to gain from it an appreciation for the complexities of the interpreting process.

The Participants

In interpreted encounters, there are always three participant categories: the initiators or the source of a message, the interpreters, and the receivers or the targets of the message. Each category may consist of more than one person, although the initiator could be a video or film, in which case only the receiver and the interpreter might be present. Similarly, in this age of telecommunications, interpreters may be adding signs or voice to a television broadcast, with both initiators and receivers not in the immediate presence of the interpreter.

Initiators

Who initiates the communication? Is the initiator in a superior or inferior position? An adult or a child? A teacher or a student? Fluent or illiterate in the language of the message? Each initiator characteristic may influence the interpreting process, affecting not only the message being delivered but also the

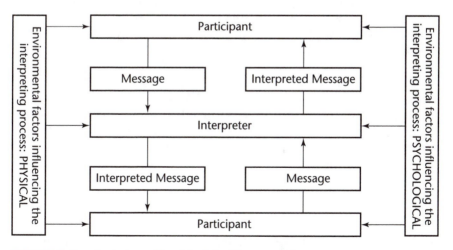

FIGURE 3-2　An Interactive Model of Interpreting

attitudes and reactions of the interpreter and the other participant(s). The initiator, in turn, is affected by the topic being discussed, the physical surroundings in which the discourse occurs, and the others' characteristics.

It seems obvious that there can only be one initiator of communication that an interpreter can transmit fully. But there are times when more than one person becomes an initiator—for example, when an audience altogether begins saying a common phrase or jeering a speaker. When two or more people speak or sign at the same time, however, interpreters encounter dilemmas that require them to either key in on what a single person might be saying, falter in their interpreting, or take action that will repair the communication process so that the interpreting can proceed effectively.

Receivers

To whom is the message addressed? Is it to an individual or a group? Are the initiator and the receiver(s) of the same or different ages? Genders? Social standings? Variations in those receiving the message affect both the process of interpreting and the nature of the interpreted message. Their characteristics and their reactions during an interpreted session influence the interpreter.

A message may not necessarily be directed to the persons observing the interpreter; a lecturer may be addressing an audience of deaf and nondeaf people without being conscious of the deaf contingent, despite the interpreter's conspicuousness. Signed messages also can affect receivers who are not the direct target, as in the case of a play being interpreted in sign language. Interpreters are visible to the entire audience, but they can perceive the sounds that the audience makes and, depending on the lighting in the theater, may or may not be aware of visual reactions to the play such as restlessness or captivated attention. Often, however, nondeaf and nonsigning members of the audience become participants in the interpreted communication, as illustrated in the following anecdote:

> I was interpreting a play, *Division Street.* Two of us were working, one on either side of the stage. The cast included one character who spoke only in song lyrics from the late '60's and the early '70's [*sic!*]. Both of us were comfortable and experienced in signing songs. Every time a song lyric appeared in the dialogue, we put it in quotes and signed it. The night of the performance, while the hearing audience roared with laughter each time this character spoke, the D/deaf people in attendance merely looked more and more frustrated and even hostile. One D/deaf person announced to her friends, "The interpreter is lousy; *that's* why we're not getting it!" I saw this, and during the intermission found that my partner was having the same experience with the translation and the audience. (McIntire & Sanderson, 1995, p. 97)

The laughter of the audience affected how the deaf people were perceiving the interpreting and, consequently, how the interpreters viewed their own effectiveness.

The Interpreter

The interpreter's background—education, experience, physical characteristics—contribute substantially to the interpreting process. In turn, interpreters are affected by initiators, receivers, and the environment. In our model, interpreting is multidimensional and dynamic.

The dynamic aspect of interpreting requires that interpreters have the ability to handle its real-time demands. Time is of the essence. Interpreters typically cannot revise their work before others see or hear it. They must constantly be on the alert for environmental, linguistic, and cultural factors that might have an impact on what they are saying or signing. How these factors might play themselves out is illustrated in the box titled "The Context of a Sign." In this

---

The Context of a Sign

A good interpreter attempts to interpret in a manner that best fits in with the task at hand. The audience, the context of an utterance, the sophistication of the communication, and other factors will influence the words and signs chosen to express a message in a target language. This is illustrated in the following account of how one interpreter described to us how she conveys the meaning of the sign DEAF-SCHOOL:

> If I am interpreting to a group of teachers of the deaf and a deaf person signs THEY DEAF-SCHOOL GROW-UP, I will likely say something like "They grew up in a deaf school" because the teachers should understand the cultural significance of residential schools. Also, I would say "deaf school" because the term means a lot to the signer who might be attempting to establish a Deaf culture framework for his speech. Signing DEAF-SCHOOL is the deaf person's way of establishing cultural identity. But if the same deaf person was delivering a talk to a group of health inspectors in a building unrelated to education, I might be more inclined to say "school for the deaf" or "residential school for the deaf." The term *deaf school* is not in the consciousness of most health inspectors. By saying "deaf school" to them, I take the chance that they might misunderstand what it is the deaf person is saying as they struggle to comprehend the meaning and implications of this term.

illustration, the interpreter describes how the nature of her audience and the location of the assignment influence her choice of words when interpreting the sign DEAF-SCHOOL. The multidimensional and dynamic aspects of interpreting are entwined, and good interpreters need much adroitness in order to handle them.

Just as there may be more than one initiator or receiver, there also may be more than one interpreter interpreting at the same time. This occurs often at international meetings where the audience contains persons with different language backgrounds. Relay interpreting is another circumstance involving more than one interpreter. These multiply interpreted situations raise issues of cooperation and of diversities in the interpreters' backgrounds. They add complexities to an already complex enterprise.

The Message

Messages can be divided into at least four parts: purpose, content, form, and paralinguistics. Interpreters must consider purposes, at least for the clues they give to the message's meaning. An interrogation by the police, a sermon by a priest, a negotiation over the price of a house—all carry with them specific purposes. Also important is knowing whether the speaker is trying to tell a joke, confirm a fact, convey a sense of uncertainty or a sense of perfect confidence, and so forth. Knowledge of these purposes helps the interpreter shape the delivery of the message.

The content can include almost anything, although most can be subsumed under (1) information and description, (2) imperatives, (3) emotional expressions, (4) questions, and (5) casual comments. A remark about the weather that is intended to establish rapport is interpreted differently from information given by a mechanic about repairs needed by a car. The content of a message may be familiar or unfamiliar to the participants, abstract or concrete, and may involve common, technical, or slang terminology. Unfamiliar terminology is especially serious in speech because the technique for handling such terms is to fingerspell them. Will the deaf person understand the fingerspelled word? Will too much fingerspelling lead to interpreter fatigue as well as that of the deaf participant, who must be more cognitively alert in order to understand the fingerspelling?

The form of communication may be speech-to-sign or sign-to-speech. Interpretation may be *simultaneous*—in which the interpreter attempts to keep pace with the speaker/signer—or *consecutive*—in which the interpreter waits for the speaker to complete a substantial chunk of the message before transmitting it. The forms of the messages, both those delivered to the interpreter and those the interpreter transmits to the receivers, enter significantly into interpreted communication.

Paralinguistics—the way in which words or signs are delivered—is crucial to interpreters. Take the message, "You should rethink your position."

Was this said in a concerned manner? Sarcastically? Matter-of-factly? Aggressively? When spoken, the words emphasized convey very different meanings. Consider the differences between the following:

You should rethink **your** position.

You **should** rethink your position.

You should **rethink** your position.

To be accurate, interpretations must reflect the intentional and emotional qualities associated with messages.

The Environment

We subdivide the environment into psychological and physical components. In addition, we consider the input to the interpreting environment from administrative decisions.

Psychological.   The psychological setting refers to what brings the participants together and their mind sets. Is the deaf person buying a car? Obtaining a medical examination? Attending a class? Testifying in a criminal proceeding? The mind set in each case will differ, as will the emotional concomitants. The meaning of a phrase—even something as simple as "Be seated"—is dependent on the setting.

The interpreter adds to the psychological environment, influencing how participants will interact. Is the interpreter known to one or all of the participants? It is normal to prefer to be with certain people, and there is no reason to expect that participants think differently. For example, in an emergency situation, a hospital or a referral agency typically calls a name from a list of interpreters kept on file. Because those initiating the call often have no familiarity with either the interpreters or the patients, they cannot prejudge whether the chosen interpreter will be compatible with the patient's communication needs. Professional interpreters, as discussed in later chapters, are aware of their own stimulus value and do what they can, including removing themselves from an assignment, to overcome any barriers that may arise because of personal relations among the participants.

Gender, for instance, may be a factor that inadvertently affects the interpreting situation, as when a woman may refuse to speak openly about sexual matters during marriage counseling if the interpreter is a male. In many smaller communities, interpreters and deaf people intermingle frequently, a fact that could inhibit disclosures of potentially embarrassing information. Interpreters and those who engage them should be aware of the contributions to the psychological environment.

The place where interpreting occurs can be expected to alter perceptions of messages. Consider the differences between platform, courtroom, classroom, and employment interpreting, to name a few examples. Each setting brings into play a variety of cultural features that may alter the meaning of messages.

Physical.   The physical setting contributes to the effectiveness and accuracy of interpreted communication. An interpreter in a school may be positioned near the teacher or off to one side of the classroom, depending on deaf students' and teachers' desires, the setup of the classroom, and the nature of the instructional activity. Stewart and Kluwin (1996) discuss the importance of positions; they point out, among other things, that where interpreters stand affects their ability to hear what is being said, and that deaf students might prefer the interpreter to be near the teacher so that they can supplement signed information with visual information gained from the teacher.

Administrative.   Administrative decisions can impose restraints on interpreters that affect the quality of their work. A school system may require that signing be in a manual code of English. It may call for consecutive or simultaneous interpreting. What will be required and who decides are questions that regularly confront interpreters. An ongoing assignment, as in educational interpreting, creates circumstances different from single encounters. Additionally, employment and remuneration matters may affect interpreters' morale, the energy they expend on an assignment, and their concentration on it.

One particularly aversive administrative decision is to recruit interpreters whose skills are not equal to the task at hand. If the ensuing communication results in misunderstandings, the person making the assignment may be as much at fault as the interpreter. Conversely, good administrative decisions facilitate the overall interpreting process. Especially beneficial are those decisions that seek to upgrade interpreting standards through recognition of appropriate certifications like those issued by the Registry of Interpreters of the Deaf.

Agencies may have regulations that hinder good communication. For example, an agency might be unwilling to compensate interpreters for the time needed to establish rapport with their participants and make some interpreting decisions prior to an assignment. Good practice specifies that, when possible, interpreters and participants meet before an interpreted session to consider such matters as the type of signing desired and the placement of the participants. Attempting to select among options while the interpreting is in progress can create serious distractions that stifle attempts to deliver competent interpretation.

Interactions
These elements—initiator, receiver, interpreter, message, and environment— interact to create additional factors not derivable from knowledge of each

separately. The status of the participants, for example, imparts meaning. The way a doctor talks to a client in his office likely differs from the way the same doctor might address a group of medical students in a classroom. An adult's language changes when speaking to a young child. Persons in authority speak to those they direct differently than they address those they consider their equals or superiors. Thus, cultural features intrude.

The setting provides contextual clues to the meaning of a message: the same humorous remark during a sermon conveys quite another meaning when expressed by a psychiatric patient. Accurate interpretation demands reflection of such nuances—features that emerge because of interactions among the communication elements. An example of such an interaction will be found in the box titled, "When Messages Get Stuck." What a particular sign conveys depends heavily on who uses it and where it appears.

When Messages Get Stuck

Understanding the message requires a firm grounding in the linguistics and culture associated with the language in which the message is expressed. At one secondary school, the sign STUCK was used by the students also to mean, "I defeated you." When used this way it symbolized a lack of respect for authority. In a sense, it was a powerful culture-specific expression of disrespect. One researcher relates its use in a school:

> The deaf students have strong intuitions about when, where, and how to use STUCK. They recognize that this sign is distinct from the sign in its traditional meanings or even such derived meanings as "pregnant out of wedlock." They are also aware that until recently the staff did not fully understand the meaning of this use of STUCK. During the period in which the sign was used most rampantly at Northfield, staff members assumed that it meant something similar to "pregnant," although they report being puzzled about how this meaning made sense in the context of the actual use. One teacher recalled thinking at the time, "Why are they saying pregnant? I'm not pregnant!" When it became obvious that "pregnant" did not quite capture the meaning of STUCK, the staff members concluded that whatever it meant it was not nice. Consequently, many outlawed STUCK in their classrooms, and some even went so far as to forbid STUCK in their presence anywhere. STUCK eventually spread to the mid-school deaf education program, where it was determined by the teachers to be a "dirty sign" and forbidden. (Wilcox, 1989, pp. 150–151)

Interpreters must consider (1) how the message is going to be interpreted, simultaneously or consecutively; (2) the signing space to be used—a large space for stage interpreting or a small one for one-to-one situations; (3) physical factors like lighting and noise levels; (4) audience feedback—facial cues and body language—to assess if the message is being received accurately; and (5) ongoing lexical, syntactic, and semantic decisions. At the same time, interpreters encounter such conditions as those arising from overlapping utterances. In day-to-day discourse, participants usually take turns speaking. But what does the interpreter do when two participants send messages at the same time? These situations confound the simple, linear model of interpreting and, more important, confront interpreters with stressful situations.

The possibilities generated by interactions of the factors make models attractive because they specify what is relevant, thereby reducing the confusion aroused by innumerable potentially significant variables. Models also have a more valuable contribution to make in examining an interactive process: they generate predictions of outcomes from concatenations of the elements that might otherwise be overlooked.

Sources of the Interactive Model of Interpreting

The Interactive Model's constituents draw partly on our experiences and partly on the published work of others—Cokely's (1992) Sociolinguistic Model, Colonomos's (1992) model of the interpreting process, Humphrey and Alcorn's (1994) review of philosophical approaches to interpreting, McIntire and Sanderson's (1995) application of bilingual–bicultural thinking, and Witter-Merithew and Dirst's (1982) and Frishberg's (1990) surveys of sign language interpreting. To each, we gratefully acknowledge our indebtedness. Their pioneering efforts have greatly assisted our own thinking in formulating the model that undergirds this book.

OTHER MODELS OF INTERPRETING

As stated earlier, our Interactive Model of Interpreting draws from our own experiences and the thoughts and models of others. All models contribute to our appreciation of the intricacies of interpreting. Taken together, they broaden our understanding of the process, suggest points to be covered in the preparation of interpreters, lead to useful ideas about how to practice, and highlight potentially fruitful areas for further research and deliberation. We present only brief summaries here; the reader is referred elsewhere for further explication of each model.

Interpretive Model

The sentence "The interpreter signs what is spoken or voices what is signed" may seem obvious, but to proponents of the Interpretive Model it is not (Seleskovitch, 1992). To do their work successfully, interpreters must thoroughly understand what is said or signed. Hearing the words and seeing the signs may not be adequate because the interpreter must understand the words and signs in order to express their meanings correctly in the other language or language form.

The interpreter's language facilities set the interpreting limits. As an example, try interpreting the excerpt from a lecture on calculus in the box titled "A Bit of Calculus." If interpreters are not familiar with calculus, how can they correctly put its sentences into sign? They cannot. If the interpreter cannot sign the sentence, the inadequacy will not be found in ASL, for it has been repeatedly demonstrated that whatever is spoken can be signed. A sign can be found for each word in the example, or the words can be fingerspelled, but such signed interpretation is not ASL and will not accurately convey the meaning. More than grammar will need to be modified.

Similarly, the interpreter must be able to understand the deaf person's signs in order to voice them accurately. ASL, which is used by Deaf people in the United States and Canada, is *not* "English on the hands." It is its own language. ASL is extensively nuanced, with the same sign having different meanings depending on the context in which it is used, the facial expression and other nonmanual signals that accompany it, the force with which it is made, and other expressive details—details only in the sense that they modify its meaning in subtle ways.

According to the Interpretive Model, the key to successful interpreting is not to seek word-for-word correspondences, regardless of the languages being interpreted, but to convey in one language the *sense* of the other one. Interpreting involves understanding what thoughts and feelings speakers and signers are expressing in their languages, and then conveying those thoughts and feelings in the other language.

A Bit of Calculus

The differential coefficient of a function is equal to the gradient of the tangent at a point on the curve that represents the function. This gradient may be positive or negative; therefore, the differential coefficient may also be positive or negative.

Interpreters are not automatons; they are *creators* (Coppock, 1992). When they merely attempt to find equivalent words for signs and vice versa, they often miss the point of the message. To convey meaning, they must restructure the thoughts and feelings expressed in one language into sometimes dissimilar expressions in the target language, and that restructuring takes time.

The Interpretive Model uses *meaning* and *sense* in somewhat different ways than are usually construed in common parlance:

> Sense emerges from the language structures of a speech but language structures are not sense. You need language to achieve sense just as you need a key to enter your home but once inside you put your key aside—your key is not your home—though without the key you would be stranded. The same applies to language meanings, they are prerequisites to sense; without the knowledge of languages we could not attain sense but words or sentences as such do not make sense . . . . To understand sense successful interpreters make use of extra-linguistic information such as the setting or the speaker's mimics and gestures and of their own background and contextual knowledge complementing language meanings. (Seleskovitch, 1992, p. 3)

Therefore, according to the Interpretive Model, language is both an entity existing in long-term memory and an activity. The activity partakes of the underlying meanings of utterances and of situations that reside in long-term memory. A particular message involves more than the immediate act of communicating; it calls upon the stored associations connected by experience with the elements of that message and held in long-term memory.

For the Interpretive Model, *sense* is synonymous with *nonverbal memory*. It uses that tautology to arrive at an intriguing theoretical formulation: languages are stored as sense impressions, either visual or auditory, but spoken words combine with cognitive elements to form nonverbal representations that remain as such until converted back into words or signs.

A major proponent of the Interpretive Model derides linguistic models as "developed not with a view to accounting for the way people actually use language but with a view to determining what language is" (Seleskovitch, 1992, p. 7). The problem for interpreters is the assertion that translations can be made without understanding a speaker's intent. Pointing to the early failures of machine translation, Seleskovitch adds, "We may say that linguistic theories that considered language as an inseparable whole (sounds + concepts) have had disastrous consequences for over fifty years for the model, practice and teaching of interpreting and translating" (Seleskovitch, 1992, p. 8).

Turning to sign languages, which seldom play a role in the conceptualization of general interpretation and translation models, Seleskovitch writes:

It seems to me that the difficulty sign languages experienced all over the world to be recognized as languages is based on this general misconception of what language is when in activity. As is still the case today in many studies on oral interpreting and written translating, speculations on sign languages have ignored the vast and complex mass of information added to language forms by human individuals when generating and understanding speech. Considering sounds, print or gestures to be one with corresponding concepts has done much harm to the Deaf and to sign languages and has led translation theory astray. (Seleskovitch, 1992, pp. 8–9)

Clearly, how one views language will have a significant impact on the way sign language interpreters are prepared.

Communication Model

Another view of interpreting looks at interpreters as language conduits, as mechanical and immune to those factors, such as the emotional state of the participants, that fall outside of the actual reception and conveyance of a message. This model held the field of sign language interpreting during the 1970s and significantly influenced the way interpreters took to their tasks. Two interpreters who experienced this change made the following observation:

We were told that we didn't have to understand what was said; all we had to do was to sign it. We were taught that possibly the worst sin possible would be to "step out of role"—that we were to be invisible, to have absolutely no impact on the situation. (McIntire & Sanderson, 1995, pp. 95–97)

An earlier interpreting textbook advanced this mechanical conceptualization by drawing the analogy that interpreters are like a telephone link (Solow, 1981). This perspective was so popular in the late 1970s that one of us used to compare the interpreter function to a hearing aid: it provided greater access to sound but in no way did it interact in the communication process. Needless to say, that attitude has been replaced by one that includes interpreters as participants in communication and not simply as communication channels.

The Communication Model draws on communication analysis. A message is first coded for transmission—a process called *encoding*. The *code* may be English, ASL, or nonlanguages such as gestures, facial expressions, or grunts. The message is then transmitted over a *channel* (e.g., speech or writing). When received, it is *decoded* (i.e., put into a form accessible to the receiver). Any signal that interferes with transmission of the message is labeled *noise* (Ingram, 1974). These are concepts familiar to engineers who develop and analyze communication systems.

In the case of interpreted communication, the interpreter is both the recipient of a message and a channel. Initiators pass their messages to the interpreter, who must first decode them, then encode them into other codes different from the one transmitted to them, and then send them to receivers who decode them. Interpreters must overcome noise in receiving a message but may contribute noise in transmitting it. Noise may consist of misleading gestures and facial expressions, as well as misconstrued aspects of the original message.

Interpreters treat all forms of communication without passing judgment on their relevance to the discourse. They interpret not only everything that nondeaf people might be saying aside from the ongoing discourse, but also what the deaf people might be signing to one another aside from the principal message. As one textbook on interpreting states:

> [T]hings that are signed in the presence of an interpreter and a hearing (nonsigning) client must be interpreted into spoken language . . . . On occasion and if deemed appropriate to the dialogue, an interpreted "comment" between deaf people may at first be found to be disconcerting to deaf people when they realize that their formerly private talk is now public, but they will appreciate the reciprocal access to communication that interpreting affords. (Frishberg, 1990, pp. 69–70)

In other words, if during a class lecture one deaf student turns to another deaf student and signs that what the teacher is saying has been said before, the interpreter would voice that comment for the benefit of the nondeaf, nonsigning audience.

The emphasis in the Communication Model is on the process itself. Still, the model does not discount entirely points made by the Interpretive Model. It stresses the psychological processes—particularly memory—to the same degree as the Interpretive model. The Communication Model implies a nearly simultaneous transmission, via the channel, of the source message, whereas the Interpretive Model focuses on the delay, usually brief, between the reception of the message and its transmission in a converted form.

The resounding point about the Communication Model is its philosophical base: interpreters assume "no responsibility for the interaction or communication dynamics taking place between clients" and instead assume "almost a robot-like role in the communication process" (Humphrey & Alcorn, 1994, p. 205). In terms of educating interpreters, the Communication Model does not believe interpreters need to make use of context and culture; hence they have no reason to spend time learning about these aspects. Instead, it emphasizes linguistics, which is consistent with its main feature—the mechanical concept of interpreting.

Sociolinguistic Model

According to the Sociolinguistic Model, the Interpretive and Communication Models leave out potentially crucial elements: the human interactions among the participants. Is the interpreter only a human translating machine, converting spoken words to sign and signs to words? Or does the interpreter intervene, consciously or unconsciously, in the colloquy? These questions do not imply such overt acts on the part of the interpreter as injecting opinions, reacting with personal emotions, or directing the conduct of the interaction, although such behavior could occur. The very presence of a third party, the interpreter, may affect the way in which the two or more other participants interact. A dramatic instance would be the mental health interview, in which the deaf client feels constrained about expressing emotionally laden material in the interpreter's presence.

The Sociolinguistic Model of interpreting covers these factors in what was termed by one of its proponents, Dennis Cokely, "a sociolinguistically sensitive and accurate model" of interpreting (Cokely, 1992, pp. 19ff). The Sociolinguistic Model and the Interactive Model both call upon the interpreter to recognize the setting, the participants, the purposes, and the message. Such recognition must be nearly instantaneous, or the interpreter risks misconstruing a message (Brown & Fraser, 1979).

The Sociolinguistic Model indirectly implies the presence of a sender and a receiver of a message. It also treats interpreting as linear, although it likely involves parallel processing, with some aspects occurring simultaneously rather than sequentially: "[I]t is probably more accurate and helpful to think of the process as one in which there is multiple nesting of stages" (Cokely, 1992, p. 128). An example of this multiple nesting occurs when an interpreter, while producing a message in a target language, simultaneously receives and analyzes a message in the source language. This example of the multifaceted nature of interpreting is presented in Cokely (1992) and is essential to our own exposition of the interpreting process.

Cokely divides an interpreting sequence into the following categories:

- *Message reception:* The sequence begins with the interpreter receiving the message and it points to the obvious fact that the interpreter will err if the message is not correctly perceived.
- *Preliminary processing:* This is the initial recognition of the message, the stage during which meaningless and meaningful elements are sorted out.
- *Short-term message retention:* The incoming message must be stored until sufficient portions of it are received to reach the next stage.

- *Semantic intent realized:* This is the stage at which the interpreter grasps what the speaker intends to communicate.
- *Semantic equivalence determined:* This is the process of finding the appropriate translation in the language or mode into which the message is to be transmitted.
- *Syntactic message formulation:* This is the selection of the appropriate form for
- *Message production:* This is the last step in the interpreting process.

The Sociolinguistic Model looks to the interpreter's internal processing to assist in analyzing interpreting errors. By determining the stage at which an interpretation goes astray, interpreters can improve their performances. If errors are occurring in *message reception*, the interpreter might conceivably have a hearing loss or may be placed in a location that makes it difficult to hear the speaker or see the signer. If deficiencies occur in *preliminary processing* or *short-term retention*, the interpreter needs to improve short-term memory. Such analyses can be useful to interpreter educators, who can use it as a tool to uncover problems with particular students' performances.

The Interpreting Process Model

The Interpreting Process Model has two main components that are focused on the skills needed for (1) the analysis of the source message and (2) the composition of the target message. For both of these components, Colonomos (1992) has identified seven factors that will determine the success of an interpretation. These factors are:

- *Process skills:* The ability to comprehend source messages and construct messages in the target language
- *Process management:* Includes monitoring process time, chunking messages into manageable units, seeking clarification from a speaker, and other tasks
- *Linguistic and cultural competence:* The interpreter's mastery of the source and target languages and understanding of the culture of the speakers of both language
- *Knowledge:* The experiences and education that the interpreter brings to the task
- *Preparation:* All action undertaken in preparation for an interpreting task; the action can occur prior to or during the task
- *Environment:* Subdivided into external factors, such as the physical setup on an assignment and the behavior of the other participants, and internal factors, such as fatigue and emotional reactions to a topic and participants
- *Filters:* The interpreter's habits, biases, beliefs, and personalities that might prevent the rendering of a successful interpretation

The Interpreting Process Model is similar to the Sociolinguistic Model in that both of them are concerned with interpreting skills. The interaction between the participants is best explicated in both models through analysis of what each skill entails. For example, the filter factor of the Interpreting Process Model could imply a possible significant affect of a speaker on an interpreter's

---

Profile: Ben Hall

Ben Hall is the coordinator of interpreting services for the Ohio Rehabilitation Services Commission. He is an adjunct faculty member in the Interpreting/Transliterating Program at Columbus State Community College and, like most interpreters, freelances whenever possible. He is a member of the Advisory Board of the RSA Region V Interpreter Training Project at Waubonsee Community College and co-chairs the Ohio Interpreter Standards Committee, a coalition of deafness-related organizations working to establish legislation in Ohio regulating professional interpreters.

Ben holds the Comprehensive Skills Certification and the Specialist Certificate: Legal. He conducts presentations on a variety of topics, including the business aspects of interpreting, state licensing/credentialing, and the Americans with Disabilities Act. He has received numerous awards for his service as well as an Instructor of Excellence award from the Columbus State Community College. He has served the Registry of Interpreters of the Deaf in various capacities over the years and is currently its vice-president.

Here, Ben speaks about credentialing interpreters at the state level, a process that is rapidly gaining favor across the nation:

State credentialing of the interpreting profession in the United States was a concept that was slow to catch on but is exploding today. Nearly every state across the country either has some form of state regulation or is considering establishing regulation of the interpreter profession. This action shows recognition of the critical nature of communication and has led to legislation to protect both deaf and hearing individuals.

Associated with credentialing comes various testing systems and state testing regulations has a profound effect upon the Deaf community and the profession of interpreting. There are at least sixteen states with an established interpreter testing system and all of these states also recognize national certification to various extends.

Continued

Profile: Ben Hall   *Continued*

The road to credentialing was not smooth, and even the systems in place today are not satisfactory to all people. One of the guiding forces in the development of credentialing is the fluctuation of interpreting models. The effects of this force are ongoing as new models replace old ones. The shift from one model to another, and especially the advent of the interpreter as a machine model, caused confusion and mistrust among Deaf people who use interpreters and misunderstandings of the interpreting process. Each shift calls up the need to reexamine existing guidelines for credentialing.

Another factor affecting credentialing was the five-year suspension of the national examination by the Registry of Interpreters for the Deaf (RID). For many years, the National RID Certification was the only national standard recognized across the country. Between 1987 and 1992, however, RID suspended the RID National Testing System for five years, leaving consumers and interpreters without a viable means of regulating standards. This flatlined the number of certified interpreters in the country at a crucial time when Congress was deliberating the historic civil rights legislation for persons with disabilities, the Americans with Disabilities Act (ADA).

Immediately following the passage of the ADA, Dr. Robert R. Davila, assistant secretary for special education and rehabilitative services, stated that although ADA requires the use of qualified interpreters, the responsibility for determining who was a qualified interpreter was a state responsibility. This clearly placed the burden on the individual states to develop regulation defining the term *qualified interpreter.*

Assessing the quality of interpreters is not only an RID or state responsibility. During the early 1990s, the National Association for the Deaf chose to develop a separate testing system based upon the California Association of the Deaf, Interpreter Assessment Program (IAP). The reasons for this are varied, but dissatisfaction with the interpreting profession at the time was a main one. The quick growth of NAD's IAP is due in part to its structure as a state-operated test. As such, it is more acceptable to state legislatures, agencies, and the community.

While the field can expect more changes and challenges to the status quo in regulating interpreters, I believe that state regulation of the profession is appropriate and long overdue. Interpreting, as with any other profession, needs to be regulated to assure high standards.

performance if the speaker is carrying on an extended dialogue on the cruelty of abortions while the interpreter is a confirmed pro-choice advocate. Similarly, if a speaker carries on beyond the scheduled time, the interpreter might become anxious about the time crunch, especially if the interpreter has another assignment to go to shortly after the present one is completed. Anxiety of the latter sort may lead to a deterioration in performance. In this instance, a better handle on process management might have avoided the anxiety created when a speaker goes beyond the scheduled time.

Bilingual–Bicultural Model

Another perspective on interpreting that merits attention is one that assumes a bilingual–bicultural approach. Elements of this approach can be found in the Sociolinguistic, Interpretive, and Interactive Models. It even includes elements of the interpreter-as-a-helper model, which was how many interpreters were perceived by others and by themselves before the field was officially recognized as a profession.

One of the main features of the bilingual–bicultural model is its accent on interpreters' attitudes and their subsequent behavior. McIntire and Sanderson (1995) and Humphrey and Alcorn (1994) offer a discussion and a comparison of this model with other models of sign language interpreting. Though not advocating a complete return to the helper role, the bilingual–bicultural model does not accept interpreters as conduits or mediators in all situations. For example, bilingual–bicultural proponents argue that an interpreter on assignment with a terminally ill deaf person may in fact assume the role of an "ally" for this person. In effect, bilingual–bicultural gives interpreters the latitude to define their precise role on a situation-by-situation basis.

Managing this freedom becomes a principal characteristic of effective interpreting. It is not, however, to be confused with control of the other participants in an interpreting situation. Two interpreters, Marina McIntire and Gary Sanderson, attempt to clarify the difference between power and control when they describe interpreters as mechanistic and thereby as having little power during interpreting situations:

> [W]e believe that interpreters have experienced a great deal of confusion between *power* and *control*. The latter is defined (as a verb) as follows: to exercise authority or dominating influence over; to direct; to regulate. Surely, *this* is what we didn't want to have when we shifted from helpers to machines. Rather than denying personal power, we should have been concerned about avoiding behaviors and attitudes that were aimed at *controlling* D/deaf people's lives. For example, interpreters have long felt free to ask a D/deaf person

for a copy of a paper in advance, as well as questions such as "how will you sign this or that?," "what words will you fingerspell?," and the like. Until recently, however, we were not comfortable asking hearing consumers for the same kind of information; it didn't feel polite, it didn't feel appropriate. So we attributed power to the hearing consumer, but appeared to be controlling the D/deaf person . . . . As interpreters, we need power. We need certain conditions so that we can work effectively. (McIntire & Sanderson, 1995, p. 101)

Associated with this demand for empowerment is a call for power over "more abstract and/or personal issues, such as self-confidence, respect, acknowledgment, freedom to make decisions, rapport with consumers, sensitivity to tricky situations, the ability to 'normalize' the situation despite being a fifth wheel, diplomacy" (McIntire & Sanderson, 1995, p. 102).

The bilingual–bicultural model leaves some key questions unanswered. For instance, what does it mean to say that the interpreter assumes responsibility for "cultural and linguistic mediation while accomplishing speaker goal and maintaining dynamic equivalence" (Humphrey & Alcorn, 1994, p. 210)? Nevertheless, in time we may gain a better understanding of how cultural and linguistic mediation play themselves out during an interpreted communication. The following exemplifies cultural mediation by two bilingual–bicultural proponents:

[I]n many areas of Canada it is common for individuals to take off their shoes upon entering another person's home. When an individual interprets to an audience of Americans a message presented by a Canadian who refers to removing their shoes, a bilingual–bicultural interpretation would require briefly providing the information that it is customary to remove the shoes when entering someone's home. Without doing that, the audience might misunderstand or miss the point of the illustration being given. (Humphrey & Alcorn, 1994, pp. 212–213)

We are well aware that taking one's shoes off before entering a house is not culturally specific to Canadians. Many Americans in the northern parts of the United States also remove their shoes before entering a house—a practice that might reflect an outside environment conducive to tracking dirt through the house when shoes are worn. If the point about taking one's shoes off is critical, then should not the speaker addressing an American audience clarify this point or use another expression? Not necessarily, according to bilingual–bicultural advocates.

Except for the helper aspect, other models of sign language interpreting would not allow for such cultural mediation on the part of the interpreter. The bilingual–bicultural model carries with it the danger of being viewed as parentalistic because cultural mediation will ensue when, in the judgment of the interpreter, the deaf and nondeaf people will not understand something. The interpreter's judgment may offend deaf and nondeaf participants alike. Some speakers might view such mediation as infringing on their right to dictate what it is that they want the audience to understand. Perhaps a speaker purposefully drops a unique notation about a culture without explanation because he or she intends to use the audience's lack of understanding to make a point later in a presentation. Should an interpreter risk this type of interference? Furthermore, exercising this judgment requires much expertise and familiarity with numerous culturally sensitive matters. It raises the question of each participant's role. If a deaf person's belief as a Jehovah Witness is crucial to understanding his or her remark, is it up to the interpreter to point this out to the other participants?

At this point, there is no consensus among interpreters as to the precise nature of the bilingual–bicultural model. How this approach develops in the future remains to be seen. It does, however, advise the field of interpreting that at least some interpreters feel they lack control over all the necessary means for effective interpreting. Whether its premises are accepted or not, the bilingual–bicultural approach deserves gratitude for raising the issues it has.

SIGN LANGUAGE AND OTHER FORMS OF INTERPRETING

Another question lurks in the background: How is sign language interpreting similar to and different from other forms of interpreting? Can models developed for one be applied, unmodified, to the other? If the only influences are those associated with the communication modes, then the task confronting research on interpreting are eased; it can partake of a much larger body of knowledge and speculation. If sign language and speech interpreting have substantive differences apart from signing versus speaking, then understanding sign language interpreting becomes more complicated.

Some evidence suggests these two forms of interpreting do call on different skills. Using the Stroop task, investigators compared two groups of interpreters. One responded manually and the other orally. Those responding manually showed greater interference than those responding orally. In the Stroop paradigm, response times are measured to color words—like *red, green, blue*—printed in the same or different-colored inks. Slower times in naming the ink color when it differs from the word (e.g., printing the word *red* with green ink) show that the word's meaning interferes with the perception of the color (Marschark & Shroyer, 1993). This study raises the possibility that the mode of communication may so influence interpreting that results from research on one will not apply directly to the other. If that proves to be the case, the loss to interpreter research would be great, demanding that separate studies be designed to tease out the principles of sign and speech interpreting. That is why more attention should be paid to ascertaining what role the communication mode—manual or oral—plays in interpreting.

We recognize that one contributing factor differentiating the two interpreting tasks is that users of different spoken languages can monitor one another's emotions and emphases auditorily. To do so, speakers rely on speech characteristics like those indicating the end of a message, which are common to spoken languages. But nondeaf people may not recognize that deaf persons signal the end of their speech by putting their hands on their laps or in another relaxed position. Likewise, a deaf person may not be sure when nondeaf people have conveyed the auditory signals indicating their intent to yield their speaking turn. Whereas rules speakers observe for turn-taking and additional modifications between speakers have been amply studied, similar attention has been investigated only sparsely in signer–interpreter–speaker interactions (Roy, 1992).

One area of study transcends modalities and languages, and that is in the accuracy of the message conveyed in the target language. In this area, we can draw from the vast literature available in the area of translations. Although there are differences in the processes and time constraints associated with interpreting and translating, both aim to transform a message from a source language to a message in a target language while retaining as much of the meaning and intended impression of the original message as possible. Translation theorists talk about the multidimensional aspect of accuracy. Leighton (1991), for instance, discusses the merits of full-valued translation, artistic translation, equivalent translation, and realist translation. Chukovsky (1984) examines a pragmatic measure of a translation, which he calls adequate translation, and describes it as something that "is not literally and precisely equivalent to the original, for it is based on the realization that adequacy requires imaginative recreations that achieve an equivalent effect, not a direct reproduction" (p. 66). This stance conforms well with the goal of interpreter education programs.

Although translation theorists may differ in many of their definitions of what a good translation is, implicit in many of their definition is the value of intuition. Robinson (1991) notes that good translators "choose words and phrases by reference not to some abstract system of intellectualized rules, . . . but rather to 'messages' or impulses sent by the body: a given word or phrase *feels* right" (p. xii). Our experience also indicates that good interpreters appear to have the knack of selecting signs and words that faithfully convey what a speaker is saying. This, however, does not mean that all good interpreters display a natural talent for interpreting. It does suggest that research is needed to delineate the characteristics not only of good interpreters but also of good interpretations. This information should be invaluable in helping us reexamine our models of interpreting and should contribute to improving the education of interpreters (see the box titled "Examples of Real-Life Models").

Examples of Real-Life Models

Students of interpreting should always seek to acquire the knowledge and experiences that will allow them to intellectually and intuitively select signs and words that do justice to their interpretations. To do this, they are wise to include in their circle of acquaintances masters of the languages in which they interpret. This notion is espoused by advice given to a Chinese translator:

> Somewhere nearby lives a scholar who is in love with Chinese poetry, who knows everything about it, understands everything, and is always ready to help the translator. One ought to make friends with him instead of a dictionary. (Gitovich, 1970, quoted in Leighton, 1991, p. 160)

We concur. An interpreter would do well to find a deaf adult who is able to combine sagaciously the dynamic elements of space and gestures to say things in ASL that are captivating not only for aesthetic reasons (although that may be the case) but for their clarity. Interpreters should also seek masters of the English language; those whose choice of words is guided not just by expediency but by insight into the power and beauty that words can bring to everyday language.

CONCLUSIONS

In concluding this survey of interpreting models, we find it stimulating to examine the potential for interpreter performance, education, and research that each provides.

Implications for Interpreting Performance

Realization of the difficulties inherent in providing accurate interpreting leads to the conclusion that it should be in the hands of well-prepared, highly skilled individuals. Such a conclusion, in turn, brings one to the realization that interpreting is hardly a trade. It is a profession—when it is performed properly. Consequently, it requires formal education, and its practitioners should be compensated at rates that mirror their experience, education, and skills.

Second, the preceding analyses make clear the inadequacy of word-for-sign and sign-for-word concepts of interpreting. Most models emphasize the transmission of *meaning*, not words. As will be elucidated in later chapters, a sign or word in one language may require a sentence or two in another language, in order to convey the same sense. Culture and context add important components to any message set, as viewed by most models of interpreting.

Third, the criticality of time emerges from the prior analyses. Interpreting is a real-time activity, as contrasted with translation. Seleskovitch regards interpreting, whether simultaneous or consecutive, as based on the same principles as translating. The differences are largely in timing: interpreting takes place under temporal stress, whereas translation does not have the insistent time pressures but provides opportunities to ponder particular words and phrases. The need to grasp the initiator's message—not just decode the words or some phrases—remains at the heart of both enterprises. Whether consecutive or simultaneous, interpreting does not allow time for the interpreter to consult dictionaries, discuss language options with colleagues, or reflect on the possible impact of particular formulations—things a translator of text can do. Interpreting decisions must be made on the spot. That is why advance access to the texts of speeches or to lecture notes, and similar opportunities to anticipate the likely content of verbalizations, are desirable strategies for interpreters to pursue.

Interpreting is a dynamic process, with severe demands on both long- and short-term memory. With few exceptions, interpreters almost always work behind the verbal flow; something must be signed or said before they can express it. The exceptions to this rule are rare, and when they do occur are seen for what they are— intuitively clever. One of us attended a speech consisting largely of platitudes and clichés. It was amusing—and instructive—that the expert interpreter finished signing parts of the speech *before* the speaker had uttered the words! Cleverness aside, interpreters must retain a portion of the message while they search long-term memory for the appropriate equivalence. How these cerebral feats are accomplished is not yet well-understood, but enough is realized to help interpreters improve their performances.

Lastly, how do we come to some agreement in the field about what is an adequate interpretation? In most models of sign language interpreting, the construction of an adequate interpretation will depend on the contribution of the participants, the adjustment to the environment, the function of the interpreting assignment, and many other factors. Even then, there should be no expectation that all interpretation will transmit the original message exactly. In this matter, we can draw on the work of scholars in the area of translation, where adequacy is defined not only in terms of how the original meaning is retained in the target language but also in the reaction of the participants to the message delivered. This assertion, however, does not bar the use of signs-for-word interpretation (i.e., transliteration). Such conveyances of messages allow a deaf participant to understand word for word what a speaker has said when making a motion at a meeting, or a legal wording in a courtroom, or even the meaning of a reprimand that a teacher has given to a child. In our view, communication is in the hands of all participants. Analyses of the communication needs of the participants and all other factors in an interpreting situation will help skilled interpreters to perform effectively.

Implications for Interpreter Education Programs

Interpreters need to know much more than two languages; they also need to understand the cultures, be familiar with any unique characteristics imposed by the setting, and have some familiarity with the subject matter. It helps—although it is feasible to learn and not essential to satisfactory interpretation—if they are acquainted with the other participants, have an appreciation for their discourse styles, and know their motivations in the particular communication situation.

Given all these requirements, interpreter education carries a far heavier burden than has often been assumed. This thinking raises doubts about the adequacy of relatively short-term preparation. Four-year degree programs—even master's degree programs—may appear increasingly reasonable as the conception of the interpreting process matures. We must qualify this assertion by stating that four-year programs that simply stretch the number of courses of two-year programs over a four-year period may not do enough to give students the requisite knowledge and skills associated with effective interpreting.

An interesting variation confronting interpreter educators arises from the fact that many deaf persons receive a bilingual education in ASL and English. Some deaf persons may prefer ASL interpretations, whereas others may lean toward an English-like form of signing that preserves the speaker's utterances intact. Other deaf persons may have lost their hearing postlingually and prefer signing that reflects English syntax more directly. All of this returns us to an oft-repeated theme, that deaf people are not a homogeneous group, but differ widely among themselves.

What all this means to interpreters and those responsible for educating them, as well as to those administering their activities, is that assessing interpreter performances must take into account the participants and hence the formulation of our Interactive Model of Interpreting. Ideally, interpreters should have the opportunity to meet with all participants prior to an assignment in order to resolve such basic issues as the form of the communication. In practice, interpreters are often thrust into situations and must make these decisions "on the fly." Educators can relieve interpreters of stresses arising from having to make these decisions alone by providing guidelines, but they should not set rigid policies—for example, that interpreters must always use a particular form of signing without consideration for deaf persons' wishes—and deny to interpreters and participants any flexibility in making these decisions. In this respect, we concur with the push from the bilingual–bicultural proponents toward empowering interpreters to do what is necessary.

Rigidness hinders the artistic aspects of interpreting. Each interpreter introduces to the interpreting equation a set of personal factors, such as linguistic competence, cognition, signing style, voicing capabilities, and the like. This personal aspect of interpreting demands flexibility so that interpreters may call on their own intuition and experiences to render what they believe to be accurate, intelligible interpretations.

Implications for Research

One reason that so few answers have been derived empirically for interpreting questions is that professional interpreting is a relatively new enterprise. Practitioners and theorists have not had the benefit of years of systematically recorded knowledge and experimentation to rely on. Further, the demand unleashed by federal legislation has directed attention to *doing* interpreting, not studying it.

Still, interpreting is a complex task, and determining the effects of the numerous factors that influence it is daunting. Indeed, the inadequacies of present research efforts may be affected by the lack of access to the elements that need to be studied: "The unstructured nature of non-verbal memory is probably the reason why researchers in the field of psychology and psycholinguistics have not paid greater attention to it" (Seleskovitch, 1992, p. 7). In short, such studies are difficult to conduct. The researcher has to devise tactics for exploring the functioning of the "black box"—the interpreter's central nervous system—while processing ongoing communication. Not an easy task.

As the field progresses, more research can be expected—research that will challenge assumptions, uncover problems, and open previously unexpected vistas for better practices. Speculations about the research that is likely to emerge in the near term will be found in Chapter 11, "The Future." We urge that studies of interpreting proceed with all deliberate speed. None of the stakeholders has justification for complacency with the status quo.

4

PHYSICAL FACTORS

Because interpreters transmit and receive auditory and visual signals, they must be in a position to see and hear well. Their audience, too, must be able to see and hear them. Lighting, interpreter clothing, room size, acoustics, and other environmental factors affect their communication. Interpreters also cope with bodily stresses and limitations. These physical factors in the interpreting environment can be classified as either auditory, visual, or personal, and can be subdivided as relating to the interpreter, to the participants, or to both. (Psychological factors are covered in the next chapter.)

Awareness of these physical factors—auditory, visual, and personal—is the first step toward managing them. The next steps are less clear. That is why we conclude this chapter with the question: *Who bears responsibility for managing the interpreting environment?*

THE AUDITORY FIELD

Many environmental problems appear obvious, yet they arise all too frequently. For the interpreter, the inability to hear speakers sometimes poses a problem. The reasons may be competing sound signals (noise), whether from people speaking or from other sounds, or the positioning of the interpreter relative to the speaker. In turn, the audience must be able to hear the interpreters when they voice for deaf signers.

Positioning

It is fundamental that interpreters be placed where they can hear the speakers clearly. At a round-table discussion, interpreters should be able to move about so as to hear better while still being seen. Participants whose speech is being interpreted can also contribute to effective interpreting by ensuring that their speech can be heard clearly.

Setting

When interpreting one on one, room size is usually not a problem. Only three people are involved, so it is easy for the interpreter to hear. Large auditoriums, on the other hand, can present problems, not entirely due to their size. The behavior of audiences within the auditorium can be noisy and, if they move about extensively, distracting to both speaker and interpreter. Even small groups can present these problems; two or more people talking at the same time as the main speaker make it difficult to attend to the speech. The type of room also has a bearing on the interpreter's access to visual or auditory information. Echoes occur in a room with poor acoustics. Rooms located near a machine shop, a gymnasium, a photocopying center, or along a busy street can expect an intrusion of outside noise that can create auditory discord, diminishing the clarity of the voice of a speaker or interpreter. Problems can also arise when an interpreter is positioned poorly relative to the speaker, which reduces the ability to hear what is being said.

Ambient Noise

Noises from moving chairs, papers rustling, and idle chatter must be overcome, along with loud ventilation fans, buzzing fluorescent lights, and street traffic. When voicing signs, interpreters must speak clearly and loudly enough to be heard easily over whatever interfering sounds may be present. When the audience is dispersed over a large area, interpreters should have microphones, such as those attached to clothing, that leave their hands free for signing. Interpreters, however, must be careful not to strike such microphones, which causes static; that is why some interpreters prefer microphones placed on a stand.

THE VISUAL FIELD

For interpreters, perhaps it is puzzling that large meeting rooms are called *audi*-toriums and not *visu*-toriums. Architects typically give less thought to arranging optimal conditions for listening than for seeing, and interpreters must work within whatever architectural constraints are imposed.

Positioning

Usually, interpreters can determine where they are located in the visual field. By controlling that aspect of the environment, they can overcome many difficulties. In taking their positions, interpreters should always bear in mind that deaf people must have a clear view of them. The entire signing space should be seen. Sign reception can be affected by whether the signer is standing or sitting, in a tiered room or on a raised platform, close to or far from the deaf participants. An interpreter may be confronted with a deaf woman lying on her back in a delivery room, a deaf man sitting in a jury box, a crowd of deaf spectators at a sporting event, one deaf child in a classroom with twenty normally hearing students, and so forth. Where should the interpreter stand in relation to the speaker and the deaf audience?

The general rule is: *the interpreter should stand where deaf viewers can see both speaker and interpreter.* When the interpreter is next to the speaker, the deaf person can read the interpreter's signs while more or less simultaneously observing the speaker's facial expressions, gestures, and changes in posture—all of which enrich the linguistic information being provided. In one-to-one situations, seating the interpreter slightly behind the speaker encourages the speaker to address the deaf person and not the interpreter.

In practice, however, the general rule often must be compromised. For example, when a deaf person is on the witness stand, a single interpreter cannot move between the judge and the attorneys, one of whom is questioning while the other raises objections and the judge rules on the objections. Interpreters for a panel discussion may be able to move behind whoever is speaking; doing so cues deaf participants as to who is speaking, as well as enabling them to gather paralinguistic information from each speaker. It can, however, quickly tire out even interpreters in top physical condition.

The effects of different positions on interpreting has received little research, except in classrooms. Deaf students and interpreters can be in the line of sight, on the sidelines, or in an idiosyncratic position (Moores, Kluwin, & Mertens, 1985). Line of sight has an interpreter positioned in a direct sightline between the deaf student and the teacher, enabling the deaf student to see the teacher, the board, or the overhead display with only a slight shift of gaze. In the sideline position the teacher has the central position, with interpreter and student off to one side. This configuration requires the student to look away from the interpreter to see the teacher, overhead, or board. Idiosyncratic positions occur most often in shop or physical education classes, where the interpreter must change positions frequently to accommodate the activity in which the deaf student is engaged (Stewart & Kluwin, 1996).

When voicing signs, the interpreter needs to see the signers, which usually means positioning across from them. In some situations, therefore, optimal positioning can require considerable interpreter agility or—a better arrangement—more than one interpreter. Finding a position, however, does not always ensure continuous viewing of a signer. Even in an audience of ten people, there are times when a deaf person directing a question or comment to a speaker must move so that the interpreter and the other deaf participants have a clear view of his or her signing. Likewise, a deaf speaker in the classroom, at a conference, or in another setting with many participants should be careful not to move out of the interpreter's view. In this respect, the deaf person signing is under more restrictions in movement than someone speaking orally. This is especially the case when deaf speakers interact with members of the audience and must constantly be on the alert for the view that the interpreter and deaf members of the audience have of their signing.

Lighting and Background

When interpreting before a large audience, interpreters should have steady, not fluctuating, lighting that accentuates their hands and facial features and reduces or eliminates shadows. Background is as crucial as lighting. A brightly colored background creates a bright-light source that will tire the eyes sooner than one that is more subdued. The color of the background, however, should not blend in with the color of the interpreter's skin or clothing. Contrast is important to reading signs.

A strong light behind the signer rapidly induces visual fatigue. Bright lights produce negative afterimages for everyone; this has nothing to do with deafness but is simply how the retina functions. What magnifies this physiological fact's importance is that deaf people must look continuously at whoever signs, whereas those who both see and hear can look away when someone is talking and still know what is being said. Knowing this, interpreters should not stand in front of bright-light sources.

Visual Noise

Interpreters should be alert to "visual noise"—that is, anything that distracts deaf people from concentrating on the signs: shiny objects, flickering television monitors, people moving about in deaf participants' lines of sight. Movements behind an interpreter can often be detected when the deaf participant's gaze focuses away from the interpreter. As with other noises, interpreters are often powerless to control them, but they should be aware of them and of techniques for reducing their influence.

Interpreters' Appearance

Clothing and makeup constitute a signing background over which interpreters have direct control. Although interpreters should, so to speak, dress for the occasion, they should remain unobtrusive. A formal event such as a banquet calls for formal attire; at a picnic, blue jeans or other casual clothing will suffice. The interpreter's appearance and hygiene should be an asset, not a liability. An interpreter's appearance may be governed, in part, by the RID

Code of Ethics, in which Principle 6 states: "Interpreter/transliterator shall function in a manner appropriate to the situation." (For a discussion of the ethical implications of dress, see Chapter 9.)

Solid colors are preferable to splashy patterns or black-and-white combinations, which promote negative afterimages. When possible, interpreters should choose colors that will not clash or contrast too harshly with the background against which they will be viewed. In some situations, certain clothing may not be allowed. Courts sometimes forbid women to wear slacks; loose clothing can be dangerous around machinery.

Men and women should not wear rings or other jewelry that will detract from their signs. Large dangling necklaces can annoy deaf persons who are trying to concentrate on the signing. Some interpreters wear solid-color smocks, which for a younger child also serves as a psychological reminder of the interpreter's role. It defines their role, signaling that the interpreter "should not become involved beyond the role of communicator facilitator" (Solow, 1981, p. 27). Removing the smock, however, does not mean that interpreters should become involved in social interactions; it may simply indicate that an interpreter is taking a break.

Fingernail length can be distracting both visually and auditorily; long fingernails can restrict an interpreter's range of movement. Only clear or flesh-colored nail polish should be used. Beards and mustaches should be trimmed so that they do not hinder speechreading. Long hair that hangs over the face should be put back during an assignment. Glasses, if worn, should not interfere with the visibility of facial cues and should not be left dangling on the chest when not in use; they should be secure on the face, as constantly pushing them back while signing may be frustrating and confuse participants.

Interpreters should always take hygienic measures to ensure that no odor emits from their bodies or clothing. This includes avoiding the use of perfumes and colognes that may be odoriferous to the other participants.

Participants' Appearance

Just as interpreters' appearances affect reception of their signs, so too do deaf signers' appearances affect interpreters' abilities to comprehend them. Deaf people have not been expected to make adjustments that will enhance the ability of others to read their signs, although many do this instinctively; yet it is not unusual for deaf people to comment on how the appearances of *other* deaf people make them hard to understand. The director of a Deaf sports association—whose vision was affected by Usher syndrome and who saw best against a solid, soft-colored background—often berated his fellow directors for not wearing suitable shirts to meetings. Even for persons with normal vision, the background against which signs must be read is important. Interpreters, however, can seldom do much about how others dress.

Visual Aids

It may seem foolish to say, but it needs to be kept in mind: *interpreters are useless in the dark*. (We set aside the possibilities of manual reception of signs until Chapter 6.) When speakers use slides or other visual materials necessitating that the lights be dimmed or turned off, interpreters must make arrangements to have a supplementary light illuminating them. When deaf people can view the visual materials without diverting their gaze from the interpreter for extended periods of time, they can understand the presentation better.

Not all media facilitate communication. When interpreting a television program or movie, interpreters should position themselves near enough to the screen to enable deaf viewers to see it and them at the same time. This is not meant to imply that deaf participants can understand simultaneously what the interpreter is signing and what they see on the screen. Rather, the close proximity of the interpreter and the display minimizes gaze shifting from one to the other. Nonetheless, deaf participants often miss a great deal in such presentations.

Television

Interpreting offers one solution to providing deaf persons with access to television programs. For the interpreter, there are a number of difficulties, some of which have been discussed. When two cameras are used—one trained on the speaker or the action and the other on the interpreter—the interpreter's image is usually inserted in the lower left-hand corner of the screen, although there is no particular reason for that placement.

The National Technical Institute for the Deaf (NTID) recognizes the problems inherent in interpreting on television and has prepared a guide called *Interpreting Television for Hearing Impaired Viewers* (1979). It recommends a natural-color makeup and avoiding orange and other distorting colors. To reduce glare from the studio lights, it is important to put makeup on all exposed skin, including the hands—which applies to men as well as women. Interpreters should explore what makeup enhances sign and lipreading. A subtle lipstick can be helpful, especially for oral interpreters. They seldom get a makeup artist's attention, so they should request it.

When interpreting with a deaf person or panel of deaf people and one or more speakers, the interpreter may stand just to the side of the television camera. When the camera is on the deaf person, the interpreter does not appear on screen at all, which may give the (false) impression that the deaf persons are lipreading the interviewer. Some deaf people object to that deception; they wish the interpreter to appear at all times on screen, to accommodate the communication needs of deaf television viewers.

Profile: Mary Beth Miller

Mary Beth Miller is a well-known actress, storyteller, and comedienne. She is one of the founding members of the National Theater of the Deaf and continues to captivate audiences with her artistic talent and wit. She has written a series of sign language books for children including Handtalk Zoo and Handtalk School and can be seen performing in popular videotapes such as Deaf Mosaic Comedy Club and Four For You. She has degrees from Gallaudet University, Connecticut College, and New York University.

Mary Beth was introduced to the power and aesthetic qualities of American Sign Language by her Deaf parents. Her gift for using ASL is evident in her signing on and off the stage. She had many years to hone her acting skills and learn the nuances of ASL while attending the Kentucky School for the Deaf. She continues to learn as she teaches ASL to the children at the Cleary School for the Deaf.

Mary Beth's extensive national and international performances bring her in contact with numerous hearing audiences. She calls interpreters her "voice" as she explains the skills they need to do her communication and art justice in their interpretations:

The varied facets of my professional career as a performing artist has presented many occasions for working with interpreters. Necessary for the access of the hearing people in the audience, the interpreter becomes my "voice." While that appears to be a simple concept, the processing of my performance through another individual has often caused me varying degrees of concern.

During performances my focus is on communicating with my audience. So much of my art is full of the richness of ASL and references to the Deaf cultural experience. The person interpreting the performance needs to be able to catch the subtleties that are inherently a part of my stories, anecdotes, and monologues. This can be challenging when I do improvisational pieces.

In the ideal situation, I can, essentially, forget about the interpreter. In the worst-case scenarios it becomes a matter of playing "sign and check," watching the interpreters for assurances that she is with me. The former situation makes for a relaxed performance, the latter tends to become distracting and annoying.

I recall one early experience I had during a nationally televised interview with a woman hosting a prominent news program.

Continued

Profile: Mary Beth Miller   *Continued*

I was answering a question when I happened to glance at the interpreter. I became uneasy when I realized that she clearly seemed not to be voicing what I was signing. I approached her after the interview and asked if she understood my signing. She replied that she had been told to "wing it" and she did! That experience, although surely not reflective of all interpreters, made me acutely aware, once again, that quality interpreting requires that the interpreter be committed to the ethics of the profession. This holds for interpreting in the entertainment field as well as in any other communication situation.

The indicators of professionalism that I look for when making arrangements for an interpreter during performances are:

- Native or approaching native-like abilities in ASL
- Fluent English skills
- Ability to interpret effectively in performance genres
- An understanding of Deaf culture

I routinely request female interpreters because a male voice does not represent me appropriately to the audience. I expect interpreters not to stop me for clarification during a performance, request that I sign more slowly, or become involved in "watching" the show, causing gaps in interpreting.

Ultimately, a highly skilled and effective interpreter allows the hearing members of the audience to simply sit back and enjoy the show!

Visual Factors Influencing Sign Formation

As amplification is needed to project an interpreter's voice, so increasing the size of signs compensates when much distance separates the signer from the receiver. A large audience of deaf people will require that interpreters enlarge their *sign space,* which is defined as the frame within which a signer's hands move. Another way to increase interpreters' visual range is to project their images via closed-circuit television onto a large screen that can be seen at a great distance. The drawback is that the three-dimensionality of signs is reduced to two dimensions.

Given the importance of the visual field in signing, it appears obvious that signers will modify their signing when the vision of those to whom they are signing is impaired. In one experiment, pairs of deaf signers were video-taped under normal, moderately impaired, and severely impaired visual conditions. As visibility decreased, the signer's hands moved further forward and higher, and signing rate decreased (Naeve, Siegel, & Clay, 1992). Feedback from the conversational partner would seem to influence the way in which deaf people sign. When interpreting for deaf participants seated nearby, interpreters can maintain eye contact and can catch facial and body expressions that cue the need for modifying their signing.

PERSONAL FACTORS

The interpreter's physical condition is clearly a factor in the interpreting process, but it is a factor that is too often taken for granted. Here we consider, first, the physical requirements for interpreting and then some of the physical hazards.

Physical Requirements

The hearing acuity of interpreters will determine how well they can receive another person's speech. If they have even a small degree of unaided hearing loss their effectiveness suffers. Familiarity with the voice of a speaker can also help an interpreter understand what is being said. Heavily accented people are especially difficult to understand even when they speak loudly and clearly enough.

Likewise, interpreters must see well enough to read deaf people's signs. Despite these obvious qualifications, those who engage interpreters rarely evaluate their audition and vision. We have encountered interpreters with some degree of hearing loss who, under particular circumstances, appear able to function quite well, but who cannot work effectively under ordinary conditions.

There should be concern about participants' auditory and visual abilities. If deaf participants have limited or no vision, they have the responsibility to advise the interpreter and determine what can be done to promote their communication. This is the case for deaf–blind people, a point that is addressed in a later chapter. For the sake of hard-of-hearing participants, interpreters may have to deal with assistive listening systems such as infrared and FM amplification systems. They should familiarize themselves with using these systems. One source of information is the organization Self Help for Hard of Hearing People and its monthly publication, *Shhh*.

Participants, too, face physical requirements that affect communication. Interpreters must accommodate the fatigue induced by deaf participants constantly watching signs. Many deaf people now request "eye breaks" during long meetings. Being forced to stare at the interpreter for long periods of time—even to the extent of inhibiting their eyeblinks—severely stresses deaf viewers.

Cumulative Stress Disorders

Interpreting can be hazardous to the interpreter's physique. The dangers fall under the heading of *cumulative trauma disorders,* which include tendinitis and carpal tunnel syndrome, among other potential disorders (Wisowaty, 1996). Their most prevalent cause is repetitive movement. Holding awkward poses, engaging in vigorous movements without prior warmup, and making overly energetic gestures can also injure muscles and joints.

Interpreters should be aware of repetitive-motion injuries, like carpal tunnel syndrome (CTS). CTS was first noted among assembly-line workers who repeated twisting motions of the wrist. The telltale signs of CTS are "numbness, burning, tingling or tickling sensations on the index, middle and ring fingers" and often occur at night, awaking the affected person (Stedt, 1989, p. 223). The repetitive movements of signing tend to inflame the nerves in the wrist, leading to painful, sometimes completely debilitating injuries. Interestingly, although repetitive-motion injuries occur to interpreters, they seldom afflict deaf people who use sign language as their principal mode of communication.

The best treatment for CTS and other repetitive-motion injuries is rest. As it is usually the dominant hand that is affected by this problem some interpreters have been known to switch the dominance of their signing to their other hand (see Stedt, 1989, for further discussions of the causes and treatment of CTS). Not surprisingly, as any signer would attest, fingerspelling places the most stress on the hands. It is not unusual to find interpreters who are experiencing problems with their fingers and wrist to do most, if not all, of their fingerspelling with their nondominant hand.

More recently, a controlled study was undertaken to determine the causes and extent of musculoskeletal disabilities among NTID's 60 full-time interpreters (DeCaro, Feuerstein, & Hurwitz, 1992). The initial finding was startling. About half were either totally disabled or carrying reduced workloads because of pain brought on by their interpreting. The text of the article says that "approximately 45%" were wholly or partly disabled, but a table shows that 35 of 53 interpreters who participated in the follow-up study were judged to be in such pain that they were either completely disabled or worked reduced schedules, a rate of 66%. Whether 45% or 66% have suffered damage, the finding is startlingly high. Those who were disabled reported difficulties with prepositioning (reaching controls on a car), grasping (opening a jar), and pinching (writing) tasks. Contrary to earlier studies, the NTID researchers uncovered little CTS and a large amount of tendinitis. A study of interpreters at

California State University, Northridge, found similar results—little CTS and much tendinitis (Cohn, Lowry, & Hart, 1990).

Preventing Repetitive-Motion Injuries

Interpreters can take steps to prevent cumulative trauma disorders. Reducing the length of interpreting sessions and increasing rest periods will help. Prevailing on lecturers to vary the pace of their presentations and to insert occasional pauses will give the interpreter some relief from constant motion. Furthermore, interpreters can control how much effort they exert in signing. Changing interpreting style—reducing the amount that the hand and wrist deviate from a neutral position and slowing the speed of these movements—can reduce pain and fatigue. Interpreters might find it desirable to wear a wrist support to lessen the impact of repetitive motions (Feuerstein & Fitzgerald, 1992), but perhaps not while interpreting. We add this cautionary note about wrist support because some deaf people have mentioned that they feel guilty when they see an interpreter wearing it, which adversely affects their ability to concentrate on the interpreter. Aside from signing, it is advisable that interpreters cut back on activities that exert a lot of stress on their wrists and fingers, such as playing the piano, knitting, and carpentry. They also can perform some exercises prior to interpreting that will help loosen their joints and therefore making them less prone to stress. Examples of exercises are shown in the box titled "Overuse Syndrome Exercises."

Pausing—the period of time when a speaker has stopped speaking briefly with the intention of continuing—is an aspect of speech and signing that provides interpreters with a brief rest. In signing pausing occurs when a signer holds the final handshape or in some other way stops signing while indicating the intent to continue. It should be noted, however, that pausing in interpretations tends to occur in the same location as in the source language; that is, a pause by a speaker will elicit a pause by the interpreter (Siple, 1993). Thus, the extent to which pausing can reduce repetitive motion stress is limited by the producer of the source language, although its value in reducing stress is not diminished.

For platform interpreters, enlarging the signing space and making signs larger for increased visibility increases interpreting fatigue (Solow, 1981). In some instances, interpreters might find it necessary to keep their hands slightly lower so that their faces are in clear view of those sitting below them. This lower signing is unnatural and will cause added stress on the arms and hands. The platform in an auditorium with a rising slope, in which deaf people are scattered throughout the seating, complicates interpreting, forcing interpreters to adopt signing styles that, though best suited for participants, are fatiguing. Such a situation can be alleviated by using more than one interpreter

Overuse Syndrome Exercises

The following exercises can reduce the amount of stress joints receive during an interpreting assignment. They take only about two or three minutes to complete.

- *Shoulder shrugs:* Raise and drop shoulders.
- *Forearm flip:* Gently flip or rotate forearms.
- *Rotating fists:* Rotate wrists one way and then the other 10 to 20 times each.
- *Finger spreads:* Shut and open hands, stretching the fingers as much as possible.
- *Finger stretch:* Place fingertips on a table or other flat surface and push down.
- *Head stretch:* Stretch head up several times.
- *Head turns:* Rotate head one way and then the other way about 5 to 10 times; then move head down toward the chest and then backwards 5 to 10 times.
- *Shoulder stretch:* Stretch arms above head and to the sides.
- *Hand flop:* Hold one hand up loosely while the other hand pushes it down.
- *Prayer position:* Lock fingers in a prayer position; then each hand alternately pushes the other hand back.

positioned at opposite ends of the stage. Indeed, the use of two or more interpreters may pay many dividends, not only with respect to fatigue but also with regard to the accuracy of the interpretations, the psychological support the interpreters provide for one another, and the professional development of the interpreters. This notion is endorsed by an interpreter educator who has said that "All interpreters should work only in teams except for those cases that can be justified to require only one interpreter" and who cites the benefits as the insurance of "accuracy, clarity, consistency, and professional growth" (Cerney, 1996, p. 1).

Interpreter education programs can play an important role in preventing cumulative trauma disorders. Students can be monitored to detect signing habits that will later become troublesome. Student interpreters can learn techniques to relieve strain, such as refusing back-to-back assignments that do not allow sufficient time for muscle fatigue to dissipate. Interpreter educators can encourage students to warm up before an interpreting assignment. In this way, interpreters develop habits that they can carry over to their professional practices.

Other types of conditioning include such obvious steps as ensuring a good night's sleep before an assignment and maintaining a healthy diet. Physical trauma can be avoided or at least ameliorated, something interpreters must constantly consider.

The legal and economic aspects of cumulative trauma disorders will be taken up in later chapters. For now, we merely remind the reader that the act of interpreting is but one aspect of being a professional interpreter. What an interpreter does before and after an assignment contributes much to making interpreting a rewarding career.

MANAGING THE ENVIRONMENT

When interpreters find that conditions are not conducive to effective interpreting, should they assume the responsibility for adjusting them, or should this task be left to deaf and nondeaf participants or to the sponsoring agency?

Several considerations guide interpreters' behavior in managing the environment. First, whenever possible, interpreters should visit the site where they will be working before undertaking an assignment. Preparation is the key to avoiding some, though not all, of the problems noted here. Such preparation will not always be feasible, but when it is, it can help interpreters avoid many complications.

Second, interpreters must not embarrass or annoy participants by interfering unnecessarily in the proceedings. They should consult with the participants before the event, when possible, to clarify any difficulties that can be anticipated. When such matters as positioning are involved, obtaining the participants' agreement to the arrangements is the ideal, though it is not always achievable in practice.

A third principle is that during an interpreting assignment, interpreters should maintain their focus on communication, not on their personal appearances and other concerns. Vanity has no place in an interpreter's profile. Once an assignment begins, interpreters should attend to their role in the communication process and attempt to manage the environment or their own physical appearance only if such action is absolutely necessary to maintain or facilitate communication.

The Setting, Positioning, and Ambient Noise

Interpreters should call to the participants' attention items they feel will interfere with communication—poor lighting, noisy apparatus, inappropriate positioning, lack of amplification, and so forth. If the participants do not wish to protest the arrangements, then the interpreters have discharged their responsibilities and must continue as best they can. Whether persons in charge of the arrangements are notified is a matter for the participants to decide. On the other hand, in educational settings where the participants are children, the interpreters should take a more active role, advising the teachers or administrators of any unsatisfactory conditions.

When speakers use slides or other visual materials requiring that the lights be dimmed or turned off, interpreters must request arrangements to have a supplementary light to make them visible. Such arrangements usually need to be made in advance, which is another reason for preparation before an assignment.

Not everyone is comfortable with interpreters sitting down or standing next to speakers. Some deaf people prefer that interpreters be less conspicuous, while others are concerned only that they be able to see clearly. If a deaf person asks the interpreter to change location, the request should be granted as "it is certainly the right of the Deaf person to make the decision on positioning, as long as there is agreement among all Deaf consumers" (Solow, 1981, p. 21). Conceivably, two or more deaf people might be at odds with one another about the interpreter's position. In most cases deaf people will reach agreement and inform the interpreter. If not, the impasse needs to be referred for resolution to whoever engaged the interpreter.

Inconsiderate Speakers/Signers

Rapid speakers make interpreting difficult if not impossible. They place a greater demand on the interpreter's decoding and encoding abilities and on short-term memory. Such speakers are especially difficult to interpret when they are reading from a prepared text, such as a list of names at a graduation ceremony. They should slow their speech rate and insert frequent pauses that will enable the interpreter to keep abreast of what they are saying. Does the interpreter have the right to inform them when they are speaking or signing too fast? Yes, it is the interpreter's obligation to do so, when this is necessary to effective communication. Similarly, interpreters must inform deaf people when their signs are indistinct or unrecognized, or when they are inadvertently moving in and out of their visual range. Interpreters should not attempt to bluff or guess; they should stop speakers and signers and get clarification.

Visual Noise

As with other noises, interpreters are often powerless to control visual noise but should be aware of it and of techniques for reducing its influence. Such techniques include signing somewhat more vigorously in order to capture and hold the deaf audience's attention. The interpreter also may be able unobtrusively to ask those causing the disruption to desist.

An increasing number of interpreters take assignments in noisy, visually distracting locations such as automotive plants, furniture factories, and computer-assembly shops. These interpreters may need to ask that the meeting be moved. If the request is not granted, the interpreter at least will have alerted management to the importance of environmental barriers to effective interpreting.

Who requests eye breaks? An interpreter can suggest them to deaf participants, but it is their decision. They may or may not wish to interrupt the proceedings, and this choice should be theirs, not the interpreter's. Interpreters may use a strategy called *chunking* to reduce eye strain. Chunking occurs when an interpreter pauses to capture a larger share of what is being said and then delivers the interpretation in summaries that do not attempt to keep pace with the speaker. Before adopting such a tactic, however, the interpreter should have the deaf participant's consent.

Other Situations

Particular settings may raise still other conditions that interfere with interpreting. The three principles suggested at the head of this section may not cover all contingencies, but they offer guidance to enable interpreters to decide wisely how to manage the environment in a professional manner that will enhance communication at the same time that the rights of the participants remain inviolate.

5

PSYCHOLOGICAL FACTORS

The psychology of interpreting has been a neglected topic. Yet, according to the Interactive Model of Interpreting, all participants in interpreted encounters—interpreters, deaf and nondeaf persons—contribute their own personalities to the process. In keeping with this model, we examine the psychological factors from the interpreters' and the participants' viewpoints, and then we consider how these factors interact. We examine such questions as:

- How does interpreting alter the relationship between individuals who do not share a common language or means of communication?
- How does an intermediary's presence affect their interaction?
- What about the accuracy of communication filtered through a third person?

These and many more are psychological questions of importance to interpreting, to interpreters, and to the deaf and nondeaf participants.

THE PSYCHOLOGY OF THE INTERPRETER

Interpreters are not machines. The popular ideal may be of a person who automatically converts words to signs and signs to words, without influencing or being influenced by them, but the quotidian reality is quite different. The public expects professionals to remain objective and emotionally aloof from their work. A surgeon does not blanch at the sight of blood. A lawyer will defend a murderer without feeling conscience-stricken. Interpreters, similarly, are supposed to be able to remain disinterested in what they communicate.

The Registry of Interpreters for the Deaf (RID) Code of Ethics insists that they must. But to what extent can they be? As one interpreter remarks:

> When I interpret I always have feelings about the situation, interest, boredom, occasionally anger or the urge to burst out laughing. I also have feelings about the people for whom I interpret. The problem is trying to mask these feelings. (Tipton, 1974, p. 11)

Interpreters cannot escape their emotions, their prejudices, their experiences. What they can do is to learn to keep them from intruding on their practices. They must develop control over their natural reactions—control that enables them to function in a professional manner regardless of their reactions to the situation.

Personality Characteristics

Interpreter education programs play a major role in helping interpreters achieve control over their reactions, but these programs alone cannot overcome every personality trait that interpreters bring to them and later interject into their work. In recruiting potential interpreters, education programs need to pay attention to their students' personalities as well as to their academic backgrounds and cognitive abilities. Emotional stability and the ability to control adverse reactions should be considered in selecting interpreters.

In recognizing that personality characteristics play a role in interpreting, a few studies have examined interpreters' psychological makeups. This research basically addressed two questions: Are individuals with particular personalities more likely than others to choose interpreting as a profession? What characteristics distinguish good from poor interpreters?

Anonymity as a Sign of Success

Is exhibitionism an interpreter trait? Interpreters in many settings are, after all, performers, much like actors in a drama. Should they regard themselves as such? How large a role does a desire to be the center of attention play in determining the choice of and in maintaining an interest in interpreting as a profession?

An experienced interpreter answers, "I am most successful when I can get others to ignore me" (Fink, 1982, p. 6). That one sentence applies in a variety of situations. For example, she wishes people would not strain her promise to maintain confidentiality by asking questions about her interpreting assignments. For another, she admonishes participants:

> So if you arrive late at a meeting or duck out for a cigarette, don't ask me what happened; I won't tell you. But all is not lost. Simply ask me

to interpret while you ask one of the [other participants]. That's why I am here. (Fink, 1982, p. 6)

Far from being the center of attention, ethical interpreters want the nondeaf participants to stop talking to them and to address the deaf participants, and for deaf persons to sign directly to the other participants.

The tendency of speakers to thank their interpreters might actually amount to an indictment of them, according to one authority: "Under the usual conditions, the interpreter who appropriately fulfills the requirements of the role will not be noticed, appreciated or applauded" (Frishberg, 1990, p. 8). Such austere criteria for success, however, may seem to lack appreciation for the current state of the art. The recency of interpreting as a profession and the lack of rewards that accompanies that nascent condition probably justify public acknowledgment of interpreters' contributions. Certainly, during a presentation, presenters should not in any way call attention to the interpreters, just as interpreters should maintain focus on what is being said and signed. But if they have performed well, as most professional interpreters do, it may be appropriate to thank them for their contributions.

On the other hand, a public rebuke—even if deserved—is not in order, any more than would be complaining about poor conference arrangements in front of the audience. Some things are best done in private. Perhaps in time, as interpreters appear increasingly in the lives of deaf people, all participants will act as the participants did in one assignment:

I was interpreting at a meeting at which angry people were arguing with one another. My arms got progressively tired and my eyes more and more droopy. Then one of the deaf participants declared, "The interpreter needs a break." . . . The hearing person who chaired the meeting turned to the deaf person who had spoken up and said, "Okay, tell the interpreter she can have a break." I was shocked to the core. After all those months of having people talk at each other through me, these two were talking to me through each other! I was being completely ignored. (Fink, 1982, p. 9)

Research on Interpreter Personality

Do interpreters really want to be ignored? An early study of 20 interpreters in the northeastern United States examined their responses to the Edwards Personality Preference Schedule (EPPS) in relation to their interpreting skills as rated by a group of deaf judges (Schein, 1974). The study found that a cluster of five personality characteristics accounted for the differences between more highly regarded and less highly regarded interpreters. Briefly summarized, the research concluded that successful interpreters desired to be the center of attention and independent, but were not overly anxious, sympathy-seeking, or perseverative. The study, however, had a number of flaws. The interpreter sample was small and drawn from a narrow region of the country, and the judges tended to differ fairly widely among themselves in their assessments of the interpreters. Most important, the study was done before interpreter education became widely available. Many of these interpreters began to interpret as volunteers in church or as hearing children of deaf parents (see Frishberg, 1990, for a critique of the study).

Whether or not these findings would apply to today's professionals was tested by researchers who gave various interpreting tasks to 15 male and 15 female interpreters (Rudser & Strong, 1986). The researchers sought characteristics among the various groupings of interpreters. They found that the top interpreters had deaf parents but also noted that two of the interpreters who had deaf parents were also rated the poorest. Curiously, when asked which interpreters had deaf and which had hearing parents, both deaf and nondeaf judges guessed at or below chance levels.

Improvements in assessment instruments can advance research in this area. The evaluation procedures of interpreter organizations can provide criterion measures for studies of interpreter performances, although a serious problem remains—variability among judges. The unreliability of judgments limits the validity of any effort to relate interpreter abilities to measures of personality or any other characteristic. Then, of course, there is the unreliability inherent in personality inventories. Furthermore, there is the difficulty in gathering adequate samples that would allow for generalizations to the interpreter population. One tactic to overcome the latter problem is to include a personality inventory in every evaluation conducted by interpreter organizations. In time, RID and the Association of Visual Language Interpreters of Canada (AVLIC) would have sizable samples from which to calculate correlations between performance and personality. Strong and Rudser (1985) offer further suggestions for research.

These bits of research illustrate by their sparseness the lack of attention given to a critical variable—interpreters' personalities or, more generally, their characteristics. This is a serious shortcoming because of the significant influence that interpreters have in a communication process.

Parentalism

Some interpreters started their careers in churches or interpreting for deaf family members. Providing a free service to their deaf co-religionists or their deaf parents often engendered parentalistic attitudes that may have persisted as interpreting became a profession and interpreting services expanded.

When it became obvious that sound interpreting entailed more than a command of two languages, the realization emerged that only qualified professionals can interpret effectively in many situations.

Wentzer and Dhir (1986) proffer one explanation for the naive behavior of earlier interpreters and their poor reputations:

> [C]hildren of deaf parents have very similar behaviors to adult children of alcoholics. They act as protectors and parents to their parents. When these individuals were brought into an interpreting setting, it is easy to see that the communication usually did not remain a pure exchange, but was colored by the interpreter's "best" wishes for the deaf person or parent. This situation created mistrust of the interpreters, the person who was being interpreted, and the hearing world in general. (p. 13)

Such revelations about the psychology of interpreters should not be construed as a criticism of the field. They are a necessary part of the growth of any profession. Thus, whereas the circumstances depicted in this quotation may have once been true, their prevalence today is much reduced because of interpreter education programs' efforts and the field's concerted drive toward professionalism.

Professionals walk a fine line between meeting their own needs and meeting those of their clients. Lawyers, social workers, physicians, and other members of the helping professions are not expected to donate their services routinely—and they do not. All professionals work for pay, as well as to serve their clients. What interpreters must guard against is a parentalistic attitude—that being able to hear and to sign gives them intellectual or moral superiority. Like other professionals, interpreters should respect the other participants in an interpreting situation and adjust their services to their participants' welfare—if for no other reason than their code of ethics demand it.

Cognition

Do successful interpreters have cognitive characteristics that distinguish them from less successful interpreters? The preliminary answer appears to be yes. For example, an empirical study of interpreters by Vallandingham (1991) affirms the hypothesis that "skilled interpreters . . . are efficient chunkers of linguistic information" (p. 68). He found that skilled interpreters have superior short-term memories, something that seems essential to success in the arduous task of providing simultaneous interpreting.

Although being an interpreter probably demands better-than-average short-term memory, research has not resolved questions about other cognitive abilities. For some types of interpreting—interpreting for advanced mathematics classes or in a courtroom—academic preparation is essential. "Book learning," however, can be acquired as interpreting assignments demand, but intelligence is generally conceived as a given, as an attribute a student brings to an interpreter education program. Researchers have not addressed cognition in a manner that enables interpreter education programs to use cognitive traits in their selection of applicants.

Interpreting Stresses

The preceding chapter discusses the physical hazards of interpreting. There are, however, psychological stresses that may have equal or greater impacts on interpreting. Some may be cognitive and others emotional.

Time stresses interpreters. Keeping pace with a fast-moving conversation or a fast-talking lecturer can disturb an interpreter's equilibrium. The pace not only allows no time for recovery from difficult decision making (which must occur in milliseconds if the interpreter is not to fall too far behind) but also generates confusion as one phrase piles upon another.

Marschark and Shroyer (1993) have shown that interpreters take longer to respond in sign than to respond orally, though the time differences they obtained were small. Interpreters should be aware that their performances may be slower when they are converting speech to sign than sign to speech.

One might suspect that in simultaneous interpretation the interpreter is required to provide in sign an immediate equivalent of spoken utterances and vice versa. Cokely (1986), however, argues against that idea:

> A popular but naive notion that sign language interpreters should strive for perfect temporal synchrony with the source message has persisted for a long time. [My research] provides evidence that imposing such a constraint or expectation upon interpreters results in inaccurate interpretation and an increase in interpreter errors or miscues. An analysis and count of miscues in actual interpreter performances has been compared with interpreters' lag time (i.e., the time between delivery of the original message and delivery of the interpreted message). The result shows an inverse relationship between the amount of lag time and the number of interpreter errors. This relationship has serious implications for interpreter educational programs, interpreter assessment programs, and programs intended to make consumers aware of interpreting's limitations. (p. 341)

Although Cokely found that processing time is important in order to give an interpreter the opportunity to deliver an accurate interpretation, he goes on to suggest that *too much* processing time will likely be detrimental to the accuracy of an interpreted message because of the strain it places on the interpreter's memory.

Another stress that faces interpreters is overlapping speech and/or sign—two competing messages arising at the same time. What is the interpreter supposed to do? Several tactics have been derived from an analysis of a speaker–signer interaction by Roy (1992):

- Interpreters can actively intervene, informing one of the speakers that the other is speaking. That does not occur when speakers can hear each other, but it does when one signs and the other speaks.
- Second, the interpreter can delay one message and produce it only when the other message is finished. Interpreters may use this tactic when the second utterance is made just before the first is completed; otherwise, too great a burden is imposed on the interpreter's memory.
- Third, the interpreter can simply ignore one of the overlapping speeches. If the latter ploy is chosen, the interpreter can indicate later that the message was not conveyed and that it is now the turn of that person either to repeat it or to contribute a new thought.

To facilitate simultaneous interpreting, the stress of overlapping communications can be relieved by education—by teaching interpreters tactics for managing these situations and by alerting participants to avoid interfering with the interpreter and behaving in ways that upset the process. Interpreter education will go a long way to creating a new generation of efficient interpreters who are better able to relieve the burden of situational stresses. But where will deaf persons learn how to optimize interpreting? With so many deaf students being educated in public school classes that follow curricula developed for nondeaf students, they have little opportunity to learn how best to participate in interpreted situations, vital as such information will be to their future well-being.

Turning to personal stresses, some interpreters refuse to interpret blasphemous, off-color, and scatological material. Some refuse because of their strong religious backgrounds; others are restrained by matters of taste. The RID Code of Ethics does not specifically take up this problem—and it can be a problem. For example, when one is interpreting in a psychiatric interview, the patient may curse, use gutter language, describe intimate sexual activities, and otherwise offend normal sensibilities. Not conveying that material accurately would be a disservice to psychiatrist and patient. Also, it would probably violate the interpreters' ethical code.

A miscarriage of justice has been attributed to an interpreter's failure to use street language to convey questions in a case of alleged rape. A deaf man was asked by an attorney if he wanted to engage in sexual intercourse with the woman who claimed he raped her. The interpreter signed, Were you *attracted to her?* The deaf man's yes amounted to a confession of guilt in the eyes of the jury, which considered his affirmation as wanting to fornicate with the woman (Woodward, 1977). Of course, readers will recognize that the interpreter failed to convey the *meaning* of the question by using signs that misled the client.

Everyone should recognize that what interpreters express should only be what someone has signed or said. Signing a swear word or voicing a signed profanity is the interpreter's ethical duty—one that may be far easier stated than practiced. Achieving so high a degree of objectivity about language requires a great deal of preparation and professional commitment. Interpreters should constantly monitor their own reactions to the meanings of messages. They need to uncover their own prejudices in order to avoid introjecting their attitudes into their interpretations.

Interpreter education programs cannot change their students from fallible human beings to saints. They can, however, help them gain greater understanding of themselves. The best professional interpreters have some prejudices, some likes and dislikes, preferences and distastes. That truism should concern no one, provided those attitudes do not intrude on their practices. Because unconscious motivation can affect any professional's behavior, interpreters need to practice introspection. They should endeavor to understand their own feelings—positive and negative—and probe their own motives. Of course, for practical reasons, such self-inspection cannot be left to occur while interpreting. Indeed, reflection on what one is doing can be a source of stress during an interpreting assignment, as indicated in the story told in the box titled "Hoping for the Best." Generally, self-inspection should be a part of preparation. With self-knowledge, interpreters can avoid misinterpretations and violations of their ethical responsibilities.

Hoping for the Best

Deaf and nondeaf people experience much difficulty when communicating with one another, and this is something that motivates interpreters to perform effectively. It is also something that adds to their level of stress even when they have performed to the best of their ability. One interpreter related how this can occur in a seemingly innocuous circumstance:

> I was to interpret an interview between a deaf man who was a potential student in a graduate program and the director of the program. I met the deaf man's plane, which was very late. By

Continued

Hoping for the Best   *Continued*

the time we arrived for the interview, we were several minutes late. Assuming we had had difficulty in finding his office, the interviewer said, "I see you finally found me." Given the deaf client's preference, I interpreted word for word. He looked puzzled, and after a significant pause, said, "I don't know what you mean?" Wanting this situation to go well for the deaf man, I was terrified that I was in for a grueling couple of hours. I know it wasn't my responsibility, but I didn't want to sit there and see these two fail to communicate.

Right or wrong, the interpreter claimed to be at fault for the miscommunication and was feeling very uncomfortable at this moment. The interviewer, however, put everyone at ease by explaining that he thought the deaf man and the interpreter had had trouble finding his office.

PSYCHOLOGY OF DEAF PARTICIPANTS

What characteristics of deaf participants interfere with or facilitate the interpreting process? Most deaf people recognize the essential contributions to their lives made by interpreters. Such recognition, however, does not mean that they necessarily like interpreters or that they enjoy the situations in which they must interact with other people through interpreters. The Interactive Model of Interpreting specifies that the participants' personalities contribute to the interpreting process. Thus, interpreters profit from awareness of the participants' psychologies.

The Evolution of Deaf People's Views

RID brought interpreting to the attention of people who had never before given it a thought—government officials, educators, rehabilitators, and some deaf adults. From 1964 to 1974, concerns about interpreting moved from the distant background to the forefront of the education and rehabilitation of deaf persons. No longer were deaf adults forced to ask their children, neighbors, or relatives to provide interpreting. In the decade after 1964, deaf citizens' views of interpreting evolved from seeing it as a favor and an ad hoc arrangement to viewing it as a right of citizenship and a professional service to be purchased like any other.

One such point of view is that expressed by a highly achieving, born-deaf engineer who describes the difference interpreters made in his work:

Never before in my life did I have access to an interpreter in professional meetings . . . . I remember the first time when I had an interpreter in a staff meeting; I felt as if I were on Cloud 9. I had a chill in
my spine and goose pimples all over myself . . . . I realized that the
five years I worked as an engineer at McDonnell-Douglas Corpora-
tion before coming to NTID were truly a time of isolation. The staff
meetings at McDonnell were useless to me; all of my work was done
on an individual basis with very little teamwork with other engineers.
(Hurwitz, 1991a, p. 73)

Observations support the hypothesis that deaf people's attitudes toward
interpreters are changing. Those deaf people who grew up in the days when
interpreters did them a favor—before 1964 and the professionalization of
interpreting—tend to view interpreters as friends or family members who
interpreted as an obligation. Younger deaf people, growing up with paid interpreters, especially in school settings, are more apt to see interpreters in a
different light, as professionals who deliver a paid service.

Looking back on their youth, older deaf people have generally said that
they were satisfied with interpreting—when they could get it. Their biggest
complaint about earlier times was that very often no interpreters could be
found or that agencies refused to provide them. Seldom did they recall (or
complain) that interpreting was poor.

In one of the largest studies of its kind, Crammatte (1987) interviewed 400
deaf professionals about their perspectives on interpreting. They extolled the
virtues of interpreting and did not mention any negative aspects—scarcity,
dependency, ineptness. In summing up their attitudes, Crammatte opines:

The Registry of Interpreters for the Deaf (RID) brought professionalism and ethics to the field of interpreting for persons with hearing
difficulties. The resulting spread of this service has enabled hearing-
impaired people to participate in activities ranging from PTA meetings to legislative hearings . . . . Professional interpreters are a boon
for ease of communication, and they are trained to be unobtrusive.
It may be very difficult to justify the cost of an interpreter for a single deaf worker. Sometimes the solution to this problem is a job position with dual responsibility, for example, a secretary/interpreter.
(pp. 5, 163)

A debate among some deaf people concerns their predisposition to sit as
close to the interpreter as possible so they can see the signing better and so
the interpreter is able to get feedback from their body language and facial expressions. One deaf woman relates how in university classes and at conferences she always felt compelled to sit in the front row and to pay attention

constantly to the interpreter. To do otherwise, she felt would be taken by the interpreter as an affront. She also never wanted her interpreter to stop signing lest the professor think she was not interested. She would forego going to the restroom until after the speaker had finished. She would rarely allow herself a break to make notes or relax her eyes by diverting her attention for a few minutes from the interpreter. This woman remembers well the days when she was grateful that she was able to get an interpreter, but she now finds herself trapped by this ingrained behavior.

Today, such studious allegiance to this unwritten code of attention is increasingly viewed as being of dubious relevance to the process of interpreting. Deaf people are now more inclined to sit where they please and to suffer the consequences should their choice create difficulty in understanding the interpreter. As for diverting their attention, experienced users of interpreters do so without apology.

The difficulties of interpreting are not lost on the deaf participants. Yet, more and more, deaf presenters at conferences are complaining about the inaccuracies of interpreting from spoken language to signed language, which, ironically, may be a reflection of the growing professionalism of the interpreting field and the accompanying respect it garners from participants in interpreted communication. When interpreters first began to organize themselves into a profession, many deaf people were too grateful for the interpretation they provided and hesitated to complain. Today, accuracy in interpretation is an expectation.

Rosalyn Rosen (1993), past president of the National Association of the Deaf, emphasizes the need for interpreters to convey correctly what deaf people sign. Despite the fact that she has an earned doctorate, her interpreters' choice of vocabulary and grammatical structures sometimes make her "sound like an idiot" (p. 3).

Today, many deaf people want to form a partnership with the interpreter. That is why some of them resent being called "consumers" or "clients." They regard their role as equal to that of nondeaf persons in interpreted communications; they point out that, if everyone signed, no one would need an interpreter.

Interpreters reasonably expect the other participants to show them the same respect they would give to any professional who serves them competently. Most interpreters do not expect participants, deaf or nondeaf, to treat them as "chums." A deaf leader writes, "By having an interpreter in my classes, I felt that I finally transformed from a totally passive student into an active learner in classrooms for the first time since I left [Central Institute for the Deaf]" (Hurwitz, 1991a, pp. 73–74). Note that he lauds interpreting, not interpreters. That emphasis on the service rather than on those who provide it indicates that the profession is maturing.

The reader will recall that an NAD president speaking at the birth of the RID, referred to interpreters as deaf people's "friends" (Sanderson, 1964). The more recent attitudes of deaf people seem more compatible with the ideal expressed by those interpreters who prefer to remain anonymous while they perform their professional duties.

Interpreter as Prosthesis

A variation on the tendency to depersonalize interpreting has begun to emerge among younger deaf adults. In the late 1970s, many deaf adults got their first experience with a professional interpreter. Participating actively in a meeting with a group of nondeaf people was exhilarating for them. This excitement was often shared with the interpreter, who might offer a few words of advice during a meeting or tag along with the deaf person for a meal or a drink after the meeting—actions that contradict the Code of Ethics. A few deaf renegades astute enough to assess the inappropriateness of such camaraderie with interpreters recognized that others must come to view an interpreter simply as a communication facilitator. Toward this end, they tried a number of different tactics.

One strategy was that of Pat, a deaf Canadian who frequently attended meetings with Members of Parliament and executive officers of large corporations. Before and during each meeting, he would instruct his interpreters not to introduce themselves. During meetings, he demanded that chairpersons not direct queries to interpreters. Interpreters were not to be thanked openly for their services, nor were their names to be mentioned in the minutes of a meeting. When Pat would leave a room or if he became absorbed in reading a document, he asked the interpreter to continue signing. He pointed out that nondeaf people can avert their attention from a discussion and later prick up their ears and immediately resume contact with it. When asked about his highly disciplined treatment of interpreters, he explained:

> Interpreters to me are an extension of my hearing aids or my eyeglasses. They help me get information that I do not have full access to. At the end of every meeting, I do not thank my hearing aids for allowing me to talk to the person at my side. I don't thank my glasses for helping me to read. Best of all, no one comes up and asks to be introduced to my prosthetic devices. Interpreters are another prosthetic device for me. They help me when I need them. But when I don't need them, then there is no other role for them at the meeting that I am at. I want people to ask who *I* am and what *I* do in my life. And I don't want this happening in the shadow of an interpreter. (Quoted from an interview. "Pat" is, of course, a pseudonym.)

Not all deaf people feel this strongly about the need to subordinate interpreters. Pat's proactive stance represents one segment of the Deaf community. He did what he thought was necessary to enhance the interpreters' effectiveness—not only at the meeting he was attending, but also in the long run—by shaping the perception of how other people regard interpreters.

Deaf Students' Views

A researcher queried deaf students attending schools in Alberta about their views of interpreting and summarized the main findings of the interviews:

> One, students feel powerless to influence the interpreting services they receive. If they complain—and they rarely do—they most often hear administrators telling them that if they don't like the interpreter assigned to them they can do without one. If they criticize the interpreter, the interpreter frequently resents the criticism and either tells the student to shut up or threatens to leave. Which brings us to the second theme: without an interpreter, there is no use going to class. This fact reinforces the sense of powerlessness and increases the frustration many students feel *at times*. By and large, the deaf students . . . were pleased with the interpreting services they were receiving. (Schein, 1992, p. 12)

The frustrations that these students felt are not unexpected. Interpreters are human and, like most people, are put on the defensive by criticism. For a few older deaf (or more likely, hard-of-hearing) students, using an interpreter was shameful. It implied they were weak, because their parents had harped on the need for them to speak and to lipread. Worse, interpreting set them apart from their nondeaf schoolmates, something no teenager enjoys. To teenagers the most important thing in the world is to be like other teenagers. Experience and education will probably rectify many of these attitudes.

Trust

Having confidence in the professionals on whom one depends is fundamental to good service. The trust of deaf participants should not be taken for granted. Lacking surveys of deaf people's confidence in interpreters, we cannot say with any certainty that deaf people, on average, have more or less trust in interpreters than in other professionals. In conversations with a few heads of interpreter referral agencies, we have found that deaf participants' allegations that interpreters have violated confidentiality top the list of complaints received by those agencies. How representative those complaints are we do not know. Surely, this is an area worthy of direct investigation.

Indirectly, humor can sometimes provide a revelation otherwise masked by proprieties. Such a case may be the story about the deaf bank robber, the sheriff, and the interpreter—a popular joke in the Deaf community.

> The sheriff asks the man where the stolen money is hidden. The deaf man signs and the interpreter voices, "He say he does not know what you are talking about."
>
> After half an hour of continual denials by the deaf man, the exasperated sheriff places a gun against the deaf man's head and says, "If you don't tell me where the money is hidden, I will kill you."
>
> The interpreter signs the threat, and the now-terrified deaf man responds, "I hid it under the back stairs at my cousin's house."
>
> The sheriff, sensing that something has changed in the deaf man's persistent denials, eagerly asks, "What did he say?"
>
> Quickly, the interpreter answers, "He says he's not afraid to die!"

What does this joke say about interpreting? Does it express some deaf people's doubts? Does it provide an outlet for anxieties about being misrepresented? One analysis sees it as a way to desensitize such fears and as "a socially acceptable way of conveying a cautionary message" (Schein, 1989a, p. 63). But if it reflects deaf people's underlying fears about interpreters, it is no joke.

Dependency

Deaf people's reliance on the visual mode results in a certain amount of dependence on interpreters, because much of the communication in today's world is arranged for persons who hear. Many everyday needs (to say nothing of emergency events) can only be taken care of through the auditory sense, imposing a dependency constraint:

> For most people born to hearing parents . . . dependence begins at birth. Their dependence on people who hear has its roots in the emotionally powerful and influential experiences of early childhood and the parent–child relationship. Dependence continues in the spheres of education, religion, employment, and in the acquisition of goods and services provided and controlled primarily by those who infrequently confront or even think about deafness as a life experience . . . . [Deaf people] continue to find their fate dependent, to a large extent, on the willingness of hearing people to interact with and accommodate them. (Erting, 1987, p. 131)

Although this appears to be an illuminating insight—and, like many brilliant observations, obvious once it has been stated—there have been some contrary reactions. Many deaf adults may agree that this quotation describes an important part of their life experience. But people who have served as their "brokers" find this notion unacceptable and argue that it is not true that deaf people are *forced* into dependency by the way the world is structured.

The thrust toward dependency in deaf people probably arises from a combination of two sources: early experience and the existing social structure. One source of dependency may be early and continuing experiences that neither foster nor allow the development of autonomy as a habit or personality characteristic. The other reason for dependency is embedded in the social structure and imposed on deaf people even if their characters or personalities are strongly autonomous (Moores & Meadow-Orlans, 1990).

Vernon and Andrews (1990) advance a different hypothesis to account for what they apparently regard as an immutable tendency toward dependency:

> Inherent in the relationship of deaf people to interpreters is a dimension of hostile-dependence. Hostile-dependency feelings emerge when a person must depend on another for some need yet feels angry toward that person at the same time. It is difficult for any human being to be as dependent on another as a deaf person is on an interpreter. By virtue of this relationship, tremendous control and power rest with the interpreter. Inevitably, this power leads to abuse and consequent anger. There is also the tendency of the deaf person to see the interpreter as omnipotent. Then when things go wrong, the deaf person blames the interpreter, not himself or the person whose speech was interpreted. (pp. 121-122)

Unfortunately, the statement offers no empirical data to support it; readers are left to accept or reject it on the basis of reason alone. The sweeping generalizations—deaf people are hostile-dependent toward interpreters, deaf people blame interpreters when things go wrong, and so forth—do not accord with many deaf people's own statements, like those cited in this chapter. Rather than debate the statements' validity, verification should be sought through systematic observation and experimentation. Doubtless in a group of people as large and varied as the Deaf community, almost every conceivable attitude is probably held by someone. What is worthwhile is to determine the proportions of deaf people who hold hostile attitudes toward interpreters and, when these are found to be especially prevalent, seeking ways to move them in a constructive direction.

The potential for dependency developing between the deaf person and the interpreter has been noted by some administrators and a number of interpreters. One school principal who has two interpreters in his school requires them to switch each month because "deaf students must learn not to depend upon a single person." An interpreter in another school tells of serving a deaf student with severe visual problems: "It took me three years to learn to work with her." Asked if working with the same student for so long a time is healthy, she acknowledges that it is a serious issue that did not have a ready answer. In practical terms, it seems the right thing to do. Nonetheless, the interpreter feels that psychologically it may not be in the student's long-term best interests.

Another interpreter notes that he had a student who had become overly dependent. When the student had a question, she would seek the answer from the interpreter. When he would tell her to ask the teacher, the student would reply, "No, you just tell me. I don't want to ask the teacher." After that, the interpreter literally hid from the student during cooking classes to avoid having to tell her he could not assist her with her assignments. We note, however, that such dependency does not develop in a vacuum, and probably this or another interpreter willingly provided answers in the past.

Administrators often regard deaf people as passive recipients of interpreting, rather than active participants. Too seldom do they seek deaf persons' contributions when making decisions about interpreting and evaluating interpreters. Such practices and views contribute to deaf dependency in interpreted and, we fear, other social situations.

The very essence of why an interpreter is so beneficial to deaf participants—because they provide visual access to communication—may be partly responsible for nurturing dependency on the part of the deaf participant. A deaf person must maintain eye contact with the interpreter whenever the interpreter is signing. This eye contact is also often maintained when the deaf person is signing because many deaf people monitor the interpreting of their signing to insure that their intended meaning is not misrepresented. Research in this area may lead to a better understanding of how positioning and eye contact affect the psychology of interpreted communication.

Socializing

The Interactive Model of Interpreting reminds us to give attention to the social side of interpreting. Many deaf people resent interpreters who hang around to chat after an assignment. Others hold the opposite view; they dislike interpreters who come in, do the job, and leave. Interpreters who maintain their professional demeanor before, during, and after professional assignments will earn the respect of most deaf people.

As for those deaf participants who want to socialize with the interpreter after an assignment, they often can be satisfied if interpreters recognize their desires for further contact but explain that they have another assignment, are too tired to stay, or cannot remain for some other valid reason. By acknowledging the deaf person's desire for further socialization and responding in a considerate manner, interpreters can avoid arousing antagonism. Informing

participants before an assignment begins that the interpreter has another en-
gagement immediately following can avoid hurting some participants' feelings when the interpreter hurries off. Preparing for such common situations
can prevent them from damaging an interpreter's practice.

PSYCHOLOGY OF NONDEAF PARTICIPANTS

Nothing in the literature addresses the nature of the nondeaf participants.
That makes sense, in that they share no definable characteristics—beyond not
being deaf and unable to communicate directly with the deaf participants.
Nonetheless, some speculations about their reactions can be useful, if only to
call attention to how little empirical information has been gathered.

Some nondeaf participants initially find that interpreted communication makes them uncomfortable. It is a novel situation and the ground rules
are unclear. Not knowing how to react, they tend to direct their comments
to the interpreter, which only makes the deaf participants and the interpreter
feel uncomfortable. Faced with this situation, many deaf people, like "Pat,"
have become adept at telling people to speak to them, not to the interpreter.
Interpreters can forestall such behavior if they have time before an assignment begins to explain to the nondeaf participants what to expect and how
to react.

In addition, correct positioning of the interpreter can allay the discomfort
that some nondeaf participants might feel. Seating the interpreter slightly behind the nondeaf participant lends itself to the nondeaf participant talking *to*
the deaf participant instead of the interpreter. That arrangement precludes
the influx of "Tell him," "Ask her," and other third-person references. When
they do occur, interpreters might shift their bodies slightly toward the deaf
participants and thereby present the nondeaf participants with a side view of
themselves, which cuts off eye contact and encourages direct communication
between the deaf and nondeaf participants.

To improve communication, nondeaf participants need to learn other
ground rules. Such instruction often can be given only as the occasion arises.
Few people would retain the basic requisites over the extended periods of
time between meetings with deaf participants. Those who do have frequent
encounters with deaf people can quickly learn how to participate appropriately. Ideally, deaf participants should ask nondeaf people to speak at a normal pace, to address their comments to them, not to speak while a deaf person
is signing or another person is speaking, and not to force their attentions on
the interpreter. While having the deaf person present these guidelines in a
simple, unemotional manner at the outset of the first meeting would be ideal,
many deaf people have not, themselves, learned how to manage interpreted
situations. If the interpreter foresees the need for such suggestions, the inter-

preter may suggest to the deaf participants, before the meeting begins, that instructing the nondeaf participants would be appropriate. It would then become the deaf participants' responsibility.

PSYCHOLOGY OF INTERPRETING INTERACTIONS

A question of paramount importance to interpreting is how well it functions. A young deaf woman of our acquaintance recently attended her first convention. She was appalled to find that she could understand only about half of what was being interpreted. Querying two older deaf adults, she was told that they often had similar experiences. One even said that because of this difficulty she sometimes avoided interpreted conferences. What factors operated to bring about these disconcerting circumstances? Was the interpretation at fault? Were the deaf participants lacking in essentials needed for comprehension?

Perhaps the speaker's manner of presentation defeats even the best attempts at interpretation. Or the material may be too difficult for the audience to grasp, regardless of how it is presented. As this sample of questions and potential explanations indicate, the issue is a complex one, not amenable to the usual one-variable-at-a-time experimentation. Obviously, however, the future of interpreting depends on gaining an increased understanding of how these numerous factors—the interpreters, participants, messages, settings—interact with each other.

Blame the Interpreter!

Interpreters are not immune to the reactions of the people for whom they interpret. For some of these participants, interpreters are expected to be error-free under all circumstances. Interpreters are, in effect, victims of their profession's novelty. The complex nature of interpreting has yet to be impressed on many people, including some frequent users of interpreting services. As a result, interpreters are sometimes unfairly pigeonholed into a simplistic sign-to-word and word-to-sign model that ignores the contributions of setting, linguistic competence, intelligibility of a speaker, and participants' language proficiencies. When interpreting goes awry, the interpreter may, unfairly, bear the blame.

This misconception does not go unnoticed by interpreters. To avoid reinforcing it, interpreters can take steps to improve their chances of successful performance. One such step is to prepare in advance of a speech by scanning the text. But is it fair that interpreters make such requests of speakers? Some would say no, but that attitude may be a reflection of idiosyncratic presentation styles. A presenter might ad lib much of a speech or simply feel more comfortable operating without written notes. Still, such an attitude is surprising when it comes from participants with considerable experience in interpreted situations:

> Only the other day I heard that an influential member of the local deaf community who was to give a talk at a public event had severely rebuked an interpreter who had called to request a copy of the speech in advance, saying, "don't you have any faith at all in your interpreting abilities? Interpreters shouldn't need a script to be able to work." Similarly, many hearing consumers of interpreting services feel it is a waste of time providing written drafts of texts, or taking the time for a briefing with the interpreter in advance of an interpreting assignment. This is a great pity, *both* from the point of view of the person wanting to get his message across, and from the point of view of the recipients of the message. These kinds of attitudes will change whenever sufficient awareness is developed among both interpreters and consumers. Responsibility does not lie with consumers alone. Interpreters themselves, and their organizations, must also develop clear and explicit policies in these areas, and cooperate with consumers and their organizations in order to develop higher levels of consumer awareness. (Coppock, 1992, p. 41; emphasis in original)

We concur that cooperation is important. An interpreting assignment should not be confused with a contest. The interpreter is providing a service, not engaging in a test of competence. Although all participants are entitled to their opinions, they should at least be agreed on the basic point of interpreting: to facilitate communication.

The possibility of misunderstandings, of course, is not restricted to interpreted situations. All people experience misunderstandings from time to time. Because two deaf people sign to one another or two nondeaf people speak to each other does not assure accurate communication. In either case, however, they usually monitor the communication and take steps to repair misunderstandings. In interpreted encounters, initiators bear responsibility to express themselves clearly and to take actions when they believe their messages have been misunderstood.

Who Should Be in Charge?

The magazine *Deaf Life* recently asked its readers, "Which organization should have authority over interpreters, their evaluation and certification?" ("Readers' Responses," Vol. 4, No. 7, 1991, p. 34) Surprisingly, of those who responded to this question, only 5% supported the NAD and only 19% the RID. Three out of four respondents suggested other organizations or combinations of organizations.

Lacking evidence that the responses are representative of the deaf population, the survey by *Deaf Life* cannot be accepted as evidence of the majority of deaf people's feelings. However, its dominant finding merits considera-tion: *Deaf people want to participate in deciding who will interpret for them.* They want a direct role in determining the quality of this service and in promoting its improvement.

Wanting greater assurance of quality seems a reasonable attitude for deaf people to have when contemplating a function as vital to them as interpret-ing. The consequences of maladroit interpreting can be devastating. Still, in-terpreters can argue that lay people have no input to medical licensing or to policing of physicians' practices; the same is true of other professions such as law and dentistry. Regarding the interpreter as a professional has some bear-ing on this issue, although it is obviously more complicated than a semantic decision can resolve.

Whether significant participation by deaf persons will continue, it should be pointed out that both RID and AVLIC have welcomed deaf participation from the beginnings of their organizations. The first two directors of RID, Emil Ladner and Albert Pimentel, were both deaf, assuring deaf input at the highest level of that organization. In states and provinces with certification programs, deaf people usually are represented on the governing boards and examination committees, but their representation may only be symbolic. On some certifying bodies, deaf persons make up such a small proportion of the examining com-mittee that their influence is negligible. Deaf representatives with forceful per-sonalities may be able to exert disproportionate leverage in such circumstances, but they tend to "burn out" quickly. A small number of deaf people on a large governing body may be dominated easily by the majority, and their influence is likely to be reduced to insignificant proportions. Again, this question is one that deaf people and interpreters would do well to keep foremost in their dia-logues, reviewing their positions as conditions change.

PSYCHOLOGICAL RESEARCH

Research has been undertaken that provides some insights into the interpret-ing process. Researchers at the National Technical Institute for the Deaf (Stin-son, Meath-Lang, & McLeod, 1981) presented to 20 deaf college students, in counterbalanced order, an interpreted videotape of a lecture and a print ver-sion of a second lecture. In a second experiment, 16 deaf college students viewed interpreted videotapes of the same two lectures. Students wrote what they recalled immediately after each presentation. To score their recollections, each presentation was divided into four equal segments and the number of ideas counted and divided by the total number that had been predetermined by the experimenters to be included in each quarter. Both experiments found that students recalled more from the first half than the second half of each lec-ture, regardless of method of presentation. In the first experiment, students re-called more from the printed lecture than from the interpreted one.

The experimenters faced some unusual results. Most learning studies find that people and animals recall best the first and last segments of various memory tasks, including turns in a maze, lists of items to recall, and so forth. The experimenters guessed that the scores reflected visual fatigue, and they recommended that frequent breaks in lecture material be given deaf students to

---

Profile: Brenda Nicodemus

Brenda Nicodemus holds the RID Certificate of Interpretation and the Certificate of Transliteration. She has been interpreting professionally since 1989, has served on the RID National Legislative Committee, and is now employed at the Indiana School for the Deaf. She has performed with the bilingual performance troupe Hands Alive! Her interest in languages led her to get a Master of Arts degree in Linguistics from Indiana University.

Brenda brings a rare yet desirable element to the field of sign-language interpreting—she is a researcher. She has a particular interest in the application of ASL and English linguistic research to the field of interpreting and has conducted a fascinating study of gender variation in interpretation. This study is a timely rejoinder to gender-related questions that are frequently tossed about by interpreters but all too often receive a flippant response. "There's no difference in the way male and female people interpret." On the basis of this one study we cannot unequivocally say, "Yes, there is," but we can now open the doors to further investigation. Research in this area will inform interpreter education programs of the adjustments they might have to make in monitoring and enhancing the interpretations of their students. Brenda provides us with a brief look at this work and its results:

> Communication breakdowns and mutual misunderstandings between men and women have been a behind-doors subject for years. Linguists have finally documented what we have always suspected; that men and women do communicate differently.
>
> We know that men and women exhibit unique language forms in both word choice and pronunciation. There are marked differences in the intonation patterns, discourse style, and amount of talk women and men generate. It has been argued that men and women differ in the kinds of language they use and how they use it because the sexes often fill distinctly different roles in language communities. Some speculate that the main aim of women's talk is the maintenance of social relationships, whereas men's is the exchange of information.
>
> Research on gender variation in language poses interesting questions for us as interpreters. Our business is language and

Profile: Brenda Nicodemus *Continued*

communication. Our goal is to create cross-language messages for equivalent impact: We want to express the same thing in one language that has been expressed in another language. In addition, we're a predominantly female group. The question follows: when interpreting for the opposite sex, does our interpretation reflect our gender bias?

In an attempt to examine this question, I conducted a pilot study in which five male and five female professional interpreters viewed a videotape of a Deaf man using ASL in five role-play situations. The scenarios had the Deaf man communicating with another man in face-threatening situations including teasing a friend about his weight; telling a dirty joke; and threatening to fire an employee. The interpreters were instructed to view the tape and provide as accurate an English interpretation as possible.

The results were startling. The male and female interpreters used linguistic forms characteristic of their gender. For example, in one scenario, a male interpreter said, "You're fat and real lazy!" A female, interpreting the same scenario said, "I think you're . . . you're, uh, too heavy, y'know. You're slowed down." In the dirty-joke scenario, all five male interpreters used slang and vulgar terms in their interpretation. For the same passages, the female interpreters used euphemistic terms and other less graphic descriptions. When the Deaf man role played the firing of an employee, one male interpreter said, "If things don't change, I'm going to fire you." A female interpreter viewing the same situation stated, "I'd appreciate it if you'd really try to improve and if I don't see things changing, I think, I'm afraid, I'm going to have to fire you."

The majority of female interpreters employed politeness strategies to soften face-threatening messages. Their language was indirect in both grammatical structure and word choice. In addition, the women used a variety of face-saving devices such as hedges, softeners, hesitancies, and minimizers in their communication. Male interpreters tended to be more direct and utilize less mitigating strategies.

The results of this study indicate that interpreters do exhibit gender biases in their work, and reminds us to continue our study of the complex, multifaceted event that is communication. As interpreters, we must be steadfast students of not only other people's communication, but our own personal filters. The excitement and challenge of the interpreting profession is that it inspires a lifelong study of language—our own and others.

allow the visual system to recover. However, this explanation ignores the fact that the same phenomenon occurred when students read the lecture, which presumably allowed them to pace themselves and reduce or eliminate visual fatigue. With respect to the finding that students' recollections were greater when the lecture was printed than when it was interpreted, the experimenters recommended that deaf students be given practice to improve their ability to attend to and remember interpreted lectures: "The educational implication of this idea is that deliberate practice may be involved in learning from lecture material" (Stinson et al., 1981, p. 11). They did not highlight the finding that students who had both lectures interpreted recalled 10% *less* than those who had one interpreted and one printed lecture. Perhaps they felt it reflected little more than individual differences in the two samples. The experimenters did caution against a rush to apply their results, because the experimental conditions were artificial and would be expected to vary in real applications.

Another experimental approach to tease out variables affecting interpreting was conducted by a group at LaGuardia Community College (Livingston, Singer, & Abrahamson, 1994). The study was rich in design and yielded a wealth of provocative findings, but generalization of the findings is restricted by the small sample size. The principal finding was that all of the deaf students scored higher when the presentations were interpreted and questions asked in ASL. This result held true no matter which method students said they preferred. Results did vary by ASL interpreters, but not by transliterators. Other contributing variables included students' educational levels, background knowledge of the subject, and communicative competencies. Question type (literal versus analytic) was studied, along with kind of presentation (lecture versus narrative). Unfortunately, the small sample precluded multiple-factor analysis that would assign weights to the various factors. On the basis of their experience, the researchers state "It is crucially important to understand as many as possible of the variables that must be considered when students seek interpreters for their courses so that an accurate assignment of resources can be made" (Livingston et al., 1994, p. 9).

It may be years before that understanding is achieved. The variables are numerous and may interact with one another in unusual ways. Patient accumulation of research will eventually yield a comprehensive and comprehensible picture of the significant factors and their interactions. In route to acquiring that picture, research will be needed to create measures of the variables—an effort worth undertaking. The more the stakeholders contribute, the swifter and more productive the results will be. This last statement is said in recognition of the social nature of the interpreting enterprise, which should not be overlooked in the scientific search. Researchers should welcome the active involvement of interpreters and participant representatives in their studies, a development that will most likely lead sooner to a valid psychology of sign language interpreting.

A surprising gap in the research is the absence of research about the influence of gender on the interpreting equation. (See the profile on Brenda Nicodemus on pages 94–95 for a discussion of the effects of gender in interpreting situations.) Do interpreters react to the gender of the other participants? Do the deaf and nondeaf participants respond better to male or female interpreters? Although these might be moot questions given the overwhelming number of female interpreters in the field, answers to them will take us one step closer to understanding the interpreting process.

SUMMARY

Psychologists have touched upon many factors that could prove crucial to interpreting. Unfortunately, research to date raises more questions than answers. The interpreters' personalities have scarcely been investigated as a source of interpreting effectiveness. How an interpreter's intelligence, attitudes, and emotions contribute to their practices is acknowledged to be important, but also insufficiently understood. Psychologists' studies have not tested techniques interpreters might use to overcome conflicting feelings and beliefs that might interfere with their work. Even more important, research has not produced ways to overcome personal and situational stresses affecting interpreters.

The psychology of the participants, deaf and nondeaf, also lacks the substantial body of studies that it deserves. The Interactive Model of Interpreting emphasizes the contributions to mediated communication made by all who participate in it. Because the participants all play major roles, the interpreter alone should not be the sole focus of efforts to make interpreting more effective. The preceding discussion has pointed to the obvious fact that participants' knowledge of and attitudes toward interpreting undergo continuous changes. How best to keep interpreters abreast of these changes has not been addressed sufficiently.

Finally, the interaction of personalities—the participants' and the interpreters'—has barely been touched. The studies described here warn against simple conclusions. Like most social encounters, interpreted sessions contain a number of elements whose interactions are reciprocal. The interpreter's personality influences the participants, and the participants' personalities influence the interpreter. So far, research has provided few clues that enable interpreters to predict the outcomes of these interactions, let alone to manage them.

6

VARIETIES OF SETTINGS

In keeping with the Interactive Model of Interpreting's emphases on the influencing characteristics of both the environment and the participants, this chapter looks at variations in interpreting situations resulting from a large number of factors:

- The form of interpreting—sign language and oral, individual and group, team and relay
- Differences in the participants—such as deafblind, minimal language competency (MLC), emotionally disturbed, non-English-background
- The setting—legal, medical, religious, and theatrical, but not educational, which is considered in Chapter 10, because there is so much to delineate about interpreting in classrooms as opposed to other settings, and because more interpreters work in educational programs than in any other setting.

Each variation in form, clientele, and setting introduces features beyond those already presented in the earlier chapters. Rather than being exhaustive, the discussions that follow focus on elements that distinguish each variation from the others, distinctions that pose special problems for interpreters and participants.

VARIATIONS IN FORM AND PARTICIPANTS

Not all deaf persons know American Sign Language (ASL) or prefer a visually oriented presentation. Interpreting for deafblind persons and those who do not know sign language (or do not prefer it as a means of interpreted communication) require that sign language interpreters deviate from their customary signing.

Deafblind Participants

Interpreters should have a sound grasp of the impact that varying degrees of deafness and blindness will have on the communication skills of a deafblind person. A loss of both hearing and vision creates a synergistic effect with great ramifications for the development of language or, in the case of adventitiously deafblind persons, for the accommodation of communication skills to a linguistic environment containing less sensory input. The age at onset of an individual's deafness and blindness helps an interpreter understand the type of communication a deafblind person might need. Whether the etiology is maternal rubella or genetic related, born-deafblind persons usually have the same communication needs. For adventitiously deafblind persons, age at onset provides clues about their communication needs, which, as discussed below, are highly heterogeneous across this population.

We will briefly illustrate how complications in communication arising from deafblindness is not readily generalized from one person to another. This is clearly shown in those people who have Usher's syndrome, a genetic condition that is the leading cause of deafblindness. People with Usher's syndrome are congenitally deaf and begin to experience progressive blindness around the age of 10 to 15 or later due to retinitis pigmentosa (Sherrill, 1993). Tunnel vision or a narrowing of the field of vision is common and typically becomes progressively worse as a person ages. Deafblind people with tunnel vision will most often require a particular seating arrangement when using interpreters. For some deafblind participants, normal signing will suffice as long as the interpreter is positioned far enough away so that the signed interpretation fits into their narrow field of vision. For others, the vision field might be so narrow that alternatives such as signing in the palms of the deafblind person's hands becomes necessary.

Indeed, using alternative means of communication is probably the most significant fact about interpreting for deafblind participants because *there is no one way to communicate that will satisfy them all*. This is due in part to the various degrees to which a deafblind person can hear and see. Some have both residual hearing and vision, allowing them to use what little information they are able to gain from these two senses. Some have limited use of only the ears or only the eyes. Still others have no access to the outside world through either hearing or sight. In the area of communication some deafblind people know signing, whereas others, especially adventitiously deafblind people, are able to speak orally but rely on other means of communication to receive information. To complicate matters further, some have additional disabilities that interfere with communication.

One manual that offers a "complete" guide to communicating with deaf-blind persons lists 73 distinct approaches, none of which is preferred by *all* or even *most* deafblind persons (Kates & Schein, 1980). To determine how best to communicate with a person who is deafblind, interpreters must inquire about the person's preferences at the beginning of an assignment. For example, a person with tunnel vision requires interpreters to be far enough away so their signing fits into, and stays within, a narrow visual field. Interpreters may need some time to adapt to this arrangement, and they may find it uncomfortable to remain in a fixed position while taking care to sign within a smaller-than-usual frame. Moreover, given the changes in communication requirements that can occur in a person who is losing hearing and sight progressively over time interpreters should inquire about any changes in communication preference of those deafblind people for whom they might not have interpreted recently.

It is clear that communication with deafblind people must be oriented to the sense of touch. While some deafblind people are able to see signs under certain conditions, most of them understand signs by touching the hands of the person who is signing. Modifications of signs to adapt them from the visual to the tactile mode are numerous. Though several decades old, DiPietro's (1978) *Guidelines on Interpreting for Deaf-Blind Persons* provides an informative introduction to serving deafblind persons. In the different types of interpreting for deafblind persons, both high and low technology come into play. Some examples are as follows:

- *Palm printing:* The interpreter draws letters of the alphabet in the deafblind person's hand to form words. Simple as it sounds, the method requires drawing the letters in special ways.
- *Alphabet glove:* The deafblind person wears a glove that has the letters of the alphabet in specific places on the palm and fingers. Words are tapped out by pressing on each letter's location.
- *Hand-over-hand signing:* Deafblind people rest their hands on top of an interpreter's hands and follow the movements. This method tends to be used with older persons because young children with small hands might find it difficult to discern the another person's handshapes and might not be able to synchronize the movement of their hands with that of the signer.
- *Fingerspelling in the hand:* Deafblind persons cup one hand over the interpreter's hand as the latter fingerspells. Like the preceding method, this method depends on the deafblind person's knowledge of the language being spelled and on the sense of touch.
- *Morse Code:* The interpreter taps the code on the deafblind person's palm or back of the hand. For deafblind persons whose peripheral sensitivity is lost or reduced, usually as a result of diabetes, their exposed backs—which have greater tactual sensitivity than the palms or backs of the hands—can be used.

- *Braille Card* and *Braille machines:* For those who know Braille, the interpreter can move a deafblind person's finger from one letter to another on a card containing the Braille alphabet or can use a Braille typewriter, which has six tiny balls that raise to create Braille letters that can be felt on the tips of the deafblind person's fingers.
- *Tadoma:* A technique for "tactual lipreading," in which deafblind people place their thumbs on the interpreter's lips and their fingers on the mandible and along the throat, in order to feel the vibrations and movements. With this information they distinguish between voiced (e.g., /b/, /r/, /g/) and voiceless (e.g., /p/, /wh/, /k/) phonemes. Though still popular with some deafblind people, it is losing its appeal, mainly because of concern about hygiene.

These examples do not exhaust the ways in which one can communicate with deafblind persons. Older deafblind people may be accustomed to communication methods such as Morse Code that are no longer taught. Other methods, taking advantage of newer technologies, can be expected to emerge.

Deafblind people often need input about aspects of their environment to help them fully understand the interpretation. An effective interpreter for deafblind persons will inform them about relevant auditory and visual conditions. Just as an interpreter indicates to deaf participants a sudden noise that is evident to the nondeaf participants, so an interpreter for deafblind persons might indicate that someone has entered the room or that there is a thunderstorm, in order to clarify the remarks being interpreted.

Intervenors

In Great Britain and Canada, those who meet the communication requirements of deafblind persons are called *intervenors*. The term's definition has been clouded by confusing applications. In the National (Great Britain) Deafblind and Rubella Association's journal, an intervenor is described as "the provider of information about a deafblind person's world, enabling him or her to understand their environment and make intelligent decisions." However, the article goes on to question the name:

> Intervention was chosen as a reasonably accurate means of describing a way of working with deafblind people. Intervention was not suddenly invented, it was a gradual evolution instigated by a practical need to maintain the skill levels of people who are deafblind in between more formal education. At some stage in the process it became necessary to call it something—it could easily have been enabler, mediator, or assistant. The important thing to remember is that the process did not stem from the word: rather the word was imposed on the process. ("Intervention," 1994, p. 11)

The work of intervenors frequently goes beyond serving as a communication facilitator. In Great Britain, intervenors may tutor, implement sensory stimulation programs, assist in mobility and feeding, and facilitate social interactions. Intervenors are expected to cooperate with other professionals, maintain simple records, and participate in the organization and supervision of extracurricular activities, such as swimming and field trips. While these remarks may seem to limit intervenors largely to students in educational settings, in practice intervenors serve both adults and children in any setting.

Culture

Because of the prevalence of Usher's syndrome, many deafblind people spend the first part of their lives in the Deaf community. When they lose their sight later in life, many of them still remain a part of the Deaf community because they retain signing as their preferred method of communication. Some might learn the British two-hand manual alphabet, which for them is a more convenient means of fingerspelling than the one hand manual alphabet used in ASL (see the box titled "British Two-Hand Manual Alphabet"). Moreover, deaf people are fast to pick up the two-hand alphabet when a fellow member of their community is dependent on it for communication, which significantly reduces the isolation that a deafblind person might feel in this community.

In specific geographic areas, there are deafblind communities apart from the Deaf communities. Detroit and New Orleans, for example, both have large deafblind societies because of the high incidence of Usher syndrome in their respective states. Seattle probably has the largest deafblind community in the United States because of the numerous services it provides for this

---

British Two-Hand Manual Alphabet

The two-hand manual alphabet used by deafblind people in the United States and Canada is the same as the manual alphabet used by deaf people in Great Britain, Australia, New Zealand, and some other Commonwealth countries. It is popular with deafblind people because the sense of touch plays major role in determining what letters are being formed. This makes the identification of letters easier than trying to determine the shape of a hand, which a deafblind person must do when reading the one-hand manual alphabet.

population. A deafblind-interpreting etiquette has emerged in these communities, which offers some suggestions for interpreters like the following:

- During initial encounters, gently touch the deafblind person's arm or shoulder to get attention.
- Place your hands in the deafblind person's hands and introduce yourself.
- Alert the deafblind person to who else is in the room.
- Work out signs for names and other matters likely to arise during the assignment.
- Describe the visual and auditory aspects of the environment, when these contribute to understanding what is being interpreted—for example, that there is vigorous applause or that a speaker is showing a graph to illustrate a point.
- Keep fingernails short.
- Use lotion before starting and during breaks to prevent chapped hands.
- When interpreting one to one, adopt techniques to reduce your fatigue.
- Determine if you are also to act as a sighted guide.
- Sit or stand on the same level as the deafblind person.
- Statements that require sight for comprehension, such as "Place the book over here," might be rephrased to "Place the book on the front table."

These suggestions convey a sense of what interpreting for a deafblind person may entail. Interpreters may also join in relay interpreting, described later on, as this technique can optimize interpreting. For additional information about deafblind interpreting, consult Smith (1992) and the December 1997 publication of *RID Views*, Volume 14, Number 11.

Compensation
Does deafblind interpreting deserve higher-than-normal compensation? Added compensation would reflect greater responsibilities and skills. It would recognize the increased physical demands, like bearing the weight of another person's hands when signing, holding the same hand position for an extended period of time when palm writing or using the alphabet glove, and concentrating intently to transmit both auditory and visual information. However, the greater physical demands could be ameliorated by a team approach that would provide adequate rest between interpreting intervals. These considerations should enter into decisions about deafblind interpreters' compensation.

Oral Interpreting

Some deaf people depend on lipreading or, more appropriately, speechreading for communication. Most of these people do not know sign language or, do not know it well enough to rely on it for communicating. These people attempt to communicate in the speech modality; but when they are unaccustomed to the person speaking, or they have a poor view of the speaker, or the speaker has an idiosyncrasy that interferes with speechreading, such as a beard, they may request oral interpretation.

Like their sign language counterparts, qualified oral interpreters undergo a preparation program. RID maintains certification for oral interpreters. They must be good articulators, avoiding overly emphatic and lazy lip movements. They should be well grounded in the principles of oral interpreting (Northcutt, 1984). To assist the deaf participant's speechreading, oral interpreters use a number of strategies, such as these:

- Keeping pace with the speaker
- Avoiding lip-smacking sounds or whispers that contribute no meaningful linguistic information and would disturb those who can hear
- In the case of novel ideas, proper names, technical terms, and statistical and chemical formulae, writing or fingerspelling them

Rephrasing is a key tactic used by oral interpreters. In reproducing a spoken message, an oral interpreter avoids *homophenes* (words that look alike on the lips, such as *time* and *dime*) especially when context will not clarify what is being said. "He grabbed a bat and ran" might be rephrased "He grabbed a baseball bat and ran." The additional word *baseball* facilitates lipreading. "He thinks he's the king" might be rendered "He thinks he's so important, just like the king."

Oral interpreters may or may not also be able to sign, although many do, but all will add gestures to boost comprehension. The statement "I will never give in" can be accompanied with a sweep of the hand to the side and the palm down for emphasis. Likewise, facial expressions and body language are critical. Deaf people who depend on speechreading want interpreters to use visual indicators when needed for understanding. The expression "I couldn't care less" stands out more clearly when interpreters toss their heads and lift one shoulder. When conveying numbers, oral interpreters may draw them in the air, because many numbers cannot be deciphered by reading the lips alone. Effective oral interpreting uses supplementary visual information to enhance comprehension.

What does the oral interpreter do about deaf persons' expressions? The interpreter must respect those who prefer to speak for themselves. Voicing for oral deaf persons can be difficult, as each deaf person may have a different idea of how to say a word. Some deaf people pronounce words as they are spelled—a practice that English often does not reward. Some oral deaf persons might even use some signing in their communication. They may have been taught to speak as they sign, a habit they have difficulty holding back. So, if deaf persons ask the interpreter to voice, then the interpreter should explain that they cannot speak at the same time as the interpreter; it creates aural confusion. How these instances are managed must, of course, be decided in advance with each deaf participant.

Cued Speech Transliteration

Another form of interpreting that is reliant on the oral modality is *Cued Speech*. It is neither a sign language nor a separate language code, but a set of eight handshapes "representing groups of consonant sounds and hand placements denoting groups of vowel sounds" that are "utilized in combination with natural speech movements to present a visually distinct model of the oral utterance in its spoken form" (Fleetwood & Metzger, 1990, pp. 19, 21). These handshapes are designed to overcome ambiguities when trying to speechread.

Although hand signals are used, it is inappropriate to call Cued Speech a form of manual communication, because the hand signals by themselves convey no meaningful language. Nevertheless, many educators and members of the Deaf community mistakenly allege that Cued Speech is another way of signing, whereas oral educators see it as a supplement to an education program that emphasizes speech and listening skills.

Cued Speech originated in 1966 and, to date, has been adopted by a minute number of deaf people. Even among this small group its use is often discontinued once a deaf person becomes an adult because there is no significant group of people who can and will use it for social interactions. Those who interpret for them must take training, typically for eight weeks. Whatever the future of this method, it currently provides an adjunct to oral interpreting.

Relay Interpreting

How can an interpreter function when the deaf person has had little or no education and has no fluency in a formal sign language? The interpreter will have to be adept at pantomime and the use of nonstandard signs, and have considerable insight into the deaf person's probable communication habits—characteristics that might be difficult to divine. Lacking those qualities, the interpreter may join with a deaf person who has experience in communicating with deaf persons with minimal language competencies (MLC). The interpreter and the experienced deaf person then engage in what is called *relay interpreting*.

In relay interpreting, the MLC deaf person gestures and signs to the deaf relay person, who conveys the message to the nondeaf interpreter, who in turn voices the message to complete the relay. Messages for the target deaf person are signed by the interpreter to the deaf relay, who transmits the message through pantomime, signs, and gestures.

Relay interpreting can also occur when a deaf person refuses to sign to a nondeaf person (the interpreter) and requests that there be another deaf person present. The deaf person making the request may be a highly capable signer and might not have anything personal against the interpreter but simply has a preference in some situations, especially those that are stressful, to sign in the presence of another deaf person.

Certified Deaf Interpreter
Deaf persons working as relay interpreters may not be qualified as such, although it would certainly be desirable. In recognition of the importance of relay interpreting, RID issues a special certificate to deaf people who participate in relays—Certified Deaf Interpreter (CDI). It is available only to deaf and hard-of-hearing persons, but there is no stipulation that their native language is ASL. Still, competence in both ASL and English is crucial for all CDIs just as it is for other sign language interpreters. Beyond these two languages, CDIs are valued for their ability to understand forms of communication that may be esoteric to nondeaf interpreters in that region. Although a CDI may work solo, most of the situations that call for their use lend themselves to relay interpreting. Interpreting for emotionally disturbed persons and for deafblind people are two examples of circumstances calling for CDIs.

Home Signs and Foreign Languages
In some situations a deaf participant only uses nonstandard signs, such as those commonly referred to as *home signs*. In other situations, a deaf participant might only know a foreign sign language. Few North American interpreters are fluent, for example, in both ASL and Russian, Ukrainian, Vietnamese, or Malaysian sign languages. The interpreter may need to recruit relatives or friends of the target person to join in a relay. This is an acceptable arrangement only when there is no other option, because it raises doubts about impartiality and confidentiality in the interpreting process.

Emotionally Disturbed Persons
Relay interpreting may be helpful in interpreting for some emotionally disturbed persons who may know signs but are unwilling to communicate with a stranger. The person with whom they will communicate may be a family member or close friend, but the interpreter's presence increases the accuracy of the interpretation and provides some assurance of professionalism. After one or two relay sessions, the emotionally disturbed individual may come to accept the interpreter.

Deafblind Relay Interpreting
An unusual relay occurs in conferences attended by several deafblind persons and involving more than one deaf relay. A platform interpreter signs the

speech to an interpreter—very often one who is deaf—who then transmits it to a deafblind person by one of the methods described previously. With three or more deafblind persons in the same audience, there may be three or more different communication modes, because deafblind participants cannot share the same interpreter.

Team Interpreting

Team interpreting refers to two or more interpreters working together, not just physically but intellectually. In team interpreting, each interpreter takes a turn to ensure that fatigue does not hamper them. Typically, team interpreting involves two interpreters, each signing for twenty- to thirty-minute periods. The amount of time depends not only on the need for periods of rest, but also on the need for consistency in the interpretation. Too short a period may distract the participants, who must become accustomed or reaccustomed to a different voice or style of signing each time there is a changeover.

On the intellectual side, when team members are not actively interpreting, they can support the one who is. They can correct mis-voiced signs and fill in unheard or mis-heard speech. Team interpreting confirms the old saying that two heads are better than one. Likewise, four hands can improve on two.

VARIATIONS IN SETTINGS

The Interactive Model of Interpreting predicts that each setting will pose different issues and considerations for interpreters. Following the model, this section introduces problems and issues specific to several interpreting environments and suggests the kinds of preparation interpreters need to make in order to overcome special conditions.

Legal

Interpreters must be aware of a particular court's attitude toward interpreters. Most judges, but not all, will be sympathetic and endeavor to accommodate them. While interpreters need to be placed in positions where they can see and be seen by deaf participants, they must make their needs known in a respectful manner and at the proper time. If the court has engaged them, they should address their requests to the judge. If they are employed by an attorney, they must let the attorney make the arrangements.

Court etiquette may take precedence over interpreting ethics, as one interpreter found. Interpreting for a deaf man who was very angry and swearing profusely during his testimony, the interpreter was suddenly interrupted by the judge. Here is what transpired, in her own words:

> The judge said, "You don't use that kind of language in my courtroom." I interpreted that to the defendant, who continued to use the same language.
>
> The judge said again, looking at me, "Miss, I told you not to use that kind of language."
>
> I said, "I'm voice interpreting for the defendant using his language, his words."
>
> He said, "Young lady, I don't care what he's saying, you aren't to use that kind of language."
>
> At that point, I said, "Well, how would you like me to tell you what he's saying?" I was afraid I'd get kicked out of the courtroom for contempt because the judge was dead serious. Then the lawyer approached the bench, and the judge called a recess. We had a conference about the problem, and the judge learned to yell at the right person: the defendant. (Schmitz, 1994, p. 27)

Linguistic Prerequisites

In legal interpreting, the interpreter may encounter terms and phrases in Latin, like *duces tacem* (items relating to a subpoena) and *res ipsa loquitir* ("the thing speaks for itself"). Obviously, to interpret these expressions, the interpreter must know what they mean or, at least, be able to spell them correctly. Before accepting assignments for attorneys and judges, interpreters should consider taking a legal interpreting course, if one is offered in their region. They can study some textbooks that will familiarize them with legal vocabulary and meet with other interpreters who have worked in the courts.

Once in the courtroom, interpreters face stiff challenges to their craft, because the penalties for mistakes can be so high—to the participants. As an illustration, take the trial of four security guards charged with homicide. A great deal depended on the interpreting of a deaf witness's testimony. Did he mean to say, "Carl looked like he was choked," or "Carl looked like he was choking"? To the defendants charged in Carl's death, the translation was critical. In the same news report about that trial, the *Washington Post* related a less important, but most revealing, exchange—an exchange in which an ASL-wise defense attorney intervened to correct a misinterpretation of some difficult testimony:

> One deaf witness, describing the guards' struggle with Dupree, seemed to veer wildly off the subject. "They continued to wrestle, and then I noticed a spider," the interpreter translated.

The jury looked confused, until defense attorney Henry F. Schuelke broke in. "I am confident the witness did not see a spider. She saw a person named Spider." ("D.C. Trial Spotlights Challenge," 1992).

Though the incident may seem amusing, it exposes the hazards of simultaneous interpreting in a court of law. All parties—judge, jury, attorneys—scrutinize every word in their search for truth and justice. The interpreter must be prepared to shoulder this heavy burden on behalf of the court.

Qualifying Interpreters
The days when interpreters' qualifications were determined solely by their positive response to a judge's questions about their competencies in English and the target language may be coming to an end. The professionalization of interpreters obligates them to meet the court's requests for evidence of their professional standing. Court interpreters must be prepared to provide their relevant education, certifications, professional experiences, and references, such as names of judges and lawyers who can testify to their qualifications for the assignment. RID and AVLIC certifications frequently suffice as evidence of adequate qualifications. However, some state courts are considering setting, or have already set, their own standards. The Judicial Council of California has established the Advisory Committee for Certification of Interpreters for the Deaf, which has recommended guidelines for approval of a certification program for interpreters for deaf and hard-of-hearing persons. Other states may soon follow suit.

Interpersonal Relations and Confidentiality
As experienced interpreters know, it is not unusual for a deaf person to trust interpreters and expect them to be allies during interrogations and trials. This attitude can be extremely dangerous in legal settings, where confessions and other damaging information might be divulged by the deaf person. Police officers may use that trust in order to elicit such statements. To preclude such incidents, interpreters must advise the deaf participant that legal interpreting differs from other situations. By law, they must interpret everything as accurately and fully as possible. Interpreters are forbidden to edit what a deaf person signs.

While deaf persons also may expect their interpreters to maintain confidentiality this expectation is not always upheld in a court of law. In most state and federal courts, interpreters can be subpoenaed to disclose information obtained while interpreting, which obviously violates the confidentiality ethic. At present, interpreters in most jurisdictions do not have the same right to maintain confidentiality that is given to priests, lawyers, and physicians. Some states have taken steps to prevent this breach of interpreting ethics, and more may follow. Interpreters must remain abreast of these developments. In the meantime, they should be certain that the deaf participants understand this deviation from usual practice.

Malpractice

Interpreters should consider having themselves videotaped where the communications are not privileged. Police interrogation provides an example of the desirability of being videotaped; it parallels the use police make of videotapes and audiotapes. In one instance, an interpreter's interpretation of the Miranda warning was the sole thrust of a motion to suppress evidence. The evidence in this case was a deaf man's confession of raping a woman. The deaf man claimed that he did not understand the intended meaning of the warning because of the way it was signed to him. In deliberations of this motion, the interpreter was grilled for two hours, while experts testified about the deaf man's linguistic competence. Had the interrogation been videotaped, that record would likely have resolved the controversy quickly.

In these litigious days, interpreters would be well advised to purchase malpractice insurance. We know of no case of an interpreter being sued for malpractice—as yet. Although videotaping can provide evidence of what actually was signed, it cannot resolve quarrels about the accuracy of the signing or voicing.

Interpreting for Deaf Jurors

A new situation has arisen in the past few years. Customarily, deaf people have been denied the right to be jurors. Lawyers and judges have argued that a nonjuror, the interpreter, would be present during jury deliberations—a violation of most codes of legal conduct. That ruling was challenged in a few states, and the results have enabled deaf people—with interpreters—to serve on juries. For interpreters this change has led to new challenges. They must interpret all manner of speech, from Latin to jargon, endeavoring to convey more than the semantics.

Jurors must decide from a witness's manner if the testimony given is credible. Should the interpreter, therefore, ask to stand next to the witness box, in order to enable the deaf juror to observe the manner in which the testimony is given? To do so would be contrary to many courts' customs. Since the court engages the interpreter, the interpreter should confer with the judge about such matters.

Health-Related Settings

Opportunities to interpret in health-related situations can occur in hospitals and physicians' offices and even in homes in areas where rural doctors still make house calls. Interpreting assignments range from childbirth classes to major surgery. Regardless of where the assignment is, the lexicon may relate to anatomical descriptions, blood chemistry, cardiovascular conditions, genetic counseling, specific diseases, and many other medical topics that can challenge interpreters' vocabularies.

Interpreting in a health-related setting is not limited solely to the exchange between a deaf patient and a nondeaf doctor, nurse, or health official. Deaf people have become physicians, nurses, dentists, physical therapists, chiropractors, podiatrists, and osteopaths. To this list can be added veterinarians. Michigan State University recently graduated a deaf veterinarian who had two full-time interpreters for four years of veterinary school, and the same university now has another deaf student in veterinary studies. The increased availability of interpreting services in postsecondary institutions has contributed this boon in opportunities to deaf people.

Emotional Challenges

The interpreter in a health-related setting must be prepared for stresses, such as embarrassment, when a patient is naked or there is discussion of intimate topics; anxiety, when conveying information about severe injuries and deadly diseases; and nausea, when confronted with the sight of blood. One interpreter recounts his experience during a medical procedure, in which he carefully placed himself in the patient's view but with his back to the doctor, who was operating on the deaf patient's infected toenail:

> The doctor caught me off guard, however, when he said, "Wow, look at this!"
>
> Being accustomed to following the doctor's orders, I made the mistake of looking in his direction, and when I saw the toenail, I became lightheaded and unable to concentrate. But before I could stop working, I had to explain to the patient why I was unable to work even while I was losing my ability to work. I had to sit down and recover, temporarily becoming a patient myself. I never would have thought that could happen to me. So much for trying to be invulnerable! (Schmitz, 1994, p. 26)

Such situations make it all the more important for interpreters to prepare themselves psychologically to keep their professional distance from the participants.

Environmental Challenges

In addition to emotional stresses, interpreters may be affronted by sensory aspects of some medical environments. They may have involuntary responses to olfactory stimuli, such as burning flesh, or to the high-pitched whine of a dental drill. These environmental aspects compound difficulties that may arise from having to work in close quarters, like a physician's examining room, or in having to move about continually to stay out of a dentist's way while still remaining in the deaf participant's sight. These factors affect the ability to interpret.

Attitudinal Issues

Another side to interpreting in health-related settings to which interpreters must be sensitive are professionals' attempts to use the interpreter to gain more information about the deaf patient. This can also be a problem when professionals "assume that the interpreter will take over the role of the health care practitioner" (Frishberg, 1986, p. 116). To counter such misconceptions, interpreters and deaf participants, when able, must explain that interpreters only interpret; they do not provide information or opinions, nor do they participate in handling equipment.

Not all deaf patients and deaf health professionals want an interpreter's services. Health issues can be extremely sensitive. Interpreters should understand that how a deaf person regards them might change from one setting to another. One interpreter viewed this issue as a love/hate relationship—love, because of the access they provide, and hate, because of the implied dependency—and relates the following story:

> I remember a conversation I had with two deaf friends which seemed to encapsulate the dilemma. I asked them if they preferred to have an interpreter along when they went to visit the doctor. My one friend said that he never wanted an interpreter along, that he preferred to write everything back and forth. My second friend countered by asking what if the conversation involved an operation or serious procedure. In that case she wanted an interpreter that she knew and trusted, to be sure that all of the information was conveyed accurately . . . . Many deaf persons would rather risk not getting all the information, than risk losing control as often happens when a family member or friend interprets for a deaf person. (Kluscarits, 1995, p. 49)

Obviously, in this last instance the family member or friend who is interpreting is better thought of as a *communicator* rather than an interpreter. Nevertheless, the point made by this interpreter merits attention.

Legal Considerations

Possible malpractice by interpreters is examined elsewhere in this book. But what about the nondeaf, nonsigning practitioner who refuses to engage an interpreter when seeing deaf patients? Some health personnel reject an interpreter even when brought by the deaf patient. They need to realize that misunderstandings between themselves and deaf patients can lead to litigation

Profile: Marty Barnum

Marty Barnum is the director of the Health Care Interpreter Program at the College of St. Catherine–Minneapolis, in Minneapolis, Minnesota. Her undergraduate work was in linguistics and her graduate degrees were in Intercultural Communication and Psychology. She holds a Comprehensive Skills Certificate from the Registry of Interpreters for the Deaf (RID) and specializes in working in medical and mental health settings. She has gained an exceptional national reputation in this area. Here she shares her thoughts on the need to prepare interpreters for work in health-related settings:

> The field of interpreting has undergone some major changes. One is that we can no longer function as Jacks/Jills-of-all-trades. Specialization is here in response to changes in educational and work opportunities for Deaf people. My belief is that we must not only be proficient in language and interpreting but also in the content areas in which we will be interpreting. As linguists are quick to remind us, if we don't understand the content, we can't interpret it. At best, we can only do a transliteration.
>
> What does this mean for interpreters working in health care settings? It means we need to be "paradoctors" or "parapsychologists" just as there are paralegals. It means being educated enough in the field of medicine or psychology, not to be a doctor or a psychologist, but to be familiar with and comfortable in medical and mental health setting.
>
> I was the contract interpreter for one Deaf patient in a locked psychiatric ward a few years ago, and watched as a second interpreter entered who had been hired to interpret for a second patient. The man's diagnosis was paranoid schizophrenia, and he was there under court order as a result of stalking a woman and refusing to take his medications. I watched her walk directly up to the Deaf patient, alone, introduce herself while leaning close to him, and offer to interpret the game show he was watching on television. When he signed, "No!" she let him know she would be sitting nearby if he needed her. She then proceeded to sit in a chair about ten feet from him and read her Bible, looking over at him frequently.
>
> In a medical setting, a graduate of our Health Care Interpreter Program interpreted for an oncologist who was informing a Deaf patient and her Deaf husband that the hospital had

Continued

Profile: Marty Barnum   *Continued*

exhausted all potential treatments for her cancer, and that she should get her affairs in order. The woman and her husband left smiling, and my former student called me to discuss her concerns. She felt that the typical hearing euphemistic way of saying "You're going to die" did not translate as such to these two Deaf people, but perhaps as, "We've done all the treatments we can and now you can get on with your life." We discussed options, and she chose to talk with the oncologist about her concerns. He agreed to talk again with the couple, and reluctantly agreed to be more direct. At the conclusion of the second meeting, the couple left in tears, called their daughter home from college, and had three months together as a family before the Deaf mother died.

These are examples of the absolute need for an interpreter in a health care settings to be more than just a freelance interpreter. The first interpreter needed to know the protocol to follow in a locked psychiatric ward, the implications of paranoid schizophrenia, why the Bible is a poor choice of reading material in a psychiatric setting, and much more. In the second setting, the interpreter was wise enough to go beyond just interpreting "faithfully," and to look at the cultural potentials in the way the message was presented. She knew it was appropriate to talk directly with the doctor about the situation and to facilitate a second meeting.

Interpreters who do not have the knowledge and experience to work in health care settings, need to (1) not interpret in health care settings, or (2) get themselves educated and mentored such that they will not compromise the best interests and health of either the Deaf or hearing people for whom they interpret.

in which their failure to provide adequate communication may result in punitive judgments against them.

Who is to blame when a deaf person decides not to use an interpreter during a meeting with a doctor? Who is the responsible party? Under some state laws, service providers may be, if they do not advise a deaf patients of the right to an interpreter. Thus, they should become more proactive in offering interpreter services to their patients. The Americans with Disabilities Act (ADA), however, places the responsibility on the deaf person or family member, who must request interpreting services to be covered by the act.

Gender Matching

Another issue is the importance of gender matching in health-related interpreting. The majority of interpreters are female and the majority of deaf persons are male, so routine matchups are simply unrealistic. Although deaf participants have the right to choose a particular interpreter, they may seldom appear to consider gender in making such decisions. However, a deaf man undergoing a prostate examination and a deaf woman visiting a gynecologist may each request same-sex interpreters. The health personnel also may have preferences for the interpreter's gender. This is an area that has not been adequately studied and, again, calls up the Interactive Model of Interpreting, in which all participants contribute to the construction of meaning. In some situations and with some participants, the interpreter's gender may be a critical factor.

Mental Health Settings

Interpreters find themselves working in any number of mental health settings, including group and individual counseling sessions, grief workshops for families, Alcoholics Anonymous meetings, marriage counseling, drug therapy, AIDS counseling, counseling for child and spousal abuse, and therapy sessions with patients in a psychiatric ward. Federal legislation, like ADA and IDEA, has also increased the demand for interpreters in mental health settings.

An increasing number of deaf people are entering the mental health field. For example, Gallaudet University offers graduate programs in mental health counseling for deaf and hard-of-hearing students. Although many of the graduates probably will seek to counsel people who use signs, they may have nondeaf patients, too, and might need to communicate with a deaf patient's nondeaf associates and nondeaf family members. The deaf professionals also might want to interact with their nondeaf colleagues. Such developments will, naturally, lead to more employment for interpreters. This should have a reciprocal effect because some deaf people are likely to become more interested in a health-related profession once they witness the access to communication provided by the greater employment of interpreters.

Effects on Counseling

Communication in counseling makes unusual linguistic demands. Providing an interpreter does not fulfill the demands of mental health counseling unless the interpreter has been prepared to meet those demands. On the one hand, interpreters confront professionals' technical vocabularies and jargon, which must be presented to clients so they can understand them. But conveying a deaf patient's expressions without the emotions and any nuances that accompany them is insufficient. The deaf participants' signs must be voiced in a manner that accurately reflects both their emotional and intellectual content. An interpreter notes, "It is no secret that the most difficult aspect of interpreting is the ability to reverse the deaf person, that is, to comprehend the sign language of the speaker" (Straub, 1976, p. 16).

Interpreters may have to interpret for a psychotic deaf person who is making no sense and/or whose outward appearance does not match the message being conveyed (the latter being characteristic of schizophrenics). All aspects of this deaf person's signing must be interpreted and, when this becomes too difficult, relay interpreting with a CDI is a viable option. At other times, an interpreter might encounter a counselor who is skeptical that the interpreter is accurately conveying what the deaf person is saying. Indeed, at times the deaf person may be so incoherent that the interpreter cannot put the signs into spoken language. Without embarrassment, the interpreter should explain to the counselor what is transpiring, if it is not already obvious. Then the interpreter and the counselor can decide how best to proceed. Videotaping the deaf person's psychotic signs will enable interpreter and counselor to review the session without the time pressures of simultaneous interpreting. To seek deeper meanings, the counselor can then make inquiries of the interpreter that would not be appropriate during the session. Of course, this should be done only in a manner that protects the deaf person's rights.

Emotional Stresses

Interpreters must be emotionally stable persons to withstand stresses that arise during sessions in which participants reveal embarrassing material that is seldom exposed and behave in odd, even threatening, ways. Working in mental health settings brings interpreters face to face with any number of unpleasant incidents, including attempted suicide, incest, child abuse, drug abuse, anger, grief, violence, and hostility. Equally stressful can be discovering that the deaf patient has been misdiagnosed and is wrongly institutionalized. Deaf people have too often been misdiagnosed as mentally ill by naive practitioners, who misinterpreted their facial expressions and vigorous hand and arm movements as indications of psychopathy (see Altshuler & Abdullah, 1981; Dickert, 1988; Freeman, 1989; Jones, 1985; Ludders, 1987; Rainer, Altshuler, Kallman, & Demming, 1963; Schlesinger & Meadow, 1972; Stewart, 1981).

Given the present shortage of interpreters, there is always the possibility that an unskilled interpreter will be hired, a practice that is strongly discouraged:

> [Signers] have learned sign language because of association with Deaf people or personal interest. DO NOT use a signer in lieu of an Interpreter. They are not trained in interpreting, only in sign language. Let me give you an analogy. Using a signer to do the job of a qualified mental health Interpreter is like asking a life guard to do surgery. Be aware; signers often mean well and are willing to provide the ser-

vice free, but in the end are very damaging to long term success. Frequently these volunteers are very enthusiastic; use them to assist with written assignments or driving the Deaf person to a meeting— NEVER AS AN INTERPRETER! [emphases in the original]. (Wentzer & Dhir, 1986, p. 13)

A counselor with signing skills, on the other hand, might be adequately prepared to meet the communication needs of a counseling session. One study showed that deaf people were more receptive to mental health professionals who had some command of sign language or used an interpreter than to those who relied on writing (Brauer, 1990). However, even when a nondeaf counselor has the ability to sign, some clients may still prefer the presence of an interpreter as an insurance against miscommunication.

Attitudinal Issues

Deaf people may harbor a reluctance to use interpreters when seeking counseling. They originally may have encountered interpreters in church or other community settings and, consequently, may hesitate to expose socially unacceptable behaviors such as substance abuse, marital infidelity, or character weaknesses before interpreters they know. Trust is also an important consideration, as the deaf participant can take as long to develop trust in the interpreter as in the counselor (Boros, 1983).

Interpreters can be the targets of a deaf participant's hostility. They may not appreciate psychological reasons for communication breakdowns, as when the deaf person rejects a therapist's utterance by claiming not to understand the interpreter. The same person might misdirect anger toward the interpreters. This may lead to situations where they may be hurt by a deaf participant confusing them with the counselor. Learning how to react in such situations is essential to effective mental health interpreting.

Some mental health professionals may be reluctant to use interpreters (Brauer, 1990). Many counselors employ eye contact as a part of their therapy, and this is difficult, if not impossible, to do when working through an interpreter. That is not to say that the interpreter has ruined the counselor–client relationship. But deaf people in this situation often require unusual strategies beyond the competence of some therapists, who should, for that reason, refer their deaf clients to others. The interpreter should be mentally prepared for this occurrence and should assume no guilt.

Mental health professionals' reluctance to use interpreters has also been related to "ethical behavior, trust, confidentiality, and to possible distortions or misunderstandings in communication by either the interpreter, therapist, or the consumer" (Anderson & Thornton, 1993, p. 219). Such issues may be especially apparent during the initial session in which an interpreter is present.

As pointed out by one interpreter, inexperienced interpreters face uncertainty as to their role, and they often suffer one or more of the following:

- Experience conflict as to who arranges the setting—the therapist, the interpreter, or the consumer.
- Have negative feelings about the therapeutic approach and/or how the therapist handles the session.
- Have personal emotional feelings aroused by the sensitive content of the session and wonder how to handle situations that become very emotional.
- Worry about what to do when eye contact is made between the deaf person and the therapist, causing loss of sign communication.
- Wonder how to handle a comment made directly to the interpreter by either patient or therapist: Should it be reported to either participant? Whose responsibility is it to inform participants that all such comments will be interpreted? (Taff-Watson, 1983, pp. 188–189)

The view that interpreters introduce adverse factors into mental health settings will probably diminish as all participants gain experience with this type of interpreting and as research contributes to improved techniques. Some counselors believe an interpreter contributes more to therapy than linguistic equivalents. In family therapy, they find interpreters can help overcome family members' objections to manual communication. Parents who have always insisted their deaf child communicate orally may be amazed at the ease of communication when their child is signed to, and this helps them begin to accept ramifications of their child's deafness for communication (Harvey, 1982).

Nevertheless, there remain barriers to the employment of interpreters in psychotherapy. A survey found many therapists unwilling to use interpreters even though they recognized their value (Brauer, 1990). These respondents said interpreting was not necessarily the best way to overcome communication differences between deaf patient and nondeaf therapist. Some of the reasons given for this belief were the adverse influence of the interpreter on the deaf participant's behavior, difficulty establishing intimacy with the client, and distortions in the messages conveyed by the interpreter. Yet few therapists are skilled in ASL, and they face many obstacles to establishing effective communication with those deaf clients whose preferred (and sometimes sole) means of communication is ASL.

Gender Matching
An interpreter's gender may be significant in a mental health setting. A deaf female victim of rape, for example, may feel uncomfortable relating details of the event in the presence of a male interpreter. Equally, male patients may be reluctant to expose sexual and other intimate material when the interpreter is female. Some counselors find such attitudes to be legitimate fodder for the

therapeutic mill—an opportunity to discuss male–female attitudes with the patient. Others may prefer to match interpreter–patient gender and finesse the subject at an early point in therapy.

Geographical Considerations

Sensitivity toward the presence of particular interpreters is especially common in small towns where interpreters and deaf people often encounter one another. Any time the interpreter is known to the patient it may cause difficulty. When highly sensitive matters are expected to arise, it might be appropriate to engage an interpreter with whom the patient is unfamiliar, which often means one from outside the geographic area.

Rehabilitation and Workplace Settings

Vocational rehabilitation, social work, and similar services aim to help people find and maintain employment, resolve personal problems, and optimize their family and social relations. Early views of interpreters in the vocational rehabilitation process found a number of problems: inadequate fees, too few qualified interpreters, lack of interpreter education programs, vague or nonexistent interpreting standards, and participants' inexperience with and lack of understanding of professional interpreters (Lloyd, 1976).

Today, interpreters are viewed as essential to the rehabilitation of deaf people and as an integral part of the workplace once they have obtained a job. There is an emerging need for interpreters in business, industry, government, education, and social services. But some critics warn, "If the interpreter is doing things other than interpreting, that person should not be labeled as an Interpreter, and the job description should clearly outline the job responsibilities of the individual" (Stone & Hurwitz, 1994, p. 261).

The education components of rehabilitation are covered in the next chapter. Here we note that interpreters working in rehabilitation or industry can expect to cover a lot of territory—interview sessions with rehabilitation officers and prospective employers, counseling sessions for employees who have lost a limb or are being prepared for retraining for a new job, visits to job sites, financial discussions, employee evaluations, grievance procedures, staff parties, retirement dinners, layoff announcements, union meetings, and many other situations. Interpreters need flexibility, extensive education, and stamina to be effective in such a variety of settings and over such a range of communication demands.

Theatrical and Platform

Interpreters become more than communicators when they are placed on stage. Opportunities for them have greatly increased to interpret dramas, musical comedies, rock concerts, and even operas. These interpreters become accustomed to rehearsing, to memorizing their parts, to repeating them, and to wearing costumes and makeup. When they are 'shadowing' performers—that is, moving about the stage with them so the audience can observe actor and interpreter at the same time—they must attend to how they move relative to the scenery and the other performers, while continuing to sign. The advantages of interpreting for a stage performance over simultaneous interpreting include the time to work out the signs, to consult with others, and to practice them as well to prepare mentally for the characters whose roles they are portraying.

The complexities of interpreting the performing arts include the sophisticated ways in which interpreters are blended into the performance itself. This raises the question of whether or not the interpreter needs to have acting ability as well as competency in interpreting. The answer usually depends on the director, but interpreters most often need no more acting ability than is required for any interpreting assignment. There are, however, special language demands. Interpreters interviewed about their experiences on stage emphasize the need to add "art signs" to their sign vocabularies. *Art signs* is a term coined by Klima and Bellugi (1979); for further discussion of this aspect of signing, see Sutherland (1985).

In sign-singing, the interpreter signs songs that are being sung by performers, either recorded or live. Interpreting songs requires a special flair. It is a matter not only of finding suitable signs for words and phrases, but also of signing them in a way that approximates the song's rhythm. Emphasis must fall in the right place to convey the song's ideas, many of which depend on more than words. As with interpreting plays, an interpreter desiring to interpret a song usually devotes much time to practicing it in order to be effective.

There are four levels of song presentations. *Cold transliteration* means the interpreter is signing the song for the first time. No attempt is made to alter the words of the song, as transliteration implies a verbatim or near-verbatim signing of the song—often not a positive experience as the interpreter simultaneously critiques the signing and realizes there are better ways to sign it. In a *cold interpretation,* interpreters attempt to convey the song's meaning as they are hearing or signing it for the first time. Does the resulting interpretation coordinate well with the music? Is this even an important consideration? For some deaf people it is, while for others the meaning alone might suffice.

Both cold transliteration and cold interpretation can create problems, especially with respect to understanding the words of a song (see the box titled "Song, Signed , . . . Folly?"). The preferred song presentations are *practiced transliteration* and *practiced interpretation*. In both cases, the songs are practiced without music to ensure that they can stand alone.

Song, Signed , . . . Folly?

In the following story, an interpreter tells of having to try to render a cold translation of a song that she could not hear clearly. Although she could not sign the song, her solution for informing the deaf audience adds humor to the situation:

> I was asked to interpret at a college graduation ceremony. Graduation night arrived and there were many people in the audience. Certificates were being awarded when all of sudden this music starts. Oh man! It might have been all right because it was one of those long drawn out, slow songs. But I couldn't distinguish between words such as *love, life,* and *light!* I started signing to the music my own apology to the deaf audience, sign-singing 'I don't know what they're saying, so sorry." After the program, several hearing people complimented me on my "beautiful signing during the song." I didn't say a word to them about what had actually happened. To the deaf people, I didn't have to say a word because they told me "We understand, its okay."

With practice, interpreters are able to render songs in signs that meet the artistic intent and meaning of the song as sung by voice. To do this, interpreters rely on a number of techniques, such as these:

- Creating visual pictures through their signing, while preserving the rhythm of the music by the rate of signing
- Using a small degree of body movement, but not dancing
- Breaking compound signs to fit the rhythm of the song as in BROTHER = BOY + SAME
- Prolonging the sign's movement to show the duration of the word it represents
- Changing facial expressions appropriately
- Making nonsign body and arm movements during musical interludes
- Practicing signing each sign's gloss while mouthing the song's words
- Keeping fingerspelling to a minimum and only for emphasis
- Varying the size of signs to indicate loudness and softness of the music

Interpreting poetry, another aspect of working in the performing arts, poses a serious challenge to the interpreter's artistic ability to convey meaning

in signs. Yet difficulty in signing poetry can be overcome, as has been beauti-
fully demonstrated by Bernard Bragg, who has brilliantly conveyed Lewis Car-
roll's nonsense poem "Jabberwocky" as well as Japanese *haiku*. An appreciation
of *haiku* depends on responding to its strict metric limits. Although Bragg is a
deaf actor, his rendition of poetry in signs is a good model for interpreters who
may find themselves in the position of having to interpret poetry.

Some deaf people insist that signing songs and poetry is anathema to deaf
people, while other deaf people express a definite liking for it. The Deaf
community's attitudes defy single categorization on any issue, and they are
subject to change over time. Certainly, when personal feelings can be accom-
modated, interpreters should do so, but in many cases they will be "damned
if they do and damned if they don't."

In the performing arts, interpreters may not know whether or not there are
any deaf people in the audience. Interpreted events often occur only one time,
and deaf people can buy their tickets at the door. Nevertheless, interpreters
must prepare for interpreting the play weeks in advance—memorizing lines,
establishing a position on stage, and the like. They must then proceed to interpret even if they know that there are no deaf persons in the audience, because there is always the chance that someone might turn up after the play has
begun.

Stresses

A common stress associated with platform interpreting comes from the
speaker who reads from a prepared text, such as a list of names. At a graduation exercise, the interpreter can forewarn the master of ceremonies that fingerspelling names takes much longer than reading them. If the interpreter is
expected to keep pace with the speaker, the speaker must read slowly, leaving ample time between names. It also helps greatly if the interpreter can
study the name list before the ceremonies.

A speaker may say something that will emotionally upset the interpreter,
who must try not to show the reaction to the audience. One interpreter was
on a platform interpreting for an expert on child abuse. During the lecture,
the interpreter suddenly recalled that she had been sexually abused as a child.
The recollection stunned her. Fortunately, the lecture was being team-inter-
preted, and she was able to excuse herself to deal with her own emotions.

Occasionally, interpreters encounter an actor who resents them. The actor
believes interpreters will distract the audience and may insist they sit in the
audience or to the side of the stage. Yet when the interpreter is in front or on
stage shadowing the actor, people can watch both the performance and the
interpreters. Interpreters can explain that if they are not located in the front
of the room, the audience will be constantly turning their heads to see how
something is signed. Those turning heads can become a greater distraction
than having an interpreter suitably located at the front of the stage.

Sometimes the producer of a performance decides to place a costume on the interpreters. This occurs most often when the interpreters are shadowing the performers. Dressing up is usually not a problem and can even be fun. However, the interpreters must be alert to anything about the costume that will make it difficult for the deaf audience to follow the signs, as occurs when highly reflective ornaments are used. They must be aware that some costumes make it difficult for them to make the signs, as when a costume prevents or inhibits arms movements. Because costumes are often not put on until the dress rehearsal, the interpreters have little time to resolve such problems before the first performance, which may be the only performance. Discussing these problems with the director early in rehearsals can forestall such disasters.

Hazards aside, platform interpreting can be rewarding. It provides interpreters with excellent opportunities to display their skills before many people who otherwise would not be aware of signing and its importance to deaf people. The educational value of these occasions contributes to the pleasure that interpreters can take in the exercise of their profession.

Religious

Religious interpreting has many of the advantages and few of the disadvantages of interpreting for stage performances. The hymns are usually well known to the interpreter, as are most of the prayers, because the interpreter is often a member of that religious denomination. The proper interpretation of these typically will have been worked out long in advance and practiced fairly often. The deaf congregation, too, is usually familiar with many, if not all, parts of the service, which greatly aids the interpreter. When time permits, the minister usually will give the interpreter an advance copy of the sermon and of the announcements, especially those involving proper names. This courtesy will enable the interpreter to prepare for unusual names and phrases, and will lead to a smoother signing of the service.

But even with the best of preparation, an assignment can go awry. One interpreter related how she had received the service and hymn before an assignment and had even made plans to meet with the minister an hour before the service. The minister never showed up, and the interpreter only found out just before the service that there was to be another minister taking his place who had never worked with a deaf congregation. Although he followed the readings that the interpreter had been given, he also delivered a forty-minute presentation in twenty minutes, in a voice so low that the interpreter could hardly hear him. Needless to say, the interpreter was exhausted by the end of the service. Time, in fact, is probably the major disadvantage with religious interpreting, as most interpreters work alone in this setting. The congregation cannot be put on hold while the interpreter takes a break; for very long services, a second interpreter is recommended.

Interpreting for special religious occasions, such as weddings and funerals, usually does not cause problems, although they can arise. One interpreter recounts her first, and last, funeral assignment:

> Before the service, I went to the funeral home and met with the minister who explained to me what would happen . . . . When I arrived for the funeral, I found an open casket, which surprised me, and a milk crate next to the casket, near the head, for me to stand on . . . . I had high heels on, so of course my heels went through the holes in the crate when I stood on it. The service went on for a very long time, and I was off balance because I couldn't move my feet. I also had a long skirt on. Finally the service ended, everyone was crying, and I moved to get down. The minister gave me his hand, and I got one shoe out, but the heel got stuck in the hem of my skirt. I lost my balance, and to compensate I went the other way, which was toward the casket. My shoe came off, and I fell on the body. It was awful . . . . The minister finally got me out. Now I don't do funerals. (Schmitz, 1994, p. 27)

Emergencies

All interpreting does not take place in quiet, well-ordered settings. Interpreters sometimes find themselves in awkward, occasionally threatening situations. They may be called in the middle of the night to an accident scene, a police station, or the locked ward of a psychiatric hospital. Medical settings, as noted, can place the interpreter in emotionally stressful positions even in the best of circumstances. In all emergency situations, interpreters may have to wait around for long periods of time. Before accepting emergency assignments, interpreters need to be confident about their own ego strength and about their ability to interpret under difficult, sometimes hostile situations (see Elkins, 1995).

SUMMARY

This chapter illustrates the remarkable variety of audiences and situations that interpreters encounter. They must contend with those who are deafblind or who prefer different interpreting modes like oral or cued speech. They may interpret in a relay or as part of a team. They will find themselves in special settings—legal, health-related, theatrical, and so forth—each introducing a special set of problems.

In all of these variations, interpreters' basic task remains the same. They are to convey meaning expressed by others as accurately as possible. Doing so requires interpreters to gain much knowledge and acquire some remarkable skills. That so many interpreters do, and do it well should encourage novices preparing to follow them and, at the same time, caution them against unrealistic views of the profession they are preparing to enter.

Those who engage interpreters should not be fooled into believing that interpreting is merely signing and voicing signs. It requires special talents, knowledge, and skills. It is a professional activity that deserves full cooperation and fair remuneration. The managers of settings in which interpreters perform should be cognizant of ways that they can facilitate the interpreting tasks, because to the extent that they do, they improve communication for all of the participants—deaf and nondeaf.

7

LANGUAGE AND CULTURE

Languages are interpreters' stock in trade. What interpreters do is re-create a spoken language in a signed language or code and vice versa. They strive to re-create American Sign Language (ASL) in English and English in ASL so that the message is not altered. To accomplish that objective, they must contend with many factors—one of which is culture. This chapter discusses the implications of the intimate relationship between language and culture, and presents some techniques interpreters use to stay abreast of and to adjust to cultural-linguistic changes, whether social, geographical or temporal.

The inseparability of culture and language can be seen in the recent fall from grace of two popular terms in the Deaf community. The term *hearing impaired* has fallen out of favor with deaf people because it is medically derived and focuses on a perceived disability rather than on a group of people who share a characteristic. In the Deaf community, *Deaf* and *hard of hearing* are the preferred terms, with the former referring to those people who have a significant hearing loss, embrace the cultural values of the Deaf community, and use sign language.

In referring to the machine that sends text symbols over telephone lines, many deaf people consider it insensitive to use the term *TDD* , an acronym for Telecommunication Device for the Deaf. The Deaf community disapproves of the implication that this device is used only to benefit deaf people. Most deaf people prefer the older acronym *TTY*, which means TeleTYpe machine, or *TT*, which stands for Text Telephone, neither of which implies benefit solely for a particular group of people.

These few examples of the relationship between culture and language indicate the value for an interpreter of understanding culture in order to sign or speak in a manner that is not offensive to the other participants. Awareness of culture and the varied meanings that words and signs carry in a community is not only important during interpreting but can be used during casual conversations with the participants and other members of the community. How interpreters talk and act in their daily living and social activities influence how others will perceive them.

RESPECTING OTHER CULTURES

The term *politically correct* may soon lose favor as an indicator of what is culturally acceptable. Here we will happily substitute the old-fashioned term *polite* to convey what we mean. What sounds or looks right to one person may mislead or, worse, offend another person. What is seen as acceptable language today might not be tomorrow. ASL and English lexicons constantly expand, and the meaning of some signs and words change. Once-acceptable terms like *chairman* and *policeman* have lost favor to the gender-neutral *chairperson* and *police officer*. Sensitivity to other groups' feelings is reflected in recent changes in ASL as well. Past signs for Africa, Japan, and China were each based on a physical characteristic of the natives of those regions. This is not polite, so these signs are being replaced by signs that depict the shapes of Africa and Japan, respectively, and, for China, the flap of a Mao jacket (see Figure 7-1).

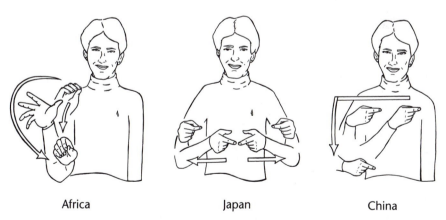

Africa   Japan   China

FIGURE 7-1   New ASL signs for countries do not reflect the physical characterisitcs of a group of people.

USING NEW SIGNS

Although the new signs show greater sensitivity to the feelings of others than the older signs, they do not permeate a community of signers overnight. It took several years for the polite sign for China to make its way into the vernacular of ASL signs, and some deaf adults still use the former sign.

What sign, then, should an interpreter use, the old or the new sign variation? Is it the interpreter's responsibility to introduce the newer, more acceptable versions of a sign to the deaf participants? While interpreting, interpreters are not in a position to endorse or teach new signs. When there is some uncertainty about which sign is suitable, some interpreters use two sign variations consecutively; as the assignment continues, the participants can indicate which sign they prefer.

Modifying nouns so that they become verbs has been a popular linguistic ploy in English. The name *Xerox* provides an example. Originally the name of a company, Xerox was made into a verb, and *Xeroxing* quickly replaced *photocopying* as the designation for what the company's machine did. In ASL signing, it underwent a similar evolution as the fingerspelled noun changed to a verb that had the hands simulating the action of the camera moving across the page in a copying machine: the "X" handshape of the dominant hand moved across the bottom of the downturned opposite hand.

All of these sign modifications tax the interpreter to remain current. New words appear frequently, and the meanings of established terms metamorphose. *The Oxford Dictionary of New Words* (Oxford University Press, 1991) contains 750 articles. It provides fascinating support to the fact that American English is changing, as the reader passes from *AAA* (antiaircraft artillery) to *zouk* (an exuberant style of popular music). Similar additions and changes are found in ASL. A newer sign for EMPOWERMENT takes the sign for POWER and thrusts it outward to indicate something gaining power (see Figure 7-2).

FIGURE 7-2   Empowerment

Fingerspelling the manual letters *A-D-A* signifies the Americans with Disabilities Act. It is imperative that interpreters keep up with new coinages as well as alterations in usage of the languages in which they interpret. Small differences in signing can lead to confusions for one age group and not another (see the box titled "Crediting Credit Cards"). Of course, such misunderstandings are neither new nor confined to sign language interpreting.

CULTURAL MISINTERPRETATIONS

Critical to interpreting initiators' messages is an understanding of their linguistic and cultural nuances. Without this understanding, interpreters and translators alike may inadvertently alter the meaning of an utterance.

Signs with sexual connotations are a frequent source of misunderstandings for which interpreters need to be alert. While teaching at a school for deaf children in Canada, one Deaf teacher used the sign for INSPIRED and was greeted

---

Crediting Credit Cards

In America, *credit card* originally was signified by a C handshape bouncing once to the side. Now it is widely signed with the dominant fist moving back and forth on the palm of the nondominant hand, simulating the action of the manual machines for imprinting a credit slip. But with improved electronics, that iconography may change again, as credit cards' magnetic strips are pulled through parallel bars on a device that then prints a paper record, replacing the manual machines. Following are the three versions for the sign CREDIT CARD:

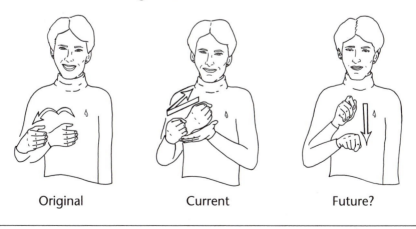

Original   Current   Future?

with muffled laughter from his class and a good-natured scolding from one of his students to keep his sexual urges private. The students had adapted this sign to mean desiring sexual gratification. They used it openly in class knowing their teachers would not know its meaning. Although a member of the Deaf community, the Deaf person had, to that point, not encountered this altered meaning of the sign INSPIRED.

In Michigan, an old sign for banana has the *Y* handshape of the dominant hand twice going down the *1* handshape of the other hand in a flipping motion. Contrast this with the sign for BANANA in most other parts of the United States, and Canada where the dominant hand forms a pinched *O* as it goes through the motion of peeling a banana symbolized by the nondominant hand's *1* handshape. The Michigan sign looks almost like the sign for condom. Given this knowledge, an interpreter might avoid using the Michigan sign when there is a possibility that its intended meaning might be misconstrued.

Another cultural nuance is seen in a sign that some deaf athletes use on the playing field to refer to a referee who appears to be obsessed with minutiae when calling infractions of a game's rules. The sign is the same as the sign BORED and is typically accompanied by a facial expression of incredulity. The athlete is not bored, as we normally take this sign to mean. Rather, he or she is exasperated that the game is being called so closely—tired of the constant stopping of the play. Few people grasp this meaning unless they have witnessed its use on a playing field.

Nyet Means No? Yes?

Chukovsky (1984, p. 106), had this to say about Russian translations of American writings, translations that miss significant nuances:

> The Russian expression "[he] used his connections" does not do justice to "pulled political wires"; "sheer raving" does not justly express "gibberish" . . . In *Cat's Cradle*, "they put prayers into action" misses the inimitable Vonnegutism, "So they gave praying a whirl"; "I had nowhere to spend the time" does not serve the American expression "so I had a night to kill"; "stupid invention of poets" falls short of "poetic crap." (p. 106)

Nuances are no less important in moving between two spoken languages (see the box titled "Nyet Means No? Yes?"). The noted American poet James Merrill recounts an amusing incident that occurred during a lecture he was giving in Italy and illustrates the importance of any interpreters' familiarity with the culture as well as the language of that culture:

I mentioned guilt in a talk I once gave in Rome, and it was translated over the earphones as gold leaf. South of the Alps guilt has only its legal or criminal sense. (Cited in Bayley, 1993, p. 32)

LANGUAGE AS POWER

Language competence can be a source of power. Deaf people have long been defined by their loss of hearing under a medical-pathological model. Only recently has there been a major movement among Deaf people to define themselves by their language. ASL is really *their* language because in the absence of Deaf people there would be little reason for its continued survival. It is through their language that Deaf people maintain their identification as a culturally distinct group.

Given the need for interpreters to have an excellent command of two languages and two cultures, the question then arises as to whether the Deaf community will enable them to gain this knowledge. ASL is dear to the hearts of Deaf people. It is their language and would simply fade away without them. As Barbara Kannapell explains:

If hearing people understand ASL, then deaf people are no longer in power using ASL. Here is what happened to me several years ago: I realized that a deaf friend of mine and I were no longer in power using ASL in front of two hearing friends. One of them knew no Sign Language, but the other one knew ASL fairly well. As my deaf friend and I began a deep personal discussion, the hearing person who knew ASL was able to understand us and felt awkward interpreting to the other hearing person what we were talking about. I did not expect her to understand our discussion in ASL or to interpret to the hearing person because hearing people are not supposed to understand the conversation of deaf people in ASL. That's how deaf people experience ASL supremacy. ASL is the only creation which grows out of the Deaf Community. It is our language in every sense of the word. We create it, we keep it alive, and it keeps us and our traditions alive. (Kannapell, 1982, p. 25)

In the early 1980s, when Kannapell wrote those words, the Deaf community was undergoing a metamorphosis from an ostracized and linguistically impoverished subcultural group to an autonomous linguistic minority proud of its cultural uniqueness. Maintaining this cultural distinction was crucial to their image of self-determination (Stewart, 1991). Even today many Deaf individuals would concur with Kannapell's sentiments about ASL. But the tide may be turning.

Teaching ASL now provides a livelihood for many Deaf people. Students studying ASL feel cheated when they find out that some of their instructors do not expect them to become fluent in ASL. By transforming the social-identification value of ASL to a monetary value, Deaf people gamble that a growing population of nondeaf ASL users will not diminish their cultural and linguistic uniqueness.

Except for children of Deaf parents and interpreters, very few nondeaf people attain ASL fluency. Does an interpreter's knowledge of ASL diminish the power that ASL gives the Deaf community? On the contrary, we believe an interpreters' knowledge of ASL increases the Deaf community's power in its interactions with the general community. We acknowledge that we would probably change our view if the number of nondeaf people fluent in ASL grew at a proportionately greater rate than the number of Deaf people using ASL, but for the time being that is an unlikely prospect.

THE INTERPRETER'S RESPONSIBILITIES

Learning another language can afford an awareness of a people and their culture. Cultural information influences the behavior of one linguistic group toward another, guiding their interactions with members of another group. For that reason, it is imperative that interpreters study Deaf culture. Interpreters, after all, are not simply tools. Their knowledge and personalities influence the intelligibility and style of their interpretations. To be maximally effective, they must be sensitive to the cultures in which the languages they are interpreting are embedded. Knowledge of a culture allows the interpreter to select words and signs that transmit a message accurately. Therein lies one more reason that interpreting can be difficult: most interpreters are not members of the Deaf community, so their knowledge of Deaf culture and expertise in ASL must be acquired—essential acquisitions.

At the same time, most, if not all, Deaf people want their interpreters to be fluent in ASL so that they may have the freedom of conversing as they wish and not having to change their signing to facilitate interpreting. For too long they have acquiesced to the fact that interpreters seldom had the skills to do justice to what they might say in ASL. Consider the following comments by Roslyn Rosen, former president of the National Association of the Deaf and now a vice-president of Gallaudet University:

> Access without equality becomes a hollow mockery of our rights as federally mandated by P.L. 94-142, [Section] 504, and the Americans with Disabilities Act, as well as assorted state laws .... Although I have a doctoral degree, years of educational experience and top-notch bilingual skills, I am practically reduced to a babbling idiot, finger-

spelling at a snail's pace and signing on a pre-school level in order to be understood by the interpreter. One such interpreter, at the end of my presentation, apologized to me, saying that although he interpreted full-time in a high school, his receptive skills were practically nil, since the deaf students were mostly passive. However, many of us have already heard the sad tales of woe by deaf mainstreamed students, who admit to becoming passive and withdrawn, rather than to face misunderstandings and humiliation by inept interpreters. (Rosen, 1992, p. 3)

In the Interactive Model of Interpreting, the interpreter is not entirely responsible for ensuring that an interpreted message is understood. The participants share the burden. If the message whether in speech or signs, is uttered sloppily, the interpreting will—indeed should—reflect it. The interpreter is not bound and should not even attempt to correct poor grammar, badly chosen examples, and other slovenly expressions. Most translators of print—who, like interpreters, are in a position to maintain or alter the intent of a passage—embrace this principle. As one translator notes, "Any writer has the right to write as his pen points and it is not our business, not even our advantage, to reshape him according to our notions of what really good writing is" (Morgan, 1956, cited in Kelly, 1979, pp. 179–180).

Nevertheless, conveying accurate interpretations is the overriding concern of all interpreters, and to this end it is helpful if they are familiar with the communication styles and nuances of the other participants. Seal (1998) illustrates this importance in her suggestions for how to interpret stories for children effectively in the primary grade setting:

Good interpreters learn to *read* their story reader. Educational interpreters must learn the different voices that a reader takes on to represent different characters and different dialects in their stories. Effective interpreters must learn to hear the *rhythm* of poetry and prose so that their bodies (not just their limbs and faces) take on or represent that rhythm. Talented educational interpreters learn to hear the rhetorical questions in their story readers and can differentiate those from questions that require a directed response from the students. (p. 65)

CULTURAL MEDIATION

If it makes sense that competent interpreters must have a comprehensive understanding of Deaf culture and ASL, then we must not forget the other side of most interpreting situations—the spoken language and its attendant culture. It cannot be assumed that, because the vast majority of interpreters are hearing and many of them grew up speaking and interacting in North American society, they will necessarily be cognizant of the entire vocabulary and structure of their native language.

Adherents of the bilingual–bicultural approach believe that interpreters should explain the cultural implications of an utterance when this is deemed essential to its understanding, and hence should practice cultural mediation. If a participant from Great Britain says, "Look under the bonnet," the direction means "Open the car's hood." Should interpreters interpose a brief explanation of the differences between British and American automotive terms? Or should they interpret the expression as "Look under the hood"? Opinions vary. Cultural mediation may be more appropriate in some situations and with some participants than others. In educational interpreting, it might be suitable at the elementary level, but not in a graduate seminar. Depending on the response of the Deaf community to the philosophical and communicative implications of cultural mediation, we may see this strategy become an integral part of interpreter education programs.

AMERICAN SIGN LANGUAGE

The association between proficiency in ASL and accurate interpreting is fundamental. ASL is the language of the Deaf community. It is a visual-gestural communication system, which functions, as do all other languages, to provide a common system of symbols and grammatical rules to facilitate the exchange of messages between its users. Sign languages incorporate the dynamic expressions of the hands, body, and face into a syntax in a spatial medium. To emphasize its lack of relationship to English, sign language linguists have stated that ASL is "a natural language with an autonomous grammar that is completely independent from the grammar of English and from the systems devised to represent English manually" (Lucas & Valli, 1992, p. 16).

Understanding the psycholinguistic and sociolinguistic aspects of ASL will help ensure that the process of interpreting results in accurate interpretations. However, an examination of these aspects is not an intent of this book, and the reader is referred elsewhere for this information (Baker & Cokely, 1980; Fischer & Siple, 1990; Klima & Bellugi, 1979; Liddell, 1980; Lucas, 1990; Sandler, 1990; Schein & Stewart, 1995; Stokoe, 1978; Wilbur, 1987). For perspectives on ASL from Deaf people and others who are not linguists, the reader is referred to a *Deaf American Monograph* series (Volume 41, (Nos. 1, 2), which contains a number of articles defining ASL.

But definitions of ASL do not account for the linguistic variety confronting interpreters daily. One familiar with the communication in the Deaf community will know that Deaf people use a variety of signing forms. To refer to these variations, linguists, over the years, have used a number of terms—Pidgin Sign English (PSE), registers, and more recently, contact signing (Cokely, 1983; Lucas & Valli, 1989; Woodward, 1973). Complicating a definition of ASL is the fact that the way a person signs is dictated by a number of factors, such as fluency in ASL and English, hearing status of the participants, context, education, and setting. Moreover, these variations can occur within a single conversation:

> [D]eaf individuals not only can sign quite differently with other deaf individuals than with hearing individuals but can also initiate an interaction in one language and radically shift when the interlocutor's ability to hear is revealed. For example, a deaf native ASL user may initiate an interaction with another individual whom he believes to be deaf or whose audiological status has not been clarified. The latter participant may well be a near-native user of ASL. Once the latter's hearing ability becomes apparent, however, it is not unusual for the deaf participant to automatically stop using ASL and begin using an English-based form of signing. (Lucas & Valli, 1992, p. 15)

Profile: Maureen Wallace

It was only after Maureen Wallace started interpreting for pay that she felt a need and an obligation to further her expertise through training and credentials. The emphasis on obligation is echoed by many interpreters who started their careers as she did—interpreting as a child for family and friends with "communication problems." She realized that the new, burgeoning field of interpreting would soon wither if she and others who had learned to sign from their Deaf parents didn't acknowledge the complex skills that interpreting required. She obtained an RID Comprehensive Skills Certificate and a Specialist Certificate: Legal in 1975 and 1976, respectively. Still, this was not enough and she earned an associate degree in sign language interpretation in 1989 and a bachelor of arts in management of human resources in 1993. She has served as the coordinator of interpreting services for the Division on Deafness, which is under the Michigan Commission on Disability Concerns, and is now a Rights Representative for the same agency.

But Maureen's story is not about interpreter certification and her advocacy of the rights of deaf people and other people with disabilities. Nor is it about her many years of interpreting in a spectrum of settings, including legal, medical, religious, deafblind, educational, vocational,

Continued

Profile: Maureen Wallace *Continued*

administrative, and the public media. Maureen's story is about the unwritten curriculum of learning to converse in two languages for herself
and for others. Talk about the prevalence of interpreters who are children of deaf adults (CODAs) is in contrast to the fact that many CODAs
do not sign well or do not have the skills to interpret professionally.
Maureen's parents were her "first interpreter trainers," as she explains:

> My parents fingerspelled words to me from the time I was a
> baby. When I began to fingerspell words, I was encouraged to
> spell clearly. As I got older, if I misspelled a word, I would have to
> fingerspell it 25 times clearly. I had to learn to speak too, and my
> parents spoke when fingerspelling. I understood everything they
> said, but they warned me that they didn't pronounce some
> words correctly. At school, my friends pointed out the fact that
> my parents' speech was different than theirs. I was "deaf tuned"
> early in life. But learning two languages at the same time didn't
> come easy. When you have to learn English as well as master ASL,
> you don't have time for idioms and play on words. Even today, I
> am still working on understanding and interpreting idioms.
>
> I had to learn how to interpret as a child and sometimes I
> learned the hard way. When I was to interpret a phone call, my
> parents would explain to me what the call was about, who to ask
> for, and to say exactly what they said. One day, I thought I would
> do "my own thing" and it wouldn't matter if I didn't follow their
> directions. I got myself in a jam doing this. When I asked my par-
> ents for help, they just said, "Honesty is the best policy." So I had
> to explain to the person on the phone, what I did, apologize, and
> then start all over again using the information my parents gave
> me.
>
> When I started doing more interpreting, I felt a need to talk
> about some situations with my parents. They would quickly re-
> mind me, "Don't talk about other people's business. You
> helped with communication! Keep your mouth shut!"
>
> My parents knew that a good interpreter had to have knowl-
> edge and skills. They encouraged me to take classes and at-
> tended seminars and workshops. They knew the power of words
> and signs and required that I read daily and do crossword puz-
> zles. I still use these methods to broaden my knowledge while
> networking with other professional interpreters. And mentoring
> new interpreters help me refine my interpreting skills.

At what point, then, does signing cease to be ASL? Such a distinction may be nebulous. If there are hundreds of variations in signing within the Deaf community then these variations simply illustrate the versatility of ASL in meeting the communication demands of different situations. Indeed, the position taken by some Deaf people is that ASL is the only label necessary to identify how Deaf and nondeaf people sign (Bragg, 1990; Kuntze, 1990). Kuntze (1990) criticizes linguists studying ASL for refusing to incorporate into their corpus of ASL grammatical aspects those features that appear to be English-influenced. This transformation in how linguists and Deaf people think about ASL expands the pool of ASL linguistic structures, making it possible that today's PSE and contact signing will be recognized as tomorrow's ASL.

ENGLISH-BASED SIGN SYSTEMS

What are interpreters supposed to do about English-based sign systems, otherwise also known as manually coded English, manual English, contrived signs, and artificial signs? More specifically, what do they do when a student they encounter is being educated in a particular type of English-based sign system such as Signed English (Bornstein, Saulnier, & Hamilton, 1983) and Signing Exact English (Gustason, Pfetzing, & Zawolkow, 1980)? If they are educational interpreters, then they might be required, as a matter of school policy, to use one or another variety. A handful of deaf adults prefer such signing in some situations. Yet the Deaf community has always had at its disposal the means to encode English in signs through the use of fingerspelling and other ASL features. When feasible, interpreters in a given situation should consult with the deaf participants as to their desires. If two or more of the deaf participants disagree, the interpreter should urge them to compromise, rather than deciding for them. The existence of other signing options imposes yet another burden on interpreters. The fully qualified interpreter will learn at least some of the English-based sign systems in order to satisfy deaf participants who request them.

THE INTERPRETER'S LINGUISTIC TOOLS

What's missing from our discussion of the role of language and culture in interpreting is a *language of interpreting*. We need terms that will allow us to talk about the tangibles and intangibles of interpreting. Scattered in the literature and "interpreter talk" are elements that give shape to what *it* is that constitute experienced interpreters' linguistic tools.

Linguistic Transfer

The encoding of English in ASL is an example of linguistic transfer. Three types of linguistic transfer of relevance to interpreters are code mixing, code switching, and lexical borrowing. They form a part of interpreters' principal tactics.

Code Mixing

In code mixing, a single language dominates, but elements of another language are used. Examples of code mixing are ASL-dominant signers inserting the English verb *to be* or adding a signed version of the suffix *-ness* when expressing a term like *deafness*. ASL does not use such forms, but some English-based sign systems do.

Code Switching

Code switching refers to alternating between one language and another—for example, between signing ASL and speaking English. Although we have defined ASL as the way Deaf people sign without reference to a specific grammar, code switching also applies when changing from ASL signing to English-based signing. It is a convenient linguistic device for incorporating English idioms into an ASL-dominant conversation and for providing the exact wording of an English phrase. It occurs in the everyday signing of Deaf people. *Conversational* and *situational* code switching are two types of code switching that are part of an interpreter's box of linguistic tools. Conversational code switching occurs when a signer switches for stylistic or rhetorical purposes. Situational code switching occurs when a signer makes a switch to another language for reasons associated with the topic, situation, and/or participants.

Lexical Borrowing

Lexical borrowing means taking words from one language and using them in another language. The terms *fingerspelled loan sign* and, more recently, *lexicalized fingerspelling* refer to fingerspelled words that have been assimilated into ASL (see Battison, 1978, for further discussion of this topic). In the assimilation process, the fingerspelling undergoes changes that take on the characteristics of signs. In restructuring, letters may be deleted, handshapes modified, locations changed, and so forth. An example of lexical borrowing is seen in the fingerspelled word J-O-B and its lexicalized ASL equivalent, J-B.

Two words that are often fingerspelled in ASL are *what* and *sure*, both of which can be expressed in ASL by signs. The fingerspelled versions serve stylistic purposes. Lexicalized fingerspelling can also occur in conjunction with signs, as in the sign LIFE#STYLE, which consists of the sign LIFE followed by fingerspelling S-T-Y-L-E. Knowledge of these lexical borrowings enhances interpreters' ability to define their own styles as well as to communicate more effectively in signs.

Processing Time

Processing time refers to the interval between an interpreter perceiving a message and conveying it. Said another way, it is the time between the input of the source language (SL) and the output of the target language (TL). *Decalage* and *lag time* are other terms used to mean the same thing as processing time.

Little in the literature deals with SL and TL in interpreted performances. Cokely (1992) examined six interpreters' performances at a conference and found that the number of their errors increased as the time between receiving and conveying a message increased. His study did not determine an optimal processing time; it might vary from one interpreter and one set of circumstances to another. Too short or too long a processing time may increase errors. An appreciation of processing time should warn those who "demand that interpreters 'keep up with the speaker' [that they] are requiring them to do the very thing that will produce inaccurate interpretation" (Cokely, 1986, p. 374).

Transliteration

Transliteration typically means matching a sign to every spoken word, or vice versa, although some authors offer convincing arguments that transliteration is not a simple matching and replacement process (cf. Winston, 1989). RID offers a Certificate of Transliteration that requires passing a comprehensive evaluation in which "the target message resulting from the transliteration process remains true and accurate with regard to the source text" and there "should be no substitutions and very few (if any) omissions" (Friedenreich, 1996, p. 24).

When interpreters transliterate, they must convey messages using sequences of signs arranged according to English syntax, which can be difficult because of the extra time it takes to sign a message in this way as compared to expressing the same message in spoken English. To overcome this problem, interpreters rely on their ability to incorporate ASL features in English word order. Although there is little research that has systematically examined the linguistics of transliteration, what has been done suggests:

[A]t least some forms of transliteration include not only English-like signing of the source message but also many features of ASL. This type of transliteration requires skills in both ASL and English in order to achieve and blend pragmatic and linguistic goals in the production of a target message. Analyzing the source message and producing a target form that is both functionally equivalent and structurally similar to the source is a complex process and requires more than the simple recoding of English words. (Winston, 1989, p. 163)

Some ASL features that research has found in transliterations are (1) repetition to indicate plurality, (2) addition of the -*mm* adverbial—nonmanual linguistic cues that accompany signs—to the sign WRITE to provide a pragmatic transliteration of the spoken expression *to mark down at random*, and (3) the use of facial and body expressions to clarify the intended meaning of a sign such as SELF-RESPECT.

The extent to which deaf and hard-of-hearing people prefer transliteration over interpretation is not known. It serves well when it is necessary to convey the exact wording of a motion made at a meeting, the terms in a legal document, and in other instances in which a sense interpretation might cause the deaf participant to misconstrue the original message. Because transliteration and interpretation differ, interpreters need mastery of both techniques.

Turn-Taking

Every culture has rules governing turn-taking in conversations. Competence in a language includes knowledge of the signals that speakers use to indicate that they have concluded their speeches and are yielding their turns. Deaf speakers drop their hands to indicate that they have finished, which corresponds to speakers dropping their voices. Interpreters can easily mark, and usually anticipate, the end of an utterance. But what do they do when a speaker and signer overlap their expressions?

This question was examined in an interpreted interview between a deaf student and a nondeaf professor (Roy, 1992). When it was necessary, the interpreter intruded in the conversation in several ways. First of all, he stopped the student with a hand signal, the equivalent of "Wait a minute." When the professor overlapped the student, the interpreter indicated the student had not finished by continuing to voice the student's signs—a tactic that did not always succeed. Another technique used by the interpreter was to hold the overlapping comment of one until the other had finished, something that can place a heavy demand on the interpreter's memory. Several points emerged from the study:

> [T]he interpreter [was] an active, third participant, with the potential to influence both the direction and the outcome of the event, and that event itself is intercultural and interpersonal rather than simply mechanical and technical. (Roy, 1992, p. 24)

Second, the interpreter tacitly acknowledged the social differences between the participants, never interrupting the professor, never saying to her, "Wait a minute," though he did interrupt the student four times in the fifteen-minute interview. Would the same order of precedence hold if the interaction took place at a Deaf club or a school cafeteria rather than in a professor's office? The answers depend on interpreter judgments made on the spot.

Interpreters at a large meeting encounter an annoying tendency of normally hearing persons to begin talking just before or precisely when another speaker stops. Because the deaf participants must wait for the interpreter to finish, they often cannot insert a comment or question, because someone else has already started talking before they can begin. In such circumstances, interpreters sometimes advise the chairperson before the meeting about this situation. Another interpreter ploy is to tell the deaf participants to signal when they wish to intervene. The interpreter can then say, as the speaker is drawing to a close, that a deaf participant wishes to say something.

Mouthing

When there is contact between a sign language and a spoken language, mouthing often occurs. It is always performed without voice. Davis (1989) identified three different types of mouthing available to the interpreter:

- *English mouthing:* The articulation of an English word, which is intended to facilitate lipreading and/or to clarify the accompanying sign
- *ASL mouthing:* Mouthing related to ASL lexical items, in order to clarify the sign, particularly in the case of ASL adverbials
- *Reduced English mouthing:* Mouth configurations between the extremes of full English mouthing and ASL mouthing

The type of mouthing depends on whether a person is interpreting, transliterating, or using English-based signing and whether a deaf participant wants to speechread all or part of a spoken utterance. In some instances, interpreters do not mouth what they hear but enhance the meaning of what they are signing with ASL mouthings. There are documented ASL mouth movements that, for example, accompany signs like FINALLY and SUCCEED (PAH); HUGE and TALL (CHA); LATE and HAVEN'T (LA LA); and FINISH (FISH). Mouthing expands interpreters' linguistic options by using elements of both ASL and English.

SUMMARY

Every interpreter has the duty to create in the target language the most accurate and most comprehensible interpretation of the source language. They have available to them a number of linguistic tools that can assist them in that awesome task. But without a firm knowledge of the two cultures that under-lie both the target and source languages, their efforts may suffer.

With language and culture being what they are, perfect interpretation re-mains an ideal that is seldom attained. Translators, whose similar work is car-ried out under less-demanding conditions than interpreters, nonetheless lament how far they often fall short of the ideal conversion of source language to target language:

> Translation at best is rarely what is called "rewarding." Things made of words get out of joint in the moving and, no matter how skillful he may be ordinarily, nor "on which rung of the ladder he stands," the translator is half doomed before he begins. (Proetz, 1971, p. 15)

Interpreters can take comfort from that view—even as they strive to prove "It ain't necessarily so."

8

THE BUSINESS OF INTERPRETING

Like lawyers, dentists, physicians, and other professionals, most interpreters interpret because it is their livelihood. Their pay is not secondary to the goodness of rendering a much-needed service—it is a primary incentive. This holds equally for part-time and full-time interpreters. That interpreting has a financial aspect raises issues that have long confronted other professionals. Whether they choose independent practice or full-time employment, interpreters must meet standards imposed by their profession and must satisfy the people for whom they interpret. With the professionalization of interpreting have come obligations as well as monetary rewards.

SUPPLY AND DEMAND

Economic factors like supply and demand affect both the cost and the availability of interpreting services. When demand exceeds supply, decisions must be made about how to allocate the supply. How are such decisions made? Does the dollar alone rule? Where does money to pay interpreters come from? Should anyone other than deaf people pay for interpreting services?

Federal Legislation

Three major federal laws have led to a substantial increase in demand for interpreting services. The first was the Vocational Rehabilitation Act of 1973, which sought to enhance job training and employment opportunities for people with disabilities. The second was the Education of All Handicapped Children Act of 1975, now known as the Individuals with Disabilities Education

Act (IDEA). IDEA mandates a free, appropriate, public education for all people with disabilities. The third, the Americans with Disabilities Act (ADA), forbids discrimination in the workplace.

Vocational Rehabilitation Act of 1973

While the founding of the Registry for Interpreters of the Deaf (RID) in 1964 gave birth to the interpreting profession, the Vocational Rehabilitation Act of 1973 helped make it a viable career option. Regulations for implementing Section 504 of the act call for "reasonable accommodations" for a person's physical and mental disabilities. For deaf people, interpreting is a reasonable accommodation. The law gives them the right to an interpreter in employment, housing, transportation, education, and health activities that use federal funds. It shifts the cost of interpreting away from the participants to the federal government or agencies using federal funds.

The shift did not occur overnight. There have been challenges in court as some colleges and state vocational rehabilitation agencies resisted covering interpreters' fees. Title I of the act provides states with grants for helping people with disabilities prepare for and obtain employment. State agencies were able to tap into these grants to pay interpreters serving deaf people enrolled in career-oriented training programs or seeking employment.

This law has had far-reaching effects, as it covers all federal agencies engaged in training and rehabilitation, as well as those providing health, welfare, and social services. As examples of the breadth of the law, the Department of Justice interprets it to mean that interpreting services must be provided in all federal court proceedings and to incarcerated deaf persons who are enrolled in a prison's rehabilitation program.

Individuals with Disabilities Education Act

In 1975, Congress passed Public Law 94-142, the Education for All Handicapped Children Act. In 1990, P.L. 101-476 reauthorized P.L. 94-142 and renamed it the Individuals with Disabilities Education Act (IDEA) to reflect the current practice of using person-first language. This law requires that, to the extent feasible, all children with disabilities must receive a free and appropriate education in the least restrictive environment—a mandate that has the effect of placing many deaf students in general classes where interpreters must be provided. Thus, it dramatically increased the employment of educational interpreters—a situation that is discussed further in Chapter 10.

Americans with Disabilities Act

The Americans with Disabilities Act (ADA) has set a legislative landmark. Passed in 1990, it is "a federal antidiscrimination statute designed to remove barriers which prevent qualified individuals with disabilities from enjoying the same employment opportunities that are available to persons without

disabilities" (*ADA Handbook,* 1991, p. 1). It applies to all employment practices, including job applications, hiring, firing, advancement, compensation,
and training. ADA requires that employers make reasonable accommodation
to enable persons with disabilities to obtain and hold employment. For deaf
persons, interpreting fulfills that requirement. If they are employed by a company with 15 or more employees, they must be provided an interpreter if one
is needed to enable them to participate actively in a meeting, a retraining program, or any other job-related function.

ADA has had a major impact on the employment of certified interpreters
in professional settings such as health-related and legal situations. Along
with the increase in demand has come increasing sensitivity toward the qualifications of the interpreter. Thus, nationally certified interpreters are in demand and enjoy the status of being at the top of most if not all interpreting
pay scales.

ADA does not guarantee that all situations will be covered, nor does it
make it more likely that the inclination of some businesses to resist providing
interpreting services will disappear. Nevertheless, since its enactment all
states have experienced a dramatic increase in the demand for interpreters.

State Legislation and Regulation

States have followed the federal government's lead in requiring interpreting for
deaf people in a number of situations. Many states have supplemented IDEA
with their own regulations assuring that a deaf student will have interpreting
in regular education classes. Some states have also established evaluation and
certification procedures to ensure that interpreters working in schools meet at
least a minimum standard.

In legal proceedings, state courts, too, have increasingly granted deaf people the right to interpreters. Closely related to giving deaf people greater access to the judicial system are the recent cases that have overturned rulings
forbidding deaf persons to serve on juries. The arguments have been that providing an interpreter violates the principles of confidentiality and undue influence in jury deliberations, because jurors might be reluctant to express
themselves candidly in the presence of someone who is not a juror. Another
reason for excluding interpreters is that the novelty of the interpreter's presence might exert too much weight on the jury's decisions. A third argument
against allowing deaf jurors has been that jurors must be able to hear wit-
nesses in order to judge their credibility, because interpreters might not convey the extralinguistic features that enter into such judgments. Recently,
however, several courts have ruled that greater harm is done by denying deaf
people their civil right to participate. In one such case, Greg Rathbun, a deaf
man from Salt Lake City, Utah, accepted a call to jury duty but requested an
interpreter. The court accepted his right to serve but insisted he should pay

for his own interpreter. Greg sued under the ADA and won. Utah courts bowed to the U.S. Department of Justice and agreed henceforth to pay for deaf jurors' interpreters.

Like all legislation, state laws change from time to time. Interpreters should stay current about laws affecting their practices. The National Center for Law and the Deaf (now housed at the National Association of the Deaf, in Silver Spring, Maryland) prepares occasional summaries of state interpreter laws.

PROJECTING DEMAND

An obvious limit on interpreter demand is the number of people who are deaf. To be useful, the number must be divided into two categories: those who know and use sign language and those who do not. The latter are largely late-deafened people who may find oral interpreters useful but who typically do not use sign language interpreters. Table 8-1 provides recent estimates for the United States and Canada. These numbers will change over time, but they provide a *tentative* basis for estimating the demand for interpreter services.

In 1991, the United States had about 1.35 million deaf people; while, in 1987, Canada had approximately 45,000. In those years, fewer than one-quarter of the deaf people in the United States (303,000) and about one-third of those in Canada (15,000) were born deaf or became deaf prior to 19 years of age and so were likely to sign. The probability that the remainder—over a million in the

TABLE 8-1   Hearing Impairment, by Degree and Age at Onset: Canada, 1987, and United States, 1991

Type of Hearing Impairment	United States Number	Percent	Canada Number	Percent
Population 3 years of age and older	235,688,000	100.00	24,806,180	100.00
Hearing-impaired	20,295,000	8.60	908,825	4.10
Deaf, all ages at onset	1,350,000	0.57	45,575	0.23[a]
Adult deaf (onset at and after 19 years of age)	1,047,000	0.44	30,490	0.15[a]
Pre-adult deaf (onset prior to 19 years of age)	303,000	0.13	15,085	0.08[a]
Prelingual deaf (onset prior to 3 years of age)	190,422	0.08	[b]	[b]

Sources: Ries (1994) and Schein (1991).
[a]Denominator is 19,736,085 for persons 15 years of age and older.
[b]Cannot calculate from data provided.

United States and 30,000 in Canada—would know sign language declines as the age at onset of their deafness increases.

These estimates do not immediately yield the projected demand for interpreters. The missing factor is the frequency with which these deaf people will use interpreters. The answers depend, at least in part, on such factors as age and occupation. Some authorities have suggested that, to properly serve the deaf population, there should be one interpreter for every 12 deaf persons (Bailey & Straub, 1992). At that rate, the United States would need 25,250 Interpreters and Canada 1,250. Neither country's present supply approximates those ideal numbers.

Elementary and Secondary Schools

Education should continue to be a major source of employment for interpreters. Although schools already employ many interpreters, it is likely that requests for their services will continue to outstrip supply for quite some time to come. On the basis of reports by local schools and state education departments of students, there were 30,341 students in the 1992–1993 school year who were under 22 years old and were receiving special education services (Schildroth & Hotto, 1994). Because some agencies fail to report, Schildroth and Hotto believe their figure underestimates the actual numbers enrolled by 35 to 40 percent of the U.S. total, yielding a gross estimate between 46,678 and 50,568. By comparison, the *American Annals of the Deaf* (Vol. 139, 1994) lists enrollments totaling 53,179—again an underestimate because many schools listed did not provide their enrollments. Not all of these students use interpreters, but many do. We can expect that the employment of interpreters in school settings will rise as school districts come to terms with their obligations to provide interpreting services and as the availability of interpreters increases.

But need for interpreters does not always lead to their employment. On some occasions, schools and parents have thought that if deaf children make it to high school without interpreters then there is no need for them to have one at that late stage in their education, even though the children might use sign language as the primary means of communication. Schools may resist hiring interpreters for budgetary reasons and opt instead to hire an aide with signing skills. Parents may resist wanting an interpreter because they are still denying the extent of their children's deafness and need for assistance in communication. One interpreter educator received a call from a school administrator asking if any of her graduates would be willing to be a communication aide. The administrator was adamantly against hiring someone to interpret and said that the parents were also against this type of support service. Instead, the administrator asked for someone who, in her own words, would "follow her [the deaf high school student] around to her classes and make her understand . . . . we definitely do not want to pay for an interpreter, we want a paraprofessional." Although the interpreter educator knew of many qualified interpreters looking for a full-time position, she felt compelled to stick up for her profession and insisted that she only knew of interpreters trained to interpret and that none of them were prepared for work as only a communication aide, whatever that job might entail.

Postsecondary Education

A report on the number of deaf and hard-of-hearing students attending postsecondary institutions found 47% of U.S. two-year and four-year schools enrolled one or more deaf or hard-of-hearing students in the four-year period from 1989 to 1993 (National Center for Educational Statistics, 1994). It should be noted, however, that the survey yielding these data defines deaf and hard-of-hearing students as those who identify themselves as such to the schools. Some do and some do not. Second, the survey did not include non-degree-granting programs, Gallaudet University, or the National Technical Institute for the Deaf. Third, not all institutions cooperate, and so some student counts are absent. Taking these three points into account, any estimate of postsecondary demand based on these data will be too low.

Even so, we can say with confidence that during that time there was a marked increase in interpreting services. Table 8-2 shows that between the 1989–1990 and 1993–1994 school years the number of students provided with interpreters grew from 7,430 to 8,100. In the same period, students using oral interpreters increased from 750 to 970. These increases—9% for interpreters and 29% for oral interpreters—should be read with the relatively short time frame in mind, which makes them impressive as expressions of trends.

What these numbers do not show is whether the supply of interpreters from 1989–1993 met the demand. Did every deaf student who requested an interpreter receive one? Nor do the estimates take into account deaf students who reject interpreting, because they either do not know how to sign, do not want to draw attention to their deafness, or do not expect sufficient benefit from interpreting. One deaf student knew he could benefit from an interpreter, after he had observed one for another deaf student in his class. Still, he refused to ask the university for interpreting services because he felt that having an interpreter would draw too much attention to himself and result in his being labeled "deaf," an identity he rejected.

Spear (1986) laments the underutilization of interpreters by persons with hearing losses and notes that in his experience they "are unaware of the benefits of using an interpreter" (p. 10). Many of these, he believes, are hard-of-hearing persons who do not know sign language. Since 1979, however, RID

TABLE 8-2   Estimated Number of Postsecondary Students Provided with Interpreters: United States, 1989–1990 to 1992–1993

Type of Interpreter Service	1989–1990	1990–1991	1991–1992	1992–1993
All types of interpreting	8,180	8,230	8,770	9,070
Interpreters/transliterators	7,430	7,440	7,970	8,100
Oral interpreters/transliterators	750	790	800	970

Source: National Center for Educational Statistics, U.S. Department of Education (1994), p. 20.
Note: Figures are rounded.

has recognized oral interpreting and has endorsed it as one means of interpreting for persons who prefer it over signed interpretation or who do not know sign language.

OTHER DEMANDS

The range of opportunities for interpreters has proliferated. They can now be seen on television signing the news, in theaters and opera houses making the performances intelligible to deaf audiences, and in government agencies providing clear communication. In 1990 Gary Malkowski, a Deaf Canadian, was elected to the Ontario Legislative Assembly. He demanded and received funding from the legislature for a full-time staff of interpreters. They interpreted not only during legislative sessions, but also during meetings with his constituents.

Another indicator of the demand for interpreters is seen in the number of calls for interpreters that interpreter-referral agencies receive. One interpreter-referral service in a major city has turned down 200 requests a month (the total number of requests received is not reported). Extrapolating from that experience, the agency estimates that more than 100,000 requests go unfilled annually throughout the nation (Bailey & Straub, 1992). Of course, extrapolating from one example cannot be expected to yield a reliable estimate of unmet national demand. Nonetheless, the 100,000 figure provides a sobering guess at the unmet demand.

NEGATIVE INFLUENCES ON DEMAND

In making projections of future demand, statisticians must remember that Congress can pass laws that limit or rescind previously granted rights, agencies can loosen regulations requiring interpreters, and courts can accept arguments that limit deaf persons' rights to interpreting services. One doctor refused to pay for interpreting services. He claimed that he and the deaf patient had always been able to communicate via speechreading and notes. In court, the patient argued that using notes and speechreading was a last resort for her and that it carried a greater risk for misunderstanding. She won her case.

Another negative factor that can influence demand for interpreters is the emergence of alternatives to signed interpretation. Real-time transcribers (like court reporters) can produce visible interpretations when their coded input is entered into a computer and projected onto a screen for viewing by an audience. A computer-based voice-to-text system is now available, although it is cumbersome at present. But technology is moving along quickly, and higher accuracy rates and greater versatility in voice recognition will occur in the near future. Even now, a hand-held voice-to-text system is on the drawing board. Whether any of these arrangements will be effective and acceptable to a large segment of the deaf population desiring sign language and not English text remains to be seen. The potential for such technology, however, should counter overly optimistic projections of demands for interpreters. For a further discussion of alternative strategies, see Chapter 11.

THE SUPPLY

Who are the interpreters? A survey of 160 interpreters at the 1980 RID convention (Cokely, 1981) found that three-quarters were female and only 2.4% were members of minority groups. Almost two-thirds wore glasses or contact lenses to correct their vision. Eight of 10 were right-handed. A little more than 6 of 10 had nondeaf parents, while the rest had one or two deaf parents. Educationally, 13% had never attended college; 26.4% had attended college for less than four years, and 60.6% had completed four or more years of college. These data might not accurately reflect the characteristics of interpreters in the field, because conferences are often attended by those who have the funds to attend or by those whose employers cover their costs. Other research has shown that a high proportion of those attending RID conventions hold administrative or instructional positions in interpreter education programs.

The RID surveyed its 1991–1992 membership and found 9.5% of the 3,070 members who replied to its survey listed themselves as members of a minority group—an increase of nearly four times over the earlier estimated racial composition of the membership. The membership remained predominantly female (almost 86% women). Information on vision, hearing, parents' hearing, and handedness was not requested. The average age (median) of those reporting was 36.9 years. Educationally, RID members had more education than those in the 1980 sample: only 8.4% had less than two years of college, 16.0% held associate of arts degrees, 26.1% bachelor's degrees, 24.1% master's degrees, and 2.7% doctorates.

In 1989, a survey of affiliated Canadian interpreters reported the same predominance of females—83.5% (Schein & Yarwood, 1990). Almost all of those who replied (95.3%) were Canadian citizens. Their median age was 32.3 years, somewhat younger than the RID members. Canadian interpreters had an average of 2.2 years of postsecondary education, though not necessarily of education directly relevant to interpreting. A corresponding average for the 1991–1992 RID respondents could not be calculated because of differences in the questions asked by the two surveys.

Where do interpreters work? As noted, the majority tend to be employed by educational programs, both in Canada and in the United States. Table 8-3 summarizes the responses of RID members to the 1991–1992 survey. Over half work in schools. Canadian interpreters spent a lesser proportion of their time in schools (40.3%), although interpreting in classrooms was the single most frequent site mentioned.

Continuing studies of the interpreter supply that plot trends are needed to guide interpreter education programs and to assist government planners. Are interpreters as a group growing older, younger, or staying about the same? The answer is important to estimating the future supply, since attrition due to retirements can be expected as members age. Is the gender difference narrowing, widening, or staying the same? What about educational qualifications: Are interpreters becoming more educated, on average? And is a substantial portion of the interpreter supply continuing to be drawn from among those with deaf parents?

Total memberships in RID and AVLIC do not give a complete account of the interpreter supply at one time in the two countries. Many educational interpreters, for example, have not joined either organization, some because

TABLE 8-3   Principal Place of Employment for Interpreters Who Are Members of RID: United States, 1991

Place of Employment	Number	Percentage
All places	2,163	100.0
College/university	680	31.4
Elementary/secondary	522	24.1
Referral agency, nonprofit	486	22.5
Referral agency, for profit	74	3.4
Self-employed	401	18.5

Source: Personal communication, Registry of Interpreters for the Deaf, 10 November 1994.

Note: Entries for those who responded to questionnaire for period July 1991–June 1992.

they do not feel qualified for certification, others because they do not seek a long-term career in interpreting. State certification programs offer the recognition some need for employment. Similarly, membership in a state or local organization satisfies other interpreters. That a large proportion of interpreters have not affiliated with any of the national, state, or local associations reflects unfavorably on the professionalization of interpreting. Identification with one's profession through membership in one or more of its organizations is an important step that interpreters should consider seriously.

In tracking the interpreter supply, it would be helpful to have statistics on attrition rates. Reasons for attrition should be investigated assiduously to determine the effects of health problems relating to interpreting, such as repetitive-stress injuries, professional burnout, and other factors that need attention. Retaining an interpreter costs society considerably less than educating one. To evaluate the interpreter supply, planners must have reasonably precise estimates of the numbers in the field; to enable stakeholders to improve interpreting conditions, they need data beyond simply knowing the numbers interpreting.

REMUNERATION

Whatever the long-term relation of supply to demand, the present imbalance places the interpreting profession in a position favorable to increasing its fees. The classic law of supply and demand states that the price of a product or service will go up when demand exceeds supply, a situation that exists today. Yet, the majority of interpreters regard themselves as underpaid (Schein & Yarwood, 1990).

Freelance Versus Full-Time Practice

Interpreters frequently agonize over choosing a full-time position versus freelancing. Either has its attractions and its detractions. Flexibility may be important to interpreters employed full-time by large corporations. The company may have many deaf workers, yet management often demands that interpreters accept such added duties as clerical tasks or teaching nondeaf employees. Interpreters in such settings confront tradeoffs that are sometimes difficult to evaluate—spending much of their time in nonprofessional activities in return for a good salary and substantial extra benefits. They may take little comfort from realizing that other professionals face similar choices when they give up their independence for the benefits of full-time employment.

For those interpreters who are employed full time, the principal complaints center on the lack of respect for their contributions. Businesses find it difficult to place interpreters in a professional hierarchy. What is the equivalent occupation: law, nursing, medicine, or what? One factor that places interpreters on the lower rung of a professional ladder is their relatively brief educational preparation. Physicians attend school for eight years, lawyers for seven, and teachers for four, whereas most interpreter education programs usually require only two years. Lack of public respect translates into low wages and salaries.

Freelance interpreters and those in private practice do not receive paid holidays and vacations, sick leave, health insurance, or pensions. These fringe benefits average about 22% of annual wages and salaries. So a freelance interpreter who is paid $50 per hour should compare that rate to $39 per hour, the equivalent amount a full-time employee receives before average fringe benefits are added. Even then, most freelance interpreters have substantial "down time", periods without paid assignments because of illness, injuries, or simply lack of assignments. Occasionally, they may not get paid for an assignment.

Freelance interpreters also must cover their expenses for travel, bookkeeping, and such. They must keep records for income tax purposes, something with which most employees do not need to bother. Because they lack fixed income, interpreters are often denied bank loans and mortgages—one more source of dissatisfaction. To be an interpreter in private practice, then, requires financial resources to cover these contingencies (see Fischer, 1995, for more information about handling the business aspect of interpreting).

On the other hand, working on a contractual basis for an interpreter-referral agency, though similar in some respects to having a private practice, has several of the benefits associated with full-time interpreting. The agency makes all the arrangements for the interpreting assignment, including handling all of the paperwork. They take care of billing. They provide information about each assignment—the participants, the setting, directions to the job site, and the expected length of time required for interpreting. Unreliable participants are easier to avoid because the agency will have a record of them. An agency will arrange for a team interpreter or a relay interpreter if necessary. In the event of a problem, the agency is an advocate for the interpreter.

One more consideration enters the choice between full-time employment and independent practice—pleasure. Freelance interpreters enjoy having no fixed commitments: their time is their own to sell or withhold as they please. The person who joins a company tacitly agrees to serving fixed hours, often in a fixed location. Freelance interpreters encounter a broader array of assignments, constantly meet new people, and encounter different topics. So in making their choices, interpreters have much to consider besides remuneration.

Is freelance interpreting a good career? Because so many interpreters choose private practice, one might suppose the answer is yes. But in reality many interpreters freelance because no full-time positions are available or because they have another full-time or part-time job that does not involve interpreting. In sum, a private practice does offer several attractions:

- Being one's own boss
- Selecting assignments and people for whom one is willing to interpret
- Developing one's own work schedule
- Working out of a home office, which offers opportunities for tax deductions

There are also disadvantages:

- Lack of opportunities to develop interpreting skills
- Sporadic income
- No employer-paid health, retirement, and other benefits
- Responsibility for finding substitutes when sick
- Must cover all costs of practice (e.g., Phone charges and transportation)
- Responsibility for collecting fees

Possibly the single most important factor in choosing private practice may be availability of people with whom the interpreter is willing to work. Freelance interpreters have a variety of settings in which to interpret—an advantage to those who thrive on variety. Some interpreters, however, might not feel comfortable interpreting in some settings and with some people. Although such prejudices might limit their earnings, the psychological benefits of being in control probably offset the potential financial restrictions.

TRENDS IN FEES

The days of the underpaid interpreter may be coming to an end as precedents for fair salaries are established. In Canada, interpreters working for the federal or provincial governments are paid the same rate as other foreign-language interpreters. In 1994, the secretary of state set that rate at C$50 an hour (about US$37.50), with a minimum guarantee of three hours. For those who pass a rigorous examination, the rate is C$675.00 per day (about US$506). In addition, the Canadian secretary of state's regulations mandate rest periods every forty minutes, so that for most interpreting assignments two interpreters are required. Similar bright spots can be found here and there in the United States, although fees are generally lower than those of interpreters who work for the Canadian government.

Pro Bono Publico

Interpreters sometimes forego remuneration. Many do not charge for interpreting religious services. Some may interpret for the performing arts only "for experience." Often, the actors in a community theater are volunteers; because everyone involved in the production is a volunteer, some interpreters likewise give their services gratis. If the theater pays its performers, however, interpreters are in a position to request payment in line with what the performers are being paid for rehearsal and preparation time.

Who Pays?

In most instances, federal and state statutes and regulations have resolved the question of who pays for interpreting. Seldom is it the deaf person. Section 504 of the Vocational Rehabilitation Act requires agencies that receive federal funds for any activity to provide deaf people with free access to that activity. Physicians pay the interpreter, if the deaf patient is covered by Medicare, because federal funds are involved. ADA requires employers to cover reasonable interpreting expenses, when required by the deaf person's job.

For agencies that do not receive federal dollars and situations that are not covered by federal laws, who pays remains an open question. Where public functions are involved, state and local governments usually can be persuaded to provide interpreter services at no cost to deaf people, if they have not already mandated such services. Most courts provide interpreters without charge to the deaf person, whether as a witness, a plaintiff, or a defendant. There are exceptions. In 1993, the Oklahoma Disability Law Center received more than a dozen complaints of judges either failing to appoint interpreters, as required by both state and federal laws, or trying to make illegal arrangements (*Tulsa World,* August 14, 1993, cited in *Silent News,* November 1993). The Center cited the case of a judge who jailed a deaf man *until the deaf man arranged for his own interpreter!*

Because interpreting is free to deaf people in so many instances, they may be upset when they find they must pay. If they engage interpreters for their personal affairs—to assist in buying a car, investigating a house for sale, or drawing up a will—then they bear the cost. In such instances, their responsibility should be made clear to them when scheduling the assignment.

More and more businesses are realizing the benefits of hiring service personnel who can sign or, even better, providing interpreters. One example is seen in the advertisements of a car dealership which announces that deaf customers can request an interpreter who is nationally certified and is experienced in new car sales and service. The authors have also encountered realtors, retail clerks, bankers, and other business personnel who have trained as interpreters.

In time, consumer education (to be discussed) should alleviate disputes about who pays and reduce deaf persons' resentment when they must pay. For the near future, prior discussions between interpreters, deaf payers, and referral agencies should be routine, in order to avoid any misunderstandings about who is responsible for paying the interpreter.

Compensating for Interpreting Hazards

Interpreters confront numerous hazards: unpaid bills, missed appointments, hostile participants. There are also actual physical hazards, such as those discussed in Chapter 4. The legal and social aspects of repetitive-motion injuries are seldom talked about but have ramifications for interpreters. Freelance interpreters have long been thought to be self-employed, hence solely responsible for their work. If they choose to have medical insurance, they must cover its cost. Until recently, it was thought that freelance interpreters could not be compensated for repetitive-motion injuries, except by their own medical insurance. That changed in February 1995, when a New York Worker's Compensation Board ruled that a freelance interpreter was an employee of an interpreter referral agency and, therefore, could claim Worker's Compensation benefits. Other states are now following that precedent and granting interpreters similar protection.

MARKETING INTERPRETER SERVICES

In discussing marketing issues, we are focusing on the broader issue of promoting the profession as opposed to the interpreter per se. Nevertheless, we acknowledge that interpreters should take steps to promote themselves, such as maintaining an up-to-date résumé, having a business card, and keeping track of expenses. They should expect to compete with one another for work. Those who are more competent and maintain higher ethical standards should do better, although charges for services will also play a role in who gets hired (see the box titled "The High Cost of Experience?"). For more about the personal aspect of marketing oneself, see Fischer (1995).

In keeping with the more general business side of professional interpreting, stakeholders should consider plans for optimal utilization of this valuable resource. Warner (1986) urges each state to develop a program for utilization of its interpreters:

> The marketing of interpreter services is a major responsibility of interpreters and interpreter organizations. If interpreter services are to evolve as an accepted vehicle for deaf people to access public agencies, those services must be sought not only by the deaf community, but also by public and private agencies. (p. 366)

Although we agree in principle that efforts should be made to increase public awareness of interpreting and of its importance not only to the Deaf community but to the general community as well, we do not agree as readily that the interpreting profession should have the sole responsibility for its pro-

---

The High Cost of Experience?

Interpreting jobs do not always go to the best qualified or most experienced interpreter. One interpreter educator who is a nationally certified interpreter and has had much experience in a medical setting described how the competition snuck up on her:

> I was meeting with a local hospital's administrators to discuss an on-call interpreting arrangement for medical interpreting services. After a lengthy discussion on availability, experience, and certification levels, we discussed rate of pay. At that point, they lost interest in me immediately. It turned out that they have talked to another local interpreter who is charging one-half of my rate. This other interpreter is a recent graduate of mine who does not yet have the highest state certification level for interpreting and is nowhere near obtaining an RID certificate. I am sure my former student didn't underbid me intentionally because it's a small, one-horse town here. She was marketing herself, albeit questionably, in the medical field.

---

motion. Governments, Deaf community organizations, and perhaps others should be involved. Among the others are educators, who, we believe, have a responsibility for preparing deaf children to be adults who are knowledgeable about their rights to have interpreters, as well as to know how to obtain these services and how to benefit optimally from them.

Marketing of any service has a number of components. Here we consider a few of the major factors: consumer education, certification and licensure, malpractice, and cost–benefit analysis.

CONSUMER EDUCATION

Given the history of professional interpreting, the need to teach consumers how best to use it becomes paramount. The education of deaf children should contain at least one unit on the correct use of interpreters, because it is a virtual certainty that they will need to work with interpreters at some point in their adult lives. The unit should emphasize that the deaf person is only one of the participants in an interpreted discourse, and it should teach the roles of nondeaf participants. The unit should be part of a larger curriculum designed specifically to provide deaf children with information they will need to become optimally functioning deaf adults.

What about deaf adults who are already out of school? Adult consumer education should cover the participants' rights and obligations, the characteristics of good interpreters and how to identify them, the history of sign and oral interpreting, and information about organizations like RID and AVLIC to which consumers can turn for updated information. Instruction should be available to them in adult education programs and in workshops conducted by organizations like the National Association of the Deaf and the National Fraternal Society of the Deaf. These organizations should undertake the continuing education of their members, since even those who will have studied the subject in school will need periodic updating to keep abreast of developments.

In addition, the curriculum should be adapted for presentation to nondeaf audiences such as school-age children, businesses, and service agencies who have extensive contact with deaf persons. The fact that many deaf children are now educated in public schools and use interpreters makes it imperative that their nondeaf classmates learn what interpreters do and how to behave in interpreted encounters. Businesses that employ a large number of deaf workers stand to benefit from having their management and other employees learn about the role of interpreters in the workplace. Service agencies, such as rehabilitation and mental health, should require their personnel to receive information about working with interpreters so they will be better prepared to serve deaf people.

CERTIFICATION AND LICENSURE

Every profession confronts the problem of identifying those it regards as qualified. Dentists, lawyers, and physicians are all licensed. In most states, so are dental hygienists, plumbers, and schoolteachers. Other professions and trades that use certification include psychotherapy, physical therapy, and speech pathology. The two approaches are not interchangeable, and they have different functions.

License

Governments or their designated agents issue *licenses.* which, as the name implies, authorize the holder to do some specified thing. Practice without it is forbidden. Educational, experiential, and procedural requirements are usually rigorous. Licensees face sanctions that the issuing government can impose in the event of abuses—sanctions that, in addition to loss of the license, may include monetary fines and even, in extreme cases, imprisonment.

Certification

A *certificate* attests that the bearer has met specified requirements and is entitled to use a designated title. With respect to occupations, states seldom issue certificates. That format is usually assigned to organizations, any of which can certify whatever they wish. Generally, the educational requirements and examination procedures for certification are less rigorous than those for licensure. Certificates typically do not have the force of law. When they do, they most often limit use of a title, such as "Certified Psychologist," "Dental Hygienist," or "Qualified Hearing Aid Practitioner." In general, the only penalty for malpractice is loss of certification.

From the consumers' standpoint, certificates and licenses usually assure them only of minimal qualifications. The holders of these documents have met some basic requirements; licenses and certificates do not promise that holders are the most competent practitioners. The assurance of even basic quality, however, is far better than having no standards at all from which to judge a potential practitioner, so consumers generally are pleased to have the guidance that these documents offer.

Appendix A lists the interpreter certifications offered through the RID. Examinations are required for each certificate. In the absence of licensing in most states, RID certification has become the standard evidence of competence. In Canada, AVLIC has fewer certification categories, but their standing in that country is similar to that of RID's certificates in the United States.

Profile: Judith Lee Carson

Judith Lee Carson has a Comprehensive Skills Certificate and has been a member of the Registry of Interpreters for the Deaf since 1965. She is chairperson of an Associate Arts degree program in ASL Studies at Vincennes University in Indiana. Prior to this position, she worked at the Indiana School for the Deaf for 23 years in various capacities. She has been active in RID since its founding, serving on both the national board and her state board. She is a strong believer in national certification because it gives "consumers an idea of the level of skill that can be expected when they hire an interpreter." In the following she comments on some of the changes that the field has undergone over the years:

> In the beginning, RID was under the umbrella of the National Association of the Deaf. As we matured as an organization, the members deemed that RID should be on its own. This did not

Continued

Profile: Judith Lee Carson   *Continued*

happen without a great deal of controversy, which seemed to follow RID with the onset of certification. Many folks were opposed to an ASL certification. Other folks were opposed to certifying a person's skill in manually coded English. Even more folks were opposed to certifying a person as an oral interpreter. Much soul searching had to occur to reach the conclusion that these areas were justifiable certification areas.

We struggled to develop a test that was fair, accurate, standardized, and valid. To this day, there are still people who do not accept the validity of the National Certification tests. I believe that what we have is a great improvement over the days when the only criteria for being an interpreter was being a child of a deaf adult or a teacher of the deaf, or a person from the church. Still, more work can be done to improve the tests. Specialization has also occurred and I feel that more specialized certifications will be developed with education and the medical field being two that should be considered. Training programs need to address the special needs of these areas.

The RID has gone through many hardships financially and in the control of its affairs. Whatever we have now will continue to grow stronger as long as the membership is actively involved. The RID is a living, breathing, viable organization that labors arduously to meet the needs of its members. Without a strong membership, no organization can succeed. Without a strong leadership to guide the membership, an organization will falter. Without a professional organization, interpreting will never remain a recognized, respected profession.

Certification Maintenance

Many professions require its membership to continually upgrade their skills and knowledge about their practice. The RID began a Certificate Maintenance Program on July 1, 1994. It asserted that such a program is necessary for interpreters to "maintain their skill level and stay abreast of the developments in the field, and assures consumers that a certified interpreter means quality interpreting services." The basic requirement is that a certified interpreter must earn nine continuing education units (CEUs) in a three-year cycle. How these CEUs are taken is carefully prescribed and covers a variety of areas, including studies that are of a professional nature, concerned with linguistic and cultural issues, both theoretical and experiential, relating to specialization (e.g., mental health, legal), and general knowledge. Alternatively, RID allows its members to earn two CEUs through an independent study.

MALPRACTICE

Although malpractice suits are not likely, they can occur. Interpreters should obtain malpractice insurance when possible, because even if they are wrongfully accused and ultimately successful in defending against such a suit, the cost of a legal defense can be overwhelming. A special insurance policy is available to interpreters who are RID members in good standing, although they need not be certified. The underwriters for this insurance policy also provide other insurance plans to cover medical, disability, and life insurance protection.

Interpreters hired by an agency are usually covered by the agency's insurance against malpractice suits. However, interpreters should not take such protection for granted. The wise interpreter asks what provisions the agency makes to defend its interpreters in legal actions against them.

Of course, a major protection against complaints is behaving ethically. Here are examples of some of the steps that interpreters might consider:

- Use discretion before accepting an assignment. Evaluate your ability to handle an assignment before accepting it. Preferably, hold appropriate certification for the assignment and be familiar with the professional knowledge associated with the area of your assignment.
- When possible, have informal discussions with participants before agreeing to an assignment, in order to determine if your skills and their expectations match.
- If proceedings are not being conducted properly, resign after explaining the adverse circumstances to the participants. If your conscience makes it hard for you to leave and you continue to interpret, you may later be included in the malpractice suit. Obtaining a transcript of the proceedings or, at least, copies of any of the participants' notes may help you defend yourself.
- If you are called on to serve in an emergency situation for which you do not feel qualified, do not accept the assignment. Gardner (1983) advises interpreters not to take at face value the designation of "emergency," because "Criminal interrogations and most medical procedures are *not* usually emergencies" (p. 13).

Like all professionals, interpreters will benefit from a healthy dose of common sense, a commitment to excellence, and honesty. As interpreting becomes more widely available and people become more sophisticated about it, malpractice suits also may become more frequent. Interpreters who are RID or AVLIC members can be disciplined by their organizations, as well as by state and local interpreter organizations. If an interpreter does not belong to such an organization, the agency providing the interpreter services can be sued. The Rehabilitation Act Amendments of 1973 and ADA require that interpreters must be qualified, but the laws and court decisions have not defined "qualified," something that will surely be clarified in the years to come. As with all pertinent laws and regulations, interpreters should be alert to such rulings when they emerge (see Fischer, 1995; Gardner, 1987; RID, 1995).

COST–BENEFIT ANALYSES

In the competition for funds within agencies and businesses, interpreters can expect to be challenged to demonstrate the effectiveness of their services in relation to their costs. Although such analyses are difficult, the task is hardly impossible. One begins by assigning a value to the communication. Instructions in lifesaving procedures for a paramedic on the job are obviously more valuable than the dialogue of a stage play. Deaf criminals cannot be convicted if they cannot understand the court proceedings and are unable to participate in their own defense. In effect, one can ask what would be the cost of depriving persons for whom the interpreting is taking place of the information being communicated. Society must determine how much intangibles like justice and participation in the management of governmental affairs are worth.

Another factor in a cost–benefit analysis is the number of persons involved. An interpreter for one student in a class costs more per student than if there are several students in the same class. So the interpreter's pay can be allocated as a fraction of the number of persons receiving the interpreted messages. It is important to note that the denominator of that fraction should not solely be the number of deaf participants. For example, in a town meeting, the total number attending are benefiting from the interpreting, not just the one or two deaf people in the audience. Without the interpreter, everyone at the meeting would be deprived of the deaf participants' opinions. We contend, therefore, that the cost for interpreting should be divided by the number of *all participants*, because all benefit from the interpretation. Insisting on that principle brings cost–benefit analyses into line with reality.

AN INNOVATIVE MARKETING PLAN

The shortage of interpreters has stimulated a Deaf attorney, Michael Schwartz, to develop a plan for using two-way television to increase the efficiency of providing interpreting services (Schwartz, 1994). The participants can be anywhere as long as they are within range of a television camera and can see a television receiver. In his original proposal, Schwartz suggests a location with many cameras and monitors, staffed 24 hours per day by qualified interpreters. Such an arrangement could be located in New York City, Los Angeles, or Kansas City. It could be called "Interpreter Central." Deaf and nondeaf participants would go to wherever a corresponding battery of television equipment is located in their area. Lawyers or physicians might have the equipment in their offices. When a deaf person appears, the lawyer or doctor would telephone Interpreter Central, which would then put an interpreter on the line. The basic idea might work with existing online interactive video capabilities. Although the principle is the same for any type of video technology, their costs and convenience of use will vary.

Such a marketing plan conquers distance, which is interpreters' greatest impediment to delivering their services efficiently. No time is wasted driving to an assignment, finding parking, and locating the correct room. Instead, interpreters can devote their working hours to interpreting. They need not fear midnight calls from hospitals and police stations, because they can handle assignments without leaving the comforts of Interpreter Central. When desired, an interpreter team can easily be assembled to manage difficult assignments.

Is this a practical addition to marketing interpreting? Will it work? Would all participants accept such arrangements? The answers to these questions await enterprising interpreters willing to undertake the first trial runs. Even if the idea has merit, there will be a period of trial and error during which flaws will need to be worked out of the system. A major consideration will be the deaf person's comprehension of two-dimensional signing and the diminished linguistic role for facial expressions and other nonmanual signals. Such a system might reduce the cost–benefit ratio but would surely alleviate the demand–supply imbalance. The idea, or a variation of it, seems worth investigating.

SUMMARY

Demand and supply are dynamic variables, changing with population shifts, with legislation, and with technological developments. Estimates of supply and demand need constant revision in the face of new data and altered circumstances. That is why we strongly recommend the continuous collection of information about both. Whether undertaken by the government or privately, that task is valuable for all stakeholders. They need the information to gauge the market properly, anticipate changes, and respond in ways that will yield optimal benefits to all concerned.

Summing up the impact of federal laws on the demand for and supply of interpreters, the President's Committee on Employment of People with Disabilities 1994 had this to say:

> Because of ADA the demand for *interpreter services* for people who are deaf or hearing-impaired has greatly improved. This has placed a tremendous strain on interpreter resources in many places, which already are stretched thin due to the scarcity of competent, trained interpreters . . . . (p. 15)
> [We recommend] expanded funding for interpreter training, better certification standards to ensure the quality of interpreter services, and encouraging schools and universities to include ASL as a standard part of their language department curricula. (p. 17)

Some states have already gone beyond the committee's suggestions. Through the Michigan Division on Deafness, interpreters in that state can obtain an assessment of their skills at one of three different levels, referred to as Quality Assurance Levels I, II, and III. Although some people in the interpreting field are reluctant to call these levels certification, they are in fact used in place of RID certification by interpreters seeking employment. The benefit of a statewide assessment program or certification is that it enables the state to impose some regulation on the hundreds of interpreters who are not yet nationally certified. They also encourage these same interpreters to continue to develop their skills in preparation for national certification.

The shortage of interpreters will not soon be alleviated. Indeed, the demand for them is likely to increase as more deaf people come to realize they are entitled to them in situations where they never before had been provided. Tracking that increase highlights the need for an ongoing demographic database that would provide more precise indicators of demand and supply for all deaf-related services. Though lacking greater precision, the present evidence justifies saying that employment opportunities are bountiful for certified interpreters and are likely to remain so, at least for the near future.

Along with requests for interpreter services and the numbers and qualifications of interpreters to fill them, compensation for interpreting, too, can be expected to change, in part reflecting supply and demand. But, as economists teach, that simple economic concept must be modified by friction in the economy. A substantial friction results from the fact that society in general, rather than deaf people, pays for most interpreting. Thus, it is wise to anticipate modifications in government support in projections of interpreter supply and demand.

Recognizing the early history of sign language, we have stressed the need to market interpreter services. The use of that phrase implies no insult to the profession. Every other profession must tangle with issues that bear directly on their members' ability to earn a fair living. The less well organized the distribution of interpreting resources, the greater will be the loss to the Deaf community and to interpreters. More efficient use of interpreting resources will benefit all stakeholders.

9

ETHICS

One of the distinguishing characteristics of a profession, as opposed to a trade, is the requirement that members of the profession abide by a code of ethics. These rules for appropriate behavior may be general, specific, or both. They state actions members must take and prohibitions against other actions. The essence of the ethical code is its commitment to the welfare of the profession and those it serves.

The best known code of ethics is the Hippocratic Oath to which physicians swear. It pledges them to refrain from practicing beyond their competence and from taking advantage of patients during their moments of vulnerability. Interpreters who belong to Registry of Interpreters for the Deaf (RID) and the Association of Visual Language Interpreters of Canada (AVLIC) are likewise bound by ethical codes—codes three thousand years younger than the Hippocratic Oath but as important to interpreters as the older code is to physicians.

THE RID CODE OF ETHICS

At the inception of RID, in 1964, the following code of ethics was set forth, which helped forge a path aimed at establishing and maintaining standards among sign language interpreters:

> Recognizing the invaluable influence of an interpreter in the life of a deaf person, we resolve to inject into the persons involved the highest ideals for which the association stands; to lend grace and sobriety to all our dealings, and to maintain poise and dignity under all con-

ditions and circumstances. We resolve to exemplify loyalty and con-
scientiousness, and to exercise patience at all times; to keep our lives
wholesome and clean; that our very presence may bring life and light
to those about us; to encourage confidence and moral ethics, lend
hope, and nourish faith, remembering that the eternal laws of God
are the only ones under which we can truly succeed. (*Workshop on Interpreting for the Deaf*, 1964, pp. 15–16)

The religious flavor of that first code of ethics arose naturally from the
background of interpreting in the United States and Canada, much of
which involved volunteers who interpreted church services. Of the 73 participants in the Ball State conference, 7 had religious affiliations, 13 were
staff members of schools for deaf students, and 16 were executives of those
schools. So school and religious people made up about half of those at
RID's founding.

By 1965 the RID Code of Ethics had undergone a major revision
(Quigley & Youngs, 1965), consisting of 12 articles. The first article required
interpreters to be "of high moral character, honest, conscientious, trust-
worthy, and of emotional maturity." The same article had a second sentence

---

RID's Code of Ethics

Interpreters/transliterators shall:

1. Keep all assignment-related information strictly confidential.
2. Render the message faithfully, always conveying the content and
   spirit of the speaker using language most readily understood by the
   person(s) whom they serve.
3. Not counsel, advise, or interject personal opinions.
4. Accept assignments using discretion with regard to skill, setting,
   and the consumers involved.
5. Request compensation for services in a professional and judicious
   manner.
6. Function in a manner appropriate to the situation.
7. Strive to further knowledge and skills through participation in workshops, professional meetings, interaction with professional colleagues, and reading of current literature in the field.
8. Strive to maintain high professional standards in compliance with
   the code of ethics.

imposing confidentiality, an interesting combination of principles. Today, the code no longer admonishes interpreters "to keep lives wholesome and clean" and "bring life and light." The present provisions for acceptable behavior are more testable, less ambiguous, and highly relevant.

In this chapter, we analyze the current RID code (see the box titled "RID's Code of Ethics"), interspersing parallels from the codes of AVLIC and the International Association of Conference Interpreters (designated AIIC because of its French name, *l'Association Internationale des Interprètes de Conférence*). The latter contrasts an organization of spoken language interpreters with the two for sign language interpreters.

The code specifies guidelines for its members' behavior. They may never think of themselves as unscrupulous or dishonest, but they might function in an unethical manner as a result of lack of awareness, insensitivity, or insufficient education and experience. The guidelines establish a framework for appropriate behavior not only to protect the interpreters, but also to defend all participants' rights. If interpreters feel they have a conflict, are uncomfortable in a situation, or doubt what action to take, they can turn to the code for clarification of their role and functions. The code brings consistency to the field, enabling participants to know what to expect of interpreters and instructing interpreters how to manage themselves.

The following discussion focuses on each of the RID code's eight provisions. It could also apply to other interpreter organizations' ethical principles, such as AVLIC's ethical code.

Confidentiality

That the first tenet concerns confidentiality accords with its importance in relations between interpreters and the other participants. Interpreters are privy to all manner of information, some of it deeply personal. While interpreting in court, they may learn about a participant's criminal past, investment holdings, sexual indiscretions, or plans to buy a house. No matter how trivial the information may seem to the interpreter, maintaining complete confidentiality is required. Frishberg (1990) has argued that interpreters must not talk about an assignment *even after it has become public*. The AIIC commands its members to keep "the strictest secrecy." AVLIC has similar strictures.

Confidentiality extends beyond not repeating what has been said or signed. In large cities, professionals can easily avoid contact with their patients and clients. In small towns, however, such social isolation is difficult, if not impossible. In a way, interpreters spend much of their time in a very small town— the Deaf community. Fink (1982) explains why it is difficult to maintain an ethical stance:

The deaf community is so small, it is very easy to figure things out with a minimum of information. Suppose I tell you I'm going to traffic court on Wednesday morning, and later you meet a deaf person who has "some legal problems to take care of on Wednesday, but nothing serious." If that person also has a dented fender on his or her car, it's not hard for you to realize who else is going to court. (p. 6)

Resisting social pressures to breach confidentiality can be difficult. Even if a deaf person's mother, with whom the interpreter is friendly, asks if the interpreter worked with her or him last weekend, the interpreter should not answer the question. Rather than lie, the interpreter might say, "You know I never discuss my work, not even who I work with. I am sure you understand." Interpreters who consistently hold that position—never discussing when, where, and with whom they interpret—spare themselves daunting experiences while remaining ethically correct.

Some settings may be especially challenging to interpreters. Schools often expect interpreters to be members of a deaf child's educational planning team (Schein, Mallory, & Greaves, 1991; Stewart, 1988). As part of a team, they might be asked about possible difficulties the child is having in class or about matters a deaf student has confided in them about troubles at home. The team may resent interpreters' unwillingness to share such information, creating a dilemma we will discuss further in Chapter 10.

Giving information about a deaf person, even to his employer at a job interview, is a breach of confidentiality. "Where does John live?" asks the employment interviewer. The interpreter should reply, "As soon as John comes in, I will interpret your question to him." That answer not only defends confidentiality, it also clarifies the interpreter's role. Nondeaf participants need to understand that whatever the interpreter contributes to the flow of information comes from, and only from, the deaf person.

Exceptions

Absolute as the principle of confidentiality sounds, it can have exceptions. What about agencies that provide interpreters? They are often supervised by an interpreter in the role of a coordinator. When not involved in interpreting, is the interpreter/coordinator bound by confidentiality? The issue becomes most significant when a participant complains about an interpreter's handling of the assignment. If interpreters cannot discuss these cases with their supervisors, how can they and the agency resolve complaints?

Interpreters who play dual roles are particularly vulnerable to the mishandling of matters relating to confidentiality. Suppose a deaf person is buying a house and the real estate agent also happens to be an experienced interpreter. During an inspection of the house, the agent interprets for the deaf person, who is questioning the owner of the house. Is the agent then obligated not to divulge any of the information gained during the discussion between buyer and seller? Or does a single role, which in this case is selling related to real estate, assume precedence? In the normal course of real estate, it is not unexpected that the agent would use the information that transpired during interpreting when talking to other buyers.

The question of dual or even multiple roles is worthy of far more scrutiny than it has received in the interpreting field. Some common combinations of roles are teacher/interpreter, secretary/interpreter, and teacher aide/interpreter. But do we also include roles not relating to work, such as colleague/interpreter or friend/interpreter? If an interpreter accompanies a deaf friend to shop for a car and acts as an interpreter when a salesperson is on the scene, is she or he supposed to stay in this role when asked for an opinion by the friend? Common sense might dictate that the interpreter is free to express an opinion because the two are friends. After all, the code only applies to professional interpreters, a point that should be made clear when interpreters are acting as friends and not interpreters.

There is also the question of how interpreters should handle a situation in which their supervisor who sets up the assignments inquires about them. The interpreter must acknowledge that the participants were met and describe any *procedural* difficulties that might have arisen during the assignment—but nothing more. Unless there is a prior agreement between all of the participants that information about the assignment will be shared, the interpreter cannot reveal any of its *content* to anybody—even the supervisor.

One agency director found that deaf participants objected to interpreter exchanges of information, even *within* the agency. The director concluded that deaf people were justified in their complaints. Now that agency forbids its interpreters to say anything about an assignment except to their immediate supervisor, and then only about professionally relevant matters.

Is confidentiality violated when interpreters exchange information about a participant among themselves? Yes, allowing interpreters flexibility to talk about situations that they have encountered violates confidentiality as much as if the person the interpreter tells is not a professional. Still, past experiences of interpreters can make significant contributions to new interpreters' education, and dialogue between interpreters can forward their professional development. They can hold discussions about assignments as long as these center on worries and frustrations, linguistic issues, interpreting strategies, and similar professional matters, and as long as the participants' identities are absolutely disguised.

Legal Status of Confidentiality

Unlike communications with clergy, lawyers, and physicians, some communications in which interpreters play a role may not be privileged. For example, interpreters can be required by a judge to reveal what took place when they interpreted. Gardner (1987) cites the following tests to determine if communications are privileged:

- They must be confidential in nature.
- Privacy must be essential to a successful and honest relationship between the parties.
- The relationship must be one which society wishes to foster.
- The injury that disclosure of communications would cause to the protected relationship must be greater than the benefit to the court of gaining the information. (p. 32)

According to the first test, for communications to be privileged, they must take place in private. Does *private,* in the legal sense, mean that the privilege does not apply if a deaf person and an attorney meet with an interpreter present? No, if one of the parties depends on sign, the meeting is still private despite the interpreter's presence. Furthermore, the interpreter does not have to be certified to maintain the privilege.

The relationships that most often meet the second legal test are: husband–wife, doctor–patient, lawyer–client, and clergy–parishioner. News reporters and their sources and nonmedical therapist–patient relationships have sometimes been treated as privileged and sometimes not. Unless in the presence of someone privileged, such as a doctor or lawyer, interpreted conversations are not privileged. Similarly, employment interviews, business discussions, meetings with accountants—all provide examples of communications that are *not* protected against disclosure in court. In situations that may be brought to court, interpreters should make clear their legal position before beginning the assignment.

The court of law even extends into those situations where a deaf person is communicating with the interpreter or a family member, because such conversations are not privileged. Interpreters can be forced by a judge—and by no one else—to repeat what a deaf person signed in private conversation. Interpreters who happen to mingle with deaf participants during lunch should strictly avoid discussing any potentially incriminating topics. Instead, interpreters should advise participants, *at the start of an assignment*, about the limits of their ability to maintain confidentiality. If interpreters believe that a deaf participant has forgotten that point and is about to confess a crime or expose something prejudicial to the court case, they should interrupt to advise the person that, although they will maintain confidentiality, they can be forced to testify in court. If the deaf person, despite the second warning, persists in giving potentially damaging information to the interpreter "in private," the interpreter can at least feel guiltless if a judge later forces exposure of what transpired during the unprivileged interchange; or the interpreter can remove himself or herself from the assignment before the information is given and thereby avoid much anxiety.

Obviously, some interpreting situations are more sensitive than others, such as when an interpreter is called to interpret while police question a deaf person. In this situation, it would be wise for the interpreter to request that the interview be videotaped. That will absolve the interpreter from breaking the ethical code, since another interpreter can be called to read the signs if the court subpoenas the videotape. Interpreters can try two other tactics: they can remind the court that they are bound by a code of ethics, and they can also point out that the process of interpreting interferes with their recollections. Indeed, many interpreters have a difficult time repeating what they have interpreted even a few minutes later. If these efforts fail, they have no choice but to comply with the court's order or face contempt charges. Important as it is for interpreters to know the boundaries of confidentiality, it is equally important that the other participants be told about them.

Wearing the badge of privileged communication is a signal of trust between the interpreter and the participants, and its value is evidenced even in the absence of interpreting services. This was the case when a real-time reporter served a board of directors' meeting at an agency serving deaf and hard-of-hearing clients. During the meeting, the executive director was asked to leave while the board had a serious discussion about a matter relating to her. The real-time reporter was instructed to delete that discussion from the meeting's minutes. Nevertheless, the director obtained a copy of the whole transcription. Such a risk has led that board to employ sign language interpreters at subsequent meetings.

Accuracy and Completeness

The principle to be accurate and complete is clear, but the tests for it are murky. If the audience is a mixture of people educated at different levels, how does an interpreter select "language most readily understood" while being faithful to the speaker? Some members of the audience might prefer that the interpreter provide a transliteration of a speech while others might desire ASL. Given these circumstances, the interpreter's most practical resolution may ignore preferences of a few while rendering interpretations that are comprehended by the majority of the participants.

Some interpreters have complained about being required to convey blasphemous and scatological speech. Adhering to the RID code, they have no choice but to convey whatever is spoken or signed, no matter how profane or how much in opposition to their own beliefs. An interpreter confesses:

> One of the most difficult interpreting assignments I ever had was to interpret an emotionally charged speech upholding the oralist phi-

losophy and downgrading all uses of sign language. While I was fuming inside, I had to match my facial expressions and mannerisms with those of the speaker. (Tipton, 1974, p. 11)

The principle does not tell the interpreter how to obey it. Most models of interpreting stress the need to go beyond delivering words for signs and signs for words. By adding references to conveying the speaker's spirit and to choosing language "most readily understood," it reinforces the necessity of taking into account the participants' cultures.

It may help to modify the principle and allow the interpreter to convey the initiator's *manifest* intent. But speakers' intentions are not always clear from their choice of words or signs. Sarcastic remarks and exaggerated statements intended to convey the opposites of their words can be particularly difficult to interpret. Chapter 7 addresses these points, so we will not pursue them further here. One more matter, however, does need to be covered here.

Most interpreters fear making a mistake while interpreting. If they convey information incorrectly, they are obligated to correct the error as soon as feasible. For example, at a meeting with an insurance agent, the interpreter tells a deaf person the agent is willing to provide coverage for a house in the amount of $125,000, but later realizes the agent said $175,000. In that case, the interpreter should immediately inform participants of the correct figure using appropriate error correction techniques.

Correcting a mistake during an assignment should also be looked upon as a means of preventing a malpractice suit. When making a correction, an interpreter should say "interpreter-error" or "interpreter-correction." Although there is no consensus in the field as to which phrase is more appropriate, interpreters do agree that saying "Excuse me" or "I meant to say . . ." is unprofessional and, especially for the nondeaf participants, could make it difficult to determine whether the interpreter is originating those words or the deaf person has signed them.

The ability to correct errors, however, varies according to the nature of the interpreting situation. For instance, what happens if a mistake is made while interpreting an address to a live audience? Immediately correcting the mistake often is not possible; the correction might confuse the audience more than it rectifies the error. But there are instances when a mistake can be rectified during the course of interpreting. An interpreter who voices "I took a boat to Jamaica" when a deaf person had in fact said "I took a cruise to Jamaica" may be in a position to insert the word "cruise" later in the discourse. On the other hand, if an interpreter voices "I worked as a sub" when the source message was "I worked as a teacher aide," then immediate correction is required.

What should interpreters do if they realize they made serious errors after a week or more has passed? Should they do nothing and hope no one has caught the mistake? Interpreters must be honest and own up to their mistakes rather than let the mistakes reflect poorly on the other participants, but they must seek practical solutions. They need to look to the seventh and eighth principles of the RID code, which call upon them to consult with their colleagues when the consequences of the error are serious and the solutions difficult to conceive. Organizations like RID and AVLIC provide interpreters with a much-needed forum for raising and resolving such problems. When consulting with colleagues in such cases, the interpreter must remember to maintain confidentiality.

Impartiality

Impartiality toward the proceedings of an interpreting situation is crucial for interpreters. Being neutral, not offering opinions, refusing to comment—these are the rules interpreters must obey while on an assignment. The historical background of interpreting for deaf people helps explain why RID feels compelled to make this principle explicit. AIIC has no such provision because conference interpreting offers little or no opportunity for interpreters to express their views.

For a friend or relative doing a favor for a deaf person, the urge to impose one's own ideas, to warn, or to encourage an action seems quite natural. Even professional interpreters might see themselves as being in a position to help participants. For example, if they are interpreting a heated debate that revolves around a fact, they might want to interrupt the participants to clarify it. Or they may find that a salesperson is misrepresenting a product to a deaf person, and they may want to caution the deaf person against buying it. The RID code discourages such *parentalistic* actions.

Several years ago a revered head of an agency with a long record of working with deaf people boasted that she often *misinterpreted* in court cases. "If I had correctly voiced what some deaf people signed, they would have gone to jail!" Coming as she did from a religious background, she saw no ethical violations in her efforts to be helpful. She had, in fact, violated her oath to the court, but not to the RID code, because she was working long before there was an RID. Still the lack of a professional code does not justify her actions.

A similar dilemma is found with some interpreters who work with deaf students and feel that they can aid them to do better academically. One interpreter who worked in a high school confided that he did not hesitate to tell deaf students for whom he was interpreting to pay attention or to give them a gentle kick under the desk if they started to doze off. Having a student's education at heart, however, is not justification for violating the RID code.

Interpreters must respect the views of other people. If one participant condescendingly snickers at the expense of another participant, the interpreter neither joins in the condescension nor expresses disapproval of the snickering. Interpreting these actions does not imply condoning them.

The RID does not specifically forbid interpreters from serving people with whom they have personal relationships. This omission leaves RID members with the burden of deciding whether or not to accept assignments involving, say, relatives or close friends. Can they maintain a professional posture in such cases? Will the fact that they are well known to one of the parties interfere with the communication process? These are questions interpreters must resolve individually, until their professional organization issues decisions about them.

Impartiality is not just reserved to acts of interpreting; the overall performance and consistency of behavior while interpreting is also critical. At a recent education conference, an RID-certified interpreter interrupted the proceedings to make a comment that she felt was relevant. This behavior contravenes the third principle. The interpreter initially asked permission to make a comment, but the speaker said no. The conference organizer (a nondeaf person) and the interpreter's supervisor (a deaf person) were present and disagreed with the speaker (a deaf person). They said that it would be all right with them if the interpreter spoke up. In defense of the interpreter, two out of three people in charge of the meeting gave permission. In our judgment, however, their permission did not mitigate the violation, because the interpreter, was there as an interpreter not as a conference attendee.

Participants can initiate circumstances that try interpreters' impartiality. In the early 1980s, deaf and nondeaf participants often asked interpreters questions relating to the discussion at hand. By virtue of their ability to sign, interpreters were called on to explain such matters as how ASL differs from English. Not being deaf but having the ability to sign created a mystique about interpreters; their signing made them ad hoc experts on deafness. Many interpreters succumbed to this flattery, but today such behavior is widely considered to be unethical.

Interpreters might regard themselves as experts on deafness, but, when engaged as interpreters, they are experts on communication only. They must obey the rules of their profession even if it means burying their lights under large bushels. As two observers have noted, sadly,

> Interpreters' reputations for being trustworthy, competent, disinterested parties has been, up to now, generally poor. Interpreters, until the last fifteen or so years, were primarily children of deaf parents and members of rather conservative religious sects who felt it their mission to reach the deaf. (Wentzer & Dhir, 1986, p. 13)

Fortunately, the work of interpreter education programs in preparing students to maintain professional standards has done much to reduce this negative impression.

The bilingual–bicultural approach (see Chapter 3) urges interpreters to become allies of deaf people. Some people may construe this as a challenge to existing notions about professional standards. Is there anything that a bilingual–bicultural interpreter would do in working with a deaf AIDS patient, for example, that might contravene the RID code? Instead of disinterestedness in such a case, should the interpreter display sympathy, take an active role in decision making, or pressure physicians about treatment the deaf patient desires? Bilingual–bicultural proponents will have to grapple with such questions as they explicate their position to interpreters and to interpreting organizations. Eventually, these organizations should react officially to these and other positions that urge a different role for interpreters than the various codes of ethics prescribe.

Discretion

The most frequent ethical violation may well be that of practicing beyond one's competence. In a survey of Canadian interpreters in 1989, over half of the 110 respondents said they did not believe their colleagues acted ethically (Schein & Yarwood, 1990). In follow-up interviews, respondents explained that they felt that other interpreters accepted assignments for which they were unqualified in the judgments of their peers (Schein, Greaves, & Wolf-Schein, 1990).

AIIC's ethical code contains a similar provision: "Members of the Association shall not accept engagements for which they are not qualified. Their acceptance shall imply a moral undertaking on their part that they will perform their services in a professional manner."

Conference interpreters usually have a fairly complete idea of what will come up, who will speak, and who will attend, but that is not the case for many sign language interpreters. They cannot always determine in advance of an assignment what skills will be needed. They must, therefore, be prepared to withdraw if unqualified.

The naive idea that interpreters should be able to interpret anything that is spoken is detrimental to the image of their profession, because they are always able to do a better job when they are familiar with the material. Consider the following quotation from a hypothetical biology lecture:

> An epicalyx is an involucre resembling the calyx but consisting of a whorl of bracts that is exterior to the calyx or results from the union of the sepal appendages.

This is actually a definition from Webster's *Ninth New Collegiate Dictionary* (1988). An interpreter would be hard pressed even to begin an interpretation of that sentence without knowing that the teacher is speaking about the leaflike parts of a flower.

What can interpreters do when such material arises unexpectedly? They might interrupt the speaker and say they are unable to convey this complex description and request it be simplified or clarified. They might fingerspell the words and phrases they do not understand. Bluffing, however, demeans the participants by implying that the interpreter understands when the audience may be equally baffled.

Interpreters who are disinclined to admit their weaknesses could benefit from the "ethics of the unthinkable"—a guideline for dealing with the reality of those times when they are not able to do the job. Some might argue that Principle 4 of the RID code addresses this when it states that interpreters should use discretion in accepting an assignment. What does it mean by *discretion?* In the words of an interpreter who has pondered this principle, it "implies that the interpreter, evaluated or not, will somehow not only know his own level of skill but be able to judge others' as well" (Tipton, 1974, p. 12).

Pointing out these ambiguities in the RID code may stimulate debate among interpreters and lead to clear-cut directives. No ethical code, no matter how detailed, can explicitly cover every situation that might confront an interpreter. That is why interpreter organizations should hold continuing discussions among their members about ethical matters. An ongoing dialogue will increasingly refine codes of conduct.

Compensation

Although interpreters have every right to earn the best wage they can, how they go about seeking higher paying opportunities must be governed by ethical conduct. Take the case of a freelance interpreter working at a university. She had committed herself to interpreting a university class for one semester. During that semester there arose an opportunity to interpret at a meeting and receive far more than her class assignment paid. Hours before the class started, she called in sick, and then went to interpret at the meeting. The university was unable to find a replacement on such short notice, so deaf students were deprived of communication. The interpreter's action was detrimental to her reputation, and she was not hired in subsequent semesters. Such actions harm the entire profession, leading school officials, in this case, to question the reliability of all interpreters. Ethical obligations transcend monetary gains.

The AIIC code does not mention payment. It does ask its members to "refrain from statements or actions prejudicial to the interests of the Association and its members," but that does not necessarily refer to compensation. The history of interpreting may account for the difference between RID and AIIC codes on this point. As discussed in Chapter 2, prior to 1964 interpreting was largely considered a favor, not a service. Interpreting was not a recognized profession. By making compensation a matter of ethics, RID may intend to overcome the opposition of those who entered the profession as religious workers and feel they should continue to donate their services.

Professional Standards

In the guidelines explicating this principle, RID refers to functioning in a manner that is appropriate for the situation. Behavior or dressing in a manner that distracts from the proceedings is discouraged. As will be noted, this ethical principle seems more a matter of satisfying physical conditions and good manners than a moral issue. However, it does have a parallel in the AIIC's caution to its members not to "detract from the dignity of the profession." The dental, medical, and legal professions' ethics do not prescribe the manner of their members' dress; yet members of these professions often appear to abide by an unwritten dress code. It may be that written concerns about appearances characterize younger professions.

This principle may also be seen as a catch-all for such unmentioned items as personal and professional relations, and individual behaviors. Does it mean that interpreters must interpret all of the conversations that they see or hear, such as the idle chatter of two audience members? The RID code says yes:

> Let us say clearly that the interpreter interprets everything. This means when the hearing participant is interrupted by a telephone call, the interpreter translates the audible portion of the call. When someone other than the deaf participant is addressed, the interpreter still translates. When the deaf students are having a bit of gossip during the lecture, the interpreter voices their side comments. (Frishberg, 1990, p. 68)

Everything means everything!

Although we support the ethical principle, we question the explanation of how it should be applied. Two nondeaf people whispering at the back of the room are inaudible to the interpreter and therefore do not get translated into signs. Should two deaf participants signing to one another at the back of a large conference room be voiced for all to hear, merely because their signing may be more conspicuous than speech and can be seen by the interpreter? Whispered speech can be controlled further by cupping a hand over one's mouth, and likewise signing can be done discreetly so that it is perceptible only to the intended audience. Thus, deaf people aware of the role of interpreters may take action to ensure that their signing is not seen, in the same way that nondeaf people prevent their speech being overheard. But for deaf people accustomed to signing openly even when they do not want to be interpreted, applying this principle can be unfair. Interpreters should exercise good judgment to keep deaf people from being mistreated because of their visual communication.

Professional Obligations and Continuing Education

RID has elected to require its members to take steps toward self-improvement. Making self-improvement an ethical requirement may seem odd, but very little research has been done on interpreting. For example, little is known systematically about the desires of deaf people and those who work with them. Experience helps interpreters when it is accompanied by appropriate feedback. Without expert appraisals, experience can merely lead to grinding in misbehaviors and misconceptions. That is why the seventh principle of the RID code prescribes formal study, along with interacting with colleagues and studying the professional literature. Interpreters need to have their knowledge updated and validated and their skills exposed to peer review.

Profile: Marilyn Mitchell

If experience yields the wisdom and prudence needed to understand two cultures, to communicate competently in two languages, and to move comfortably in two worlds, then Marilyn Mitchell's thirty years in the field of deafness has served her admirably. She has journeyed through the field as an educator, actress, writer, editor, manager, consultant, and interpreter. She has picked up a master of science degree along the way and presently holds the Registry of Interpreters for the Deaf (RID) Comprehensive Skills Certificate (CSC) and the Oral Interpreting Certificate: Spoken/Visible (OIC:V/S). She is an assistant professor and interpreter coordinator in the Department of American Sign Language and Interpreting Education at the National Technical Institute for the Deaf, Rochester Institute of Technology. She continues to use her knowledge and experiences to enhance the professional development of the interpreting field by serving RID in various capacities and the Educational Standards Committee of the Conference of Interpreter Trainers.

Marilyn knows well the struggles of interpreters who, while always being scrutinized for accuracy and professionalism in their daily work, have few places or people to turn to for support. Especially in rural areas, an interpreter may be out of contact with other interpreters for long stretches of time. Even in large urban areas, interpreters face many dilemmas that are challenging for even the best of them to tackle alone. But the plight of the interpreter can be too precarious to leave up to

Continued

Profile: Marilyn Mitchell   *Continued*

each individual to deal with. In more global terms, the advancement of the field is dependent on interpreters helping one another. Those interpreters with substantial experience are well positioned to help out those with lesser experience or, as Marilyn explains, to mentor them:

> What do interpreters need when they move to a new, unknown location? Where do interpreters go for advice when they venture into a new content area or new environment? When interpreters encounter an ethical dilemma, who can they discuss it with? How is an interpreter going to go to a Deaf club for the first time? How do recent graduates of interpreting programs experience the professional arena? If interpreters wish to observe model interpretations, then who are they to watch? These and many other questions can be answered by some type of mentorship.
>
> Mentoring has always been a part of my life, personally and professionally. A mentor teaches, coaches, counsels, accepts, affirms, models, challenges, protects, is a friend, and encourages stretching and visibility. Recently, I had the opportunity to interpret *The Phantom of the Opera,* an arena I rarely interpret in. In Rochester, New York, a referral agency has a goal of contracting interpreters qualified and inexperienced in performing arts interpreting. Because of my team interpreter, my mentor in this situation, I accepted the job and believe that I was quite successful especially because of the mentoring. This experience was only for the duration of the rehearsal and performance (a short-term mentorship), and I was able to approach the experience with confidence, trust, and knowledge. I needed my mentor to tell me the story of the play, describe who the characters were, the physical characteristics of the theater, and the contact people associated with the theater. She also got me in to watch a performance and assured me that I would be able to do the job.
>
> To give and receive mentoring, I must know what I can offer and what I need. I must understand my strengths and weaknesses and be willing to ask for and give advice. I need to know how to take a positive approach when mentoring as well as how to positively give and receive feedback. I must learn to trust and be trustworthy. And perhaps above all, I must enjoy the mentoring opportunity.

Social Relations

Another consideration for interpreters is the circumstances in which they should socialize with deaf people. It is widely held that interpreters must be proficient in both of the languages and cultures in which they interact. Their proficiency can be enhanced through interactions with deaf people, a fact not missed by those interpreter education programs that require their students to meet regularly with deaf people. This practice, when formally initiated, was rarely questioned and often encouraged by deaf people who ultimately benefited from the availability of more highly skilled interpreters.

Today, however, in younger Deaf communities, and especially in larger cities, there is some resentment among members toward a nondeaf person coming into *their* Deaf clubs to interact socially. There is an element of distrust, as one Deaf woman, who is also an ASL instructor, confided:

> I go to the Deaf club to enjoy myself—to be with other Deaf people and not have to worry about who I am with. I don't want to see people there who should not be there. This is my club, my time. They are interfering with my time and make me feel uncomfortable. They are mooching off our social lives. Too many ASL teachers are sending their students to clubs to learn to sign and I resent that. Let them bring Deaf people into their classes. (personal communication)

Another Deaf woman who is also an ASL instructor had a more positive outlook:

> I don't want hearing people coming into a Deaf club to learn to sign. But I do want people who are training to be interpreters to socialize with Deaf people, because those that do are likely to become better signers. When they become interpreters, I can understand them much better than others who do not socialize with Deaf people. I send my interpreting students to Deaf events like sports and drama shows. These events are open to the public and no invitation is needed. (personal communication)

Interpreter knowledge and proficiency must be balanced against respect for the privacy of deaf people. This ethical principle encourages the professional growth of interpreters without mentioning that interacting with deaf people is one way to achieve that objective. It makes clear, however, that there are other ways that should also be pursued, such as getting formal instruction and conferring with professional colleagues.

Punctuality

Punctuality is basic to good professional behavior. So is keeping appointments, once they have been made. As noted previously, even when it is to the interpreter's monetary advantage to do so, it is unethical to leave one assignment for another without adequate notice.

Sound Judgment

The eighth principle is somewhat legalistic, only requiring members to abide by the rules. In a sense it is a principle encouraging the interpreter to use common sense in all situations. AVLIC and AIIC have similar provisions of obedience in their codes. AIIC specifically cautions against "conduct that might bring the profession into disrepute, and particularly from any form of personal publicity."

Having reached the eighth and final principle in the RID code of ethics, we believe that there are, in fact, two levels of ethics that are used to guide an interpreter's behavior. One is a professional code of ethics, and the other is a person's own sense of moral conduct. The level of ethics that receives the most attention is the professional code, which has been described by Caccamise et al. (1980) as "a code of common sense." Perhaps today it is common sense for certified interpreters, but as with any young profession, there was a period of time before the entire membership concurred on the meaning of each of the codes. Indeed, it has been suggested that interpreters are hindered by the misconception that the RID code "merely reflects 'common sense'" and that it "can be applied effortlessly to any situation" (Rudser, 1986, p. 47).

Such misconceptions allow little room for interpreters to reflect and evaluate their ethical conduct. Yet the eighth tenet of the RID code calls for precisely that kind of personal effort to "maintain high professional standards." To be fair to interpreters, it should be noted that common sense comes with experience. Beginning interpreters may not see the difference between ethical behavior and a question of proper etiquette or behavior. To avoid making a mistake, some of these interpreters will tend to be vigilant on the side of ethics and, in a sense, adopt an interpreter-as-conduit model as guidance for their behavior.

How much interpreters agree on the application of the RID code was the subject of a study of 45 interpreters. While only one-quarter had RID certification, more than two-thirds had attended a workshop on the RID Code of Ethics (Stewart & Lindsey, 1990). They were given eight cases and asked how they would act in each, and why. As a group, they were inconsistent in their handling of the ethical problems. Perhaps more telling were the underlying reasons they gave for their decisions. Three contradictory rationales covered most of their reactions:

- The RID code is to be adhered to at all times.
- Civil responsibilities and federal laws take precedence over the RID code.
- A decision cannot be made without real-life experience involving a particular situation.

As the profession matures, its members can be expected to reach consensus not only on ethical principles, but also on when and how to apply them. At least some interpreters express a need for flexibility within their ethical code to respond appropriately to situations not anticipated by those responsible for writing the code.

BREAKING THE CODE

People are fallible, so the question that arises when any type of regulation is established for a membership is: What happens when members do not adhere to their organization's ethics? How does the profession enforce its own regulations? What steps do interpreter organizations take to enforce their members' ethical behavior? Although ethics are at the fulcrum of any profession, ethical issues in interpreting are often shunted aside at professional meetings in favor of issues like accommodations to physical factors and semantic accuracy in interpreted messages. In this respect, RID, AVLIC, and other interpreter organizations are alike. Professions generally develop strong in-groups that resist punishing members. Without enforcement, however, ethical codes do not protect the public nor do they advance the profession.

Censure

One punishment is banishing the errant professional from membership. That is the principal punishment meted out by American Psychological Association and American Speech/Language Hearing Association. Most professionals dread censure by their peers. It is strong medicine to be denied membership in a professional society. It is a blow to the ego that has potential economic consequences. People who are sophisticated enough to inquire about professional memberships will shun professionals who are not accepted by their peers.

Probably the most realistic punishment for those who act unethically is denial of employment within the Deaf community. Word of poor interpreting usually circulates quickly. Unethical interpreters are apt to find themselves with time on their hands. Interpreters who behave badly are shunned, just as those who interpret well are sought after. Such informal enforcement has sharp limitations. Some interpreters are welcomed *because of* their unethical behavior; for example, an interpreter might be preferred who gives advice, tutors, or explains things—all are roles that are not condoned by the RID code.

Preservation of ethical standards, then, depends primarily on organizational sanctions that are largely confined to censuring members and, if their behavior is sufficiently deviant, expelling them from the organization. Most commonly, the community can avoid using those interpreters known to be unethical and can urge agencies not to engage them. In cases of flagrant violations, injured parties can sue the offending interpreters. To the best of our knowledge, that step has not been taken, but it is a threat for interpreters to consider as their range of services increases along with participants' sophistication.

Protecting Interpreters' Rights

Interpreters have rights, too, and they appropriately look to their professional organization for defense of their rights when threatened. Their organizations must be scrupulous in defending them against false accusations of misconduct. At the least, an accused interpreter deserves a hearing before professional peers. Some cases may call for an outside panel of experts, drawn from among knowledgeable people who have no personal stake in the case. However, with the various models of interpreting available, selecting an impartial panel may be a problem. Consider the case of an interpreter who advocates a bilingual–bicultural approach to interpreting and decides to add information to a message in an attempt to avoid misunderstanding on the basis of cultural differences. Who determines whether the added information was a necessary part of cross-cultural mediation or an unjust intrusion on the conveyance of the original message? Discussions among interpreters about questions like this one is the only way to an agreeable resolution.

The RID has established grievance procedures that include an Ethical Practices Board, which reviews complaints that cite a specific violation of the RID code. A complaint may be made by "any person having a direct or professional interest in the occurrence specified in the complaint." All Ethical Practices Board members belong to RID, and at least one of them must be deaf or hard or hearing. Disciplinary measures include suspension or revocation of RID membership and certifications, and/or additional training in a specified aspect of interpreting.

Malpractice

The first line of protection against malpractice is to perform ethically and to have one's performance witnessed by other professionals. Team interpreting is one way of providing each interpreter with a witness. While one is interpreting, the other can watch to ensure that the interpretation is correct. These safeguards are not always possible, however, and interpreters may be unjustly accused of making errors. Interpreter organizations should defend their members' welfare along with that of the public.

If the interpreter is sued for malpractice, the law has numerous safeguards. The interpreter should have legal counsel, but obtaining such assistance can cost a great deal. Interpreter organizations may wish to offer financial support to members involved in malpractice suits. More customary protection is for the interpreter to obtain professional liability insurance. Such coverage can take the financial sting out of defending against malpractice charges.

UNCHARTED ETHICS

Ethical codes provide general principles that must be applied in specific circumstances. Over time, organizations flesh out their code's bare bones with decisions that give them direction in applying its principles. The interpreting profession's youth leaves open to question how interpreters should respond to many situations that trouble them. Here we bring up some unresolved issues, without any intent to resolve them, because such decisions are the responsibility of the professional organizations and those they serve.

Relations with Interpreter Referral Agencies

Interpreters frequently depend on referral agencies for their livelihoods. How should they relate to these agencies, particularly when sensitive issues arise? Take the case in which a referral agency is told by a deaf person that he does not want a particular interpreter to ever interpret for him. How should the coordinator of the referral agency react? Is the coordinator bound to inform interpreters so they can argue their case or begin a process of self-analysis and improvement? It is a judgment call for the agency, which must make decisions that will protect all participants, including the interpreter. Yet, how it reacts can have a profound influence on relations within the Deaf community. If the interpreter is told of the accusations, the deaf person may feel betrayed. Withholding the information from interpreters, however, deprives them of their rights.

Relations with Colleagues

AIIC specifies that disputes between members must be settled within the organization. AVLIC and RID do not have such an explicit stipulation nor do they have a mechanism for carrying it out. In the survey of Canadian interpreters mentioned earlier, a striking finding was that 43% expressed reservations about their fellow interpreters' ethical behavior. Nineteen percent had no opinion on this issue, and only 38% believed that all interpreters act ethically (Schein & Yarwood, 1990). With such a high proportion of a membership doubting fellow members' ethics, the organization's attention should be focused on this issue.

AIIC requires that its members "afford their colleagues moral assistance and solidarity." The principles that guide interpreters' behavior must be distinguished from etiquette, from socially acceptable behavior. The two concepts overlap, but they differ in significant ways. Interpreters need to recognize when an ethical principle conflicts with a socially desirable behavior, and the interpreter should not hesitate to follow the ethical path. For example, ethics require interpreters not to reveal any information they gather while interpreting; good manners, on the other hand, urge that one respond politely to questions.

Personal Appearance

Dress codes are not ethical matters, but they do involve the interpreter's appearance and sometimes the ability to function well. A neat appearance promotes a good professional image. Excessive makeup, loud or odd apparel, excessive jewelry, and uncleanness can upset an interpreter–participant relationship by bringing attention to the interpreter. As noted in Chapter 4, the interpreter has to consider dress in terms of its effect on participants' ability to read signs. Although these factors are discussed in detail as physical factors influencing interpreting, they are mentioned here in the context of etiquette and professional demeanor.

The Interpreter's Authority

Another unresolved ethical question relates to the determination of how interpreting should be performed. Take a fairly common situation:

> Alma interprets for a local school. The board has ruled that the language of instruction for deaf students will be English. When Alma begins to interpret for Jason, however, he tells her that he does not understand English well; he prefers signing that is ASL over other ways of signing. Alma is competent in ASL, but she has been told to use a specific kind of manually coded English.

What should the interpreter do in this situation? Obey school policy and frustrate Jason? Ignore school policy and satisfy him? Or request a meeting with Jason's educational team to discuss the problem?

In some earlier research interpreters gave several answers to this question (Schein, Greaves, & Wolf-Schein, 1990). Some felt the student should determine the signing form. Others noted that they were employees of the school board and must, therefore, abide by its wishes. The majority answered, quite practically, that *they* decided. After all, they said, no one supervising them would know the difference!

Both RID's and AVLIC's codes of ethics state that interpreters should communicate so that they are understood by the participants. Neither, however, addresses the issue of participants' preferences, especially when they clash with those of an agency. To explore the issue further, we need to ask if the interpreter is an employee or a professional. If the former, then it seems the question has an obvious answer: the school board must be obeyed. It follows the old principle, "Who pays the piper calls the tune." As a professional, however, the interpreter should be free to exercise independent judgment. This ethical dilemma confronts interpreters daily.

Another apparently simple situation involves what the interpreter should do when the deaf person is not paying attention. Are interpreters human machines that put out signs whenever someone speaks? If so, they should be unconcerned with whether or not the deaf person is watching. On the other hand, if participant interaction is a key element in an interpreter's philosophical approach to interpreting, then a decision is not so easily rendered. As an example, take the situation in which the deaf people in the audience stop attending to the lecturer. A strong contingent of deaf people would expect the interpreter to continue interpreting, their rationale being that an interpreter is paid to interpret and should do so, regardless of what the audience is doing. But should that reasoning prevail when working with an eight-year-old child in school? Some would argue that deaf children should be on the same grounds as their classmates: if they are not paying attention, then that is the concern of the teacher, not the interpreter.

The Deaf Community's Authority

Closely related to the question of who controls the interpreting situation is that of who controls the interpreters. *Deaf Life*, a journal devoted to affairs of the Deaf community, polled its readers with the question, "Which organization should have authority over interpreters, their evaluation and certification?" The responses reported in the January 1991 issue (which did not, however, indicate how many replies were received) gave 5% to the National Association of the Deaf, 19% to the Registry of Interpreters for the Deaf, and 76% to "Other." The last category included "a licensing board made up of native signers with expertise in the interpreting process" and "a combination of organizations and businesses, including interpreters and interpreter trainers and Deaf and Hard of Hearing." Though hardly a definitive study, this straw poll suggests confusion in the Deaf community about interpreters' roles. If representative samples obtain similar results, they will indicate an important area for interpreter organizations to investigate.

SUMMARY

At the heart of every profession's code of ethics lies an obligation to do well and refrain from behavior that is unbecoming to the profession and harmful to those it serves. Being morally responsible as an interpreter means coming to terms with limitations and strengths. To interpreters, their code of ethics suggests the boundaries of their practice. To the interpreter organizations, ethics mean being responsible for each member. To oversee those responsibilities, organizations depend, in part, on feedback from those who make use of their members' services. That is one reason we strongly support the education of participants as to their rights and obligations when using interpreters. Well-informed participants enhance professional relations.

Ethics are dynamic and extend beyond the principles outlined in any organization's code. Ethics are about how one conducts one's daily personal and professional affairs and how one relates to the persons one encounters as a professional. No one code will cover every situation that may challenge a professional. We have mentioned a few situations that puzzle interpreters today. These and more dilemmas will be resolved as the field matures. For now, taking the time to examine and make explicit principles is worth the professional's effort. As Robinson (1991), a distinguished translator, writes about ethics:

[B]y concerning yourself with the rights and wrongs of what you are doing to other people (the usual meaning of "ethics"), you inevitably bring yourself around to a concern with what doing those things is doing to you, how it is shaping your character (the root meaning of "ethics," a concern for *ethos* or character) . . . . realizing that you are not a neutral instrument but a human being *acting* in a social context. (p. 217)

10

EDUCATIONAL INTERPRETING

More interpreters practice in schools than in any other setting. The 1989 report of the National Task Force on Educational Interpreting estimated that there were 2,200 educational interpreters working at the elementary and secondary levels (Stuckless, Avery, & Hurwitz, 1989). Gustason (1985) found that over one-third of graduates of programs preparing interpreters obtained employment in public schools. A survey of Canadian interpreters found the same preponderance in educational settings (Schein & Yarwood, 1990). In the United States and Canada, then, from one-third to one-half of all interpreters practice educational interpreting.

In schools in which instructors sign, interpreters serve visitors, parents, and an occasional lecturer who does not sign, and the interpreting responsibilities are usually the same as those described in preceding chapters. But in schools where teachers, nondeaf students, and most personnel do not sign, interpreters' roles and functions change, and new operating considerations emerge. This chapter discusses these matters, after a brief review of the history of educational interpreting.

EDUCATIONAL PLACEMENT BEFORE AND AFTER P.L. 94-142

Although the idea of educating deaf students in regular classes was introduced over a century ago, the practice occurred on a large scale only recently. Before 1975, deaf children in the United States and Canada were mainly enrolled in specialized settings with other students who were deaf. Such facilities were:

- *Residential schools:* Schools made up entirely of deaf students who resided at the school during the week
- *Day schools:* Schools having only deaf students who returned to their homes each evening
- *Self-contained classes:* Classes made up solely of deaf students but located in public schools educating nondeaf students.

In each of these placements, instruction was designed for deaf students and typically carried out by teachers prepared to instruct them.

The passage by the U.S. Congress of Public Law 94-142 (the Education of All Handicapped Children Act) in 1975, altered educational administrators' approach to placement. It mandates a free and appropriate public education for children, regardless of any disabilities they may have. It specifies that such education shall take place in "the least restrictive environment," a phrase that has generated heated debate over its meaning. Local school districts often construe it to require placement of students with disabilities in regular classrooms in neighborhood schools. Consequently, deaf students today are likely to be assigned to a public school in their neighborhood or county and not sent off to a school for deaf children. This placement strategy has been called *mainstreaming, integration,* and, more recently, *inclusion.* The mandate stipulated in P.L. 94-142 was reaffirmed with its replacement, the Individuals with Disabilities Education Act (IDEA).

Although no one law dictates school placements in Canada as it does in the United States, Canadian provinces have similar laws and practices that have deeply affected the educational placement of deaf students. As a result, residential school enrollments in both countries are down, some schools have closed, and the number of deaf students in regular classes has substantially increased.

Combining deaf and nondeaf students in the same classes generates a great portion of the demand for interpreters. This surge in demand for and employment of educational interpreters preceded the emergence of programs to prepare them. The discrepancies between supply and demand that have been created show no sign of abating. Even today, some school districts continue to hire persons who lack a formal education for educational interpreting—a matter that will be discussed more fully later. Fortunately, the need to prepare well-qualified personnel has been recognized by interpreter educators, all of whose programs cover some aspects of educational interpreting, while a few programs are designed specifically for the preparation of educational interpreters (Taylor & Elliott, 1994).

THE ROLE OF EDUCATIONAL INTERPRETERS

Educational interpreters are the linchpin joining deaf and nondeaf students with classmates and school personnel who do not sign. The significance of educational interpreters is guaranteed; without them, the placement of deaf students in unspecialized classes would not be feasible. As Conway (1990) writes, "Educational interpreters provide a vital communication support service to mainstreamed hearing-impaired students" (p. 136). His position is augmented by a U.S. task force on educational interpreting that describes educational interpreting as "an enabling factor" in integrating deaf students (Stuckless, Avery, & Hurwitz, 1989, p. 1). Putting the case even more forcefully, an educator writes that the "inestimable importance of classroom interpreters . . . is obvious if [deaf] students are to have access to the mainstream curriculum afforded hearing students" (McGee, 1990, p. 205).

Given the importance of interpreters in educational settings it is not surprising to note that attention is being given to their qualifications. Interpreting for school-age children is as complex a task as interpreting for adults. In recognition of this the Commission on Education of the Deaf (1988) made the following recommendation with regard to standards for educational interpreters:

> The Department of Education, in consultation with consumers, professionals, and organizations, should provide guidelines for states to include in their state plans such policies and procedures for the establishment and maintenance of standards to ensure that interpreters in educational settings are adequately prepared, trained, and evaluated. (p. xxi)

These views are not unique to North America. They are shared in European and African schools (Wolf-Schein & Schein, 1990). In New Zealand, Sefton Bartlett, an administrator of a school for deaf students, notes,

> As yet, no formal training program is provided for interpreters in New Zealand, and there is no doubt that if deaf students are to be appropriately catered for in a mainstream placement, central government will need to provide considerable financial resources for interpreter services. (Bartlett, 1991, p. 71)

His words were timely, as New Zealand has since established a program to prepare interpreters.

Job Descriptions

One way to grasp a school's image of its interpreters is to examine its job descriptions for clues to qualifications and functions. Often, no mention is made

---

of any previous education for interpreting and knowledge of sign language is often considered sufficient. A few schools do not even mention ability to sign, and most do not emphasize *quality* interpreting.

One administrator's only requirements for an educational interpreter were "good with children and works well as part of a team." Good communication with deaf students was not one of that administrator's requirements. This administrator may have assumed that all interpreters would be proficient communicators in whatever language and modality the child used. Credentialling of educational interpreters would help cover this assumption, as well as providing guidance for school districts in their search for interpreters.

Expanding the Interpreter's Role

More than in any other setting, the educational interpreter's role remains unclear. Should interpreters be burdened with tasks other than interpreting? What about their ethical responsibilities? A sociologist offers the following description of a school that provokes these questions:

> In one secondary program for deaf students, the teachers in the self-contained classes gave the interpreter a notebook and asked her to record whatever difficulties she experienced with the deaf students and pass the notes to them. The teachers would then be able to help the interpreter. Less formally, the interpreter may share successes and setbacks of the students in mainstream classes with the teachers in the self-contained classes, telling the teachers of good grades, active participation, misbehavior of students, and the like. The interpreter may also speak of the problematic behavior of the mainstream teachers . . . which mainstream teachers realize can cause some discomfort . . . . Mainstream teachers may even directly ask interpreters about the deaf youth's comprehension. Consequently, interpreters may intervene by asking teachers to repeat, encouraging the deaf students to question the teachers, informing the teachers of the difficulty experienced by the student, and the like. (Higgins, 1990, pp. 158–159)

Although there are educators and interpreters who are resolute in their belief that interpreters should just interpret, many school districts assign interpreters multiple responsibilities. One school district's job description for educational interpreter lists ten specific duties, all of which seem appropriate, but then the list adds an eleventh item, "and other duties as assigned" (Zawolkow & DeFiore, 1986, p. 27). In another instance of expanding the usual interpreter functions, Florida has drawn up an ethical code specifically for educational interpreters. It softens the RID code's proscriptions against breaching confidentiality by allowing educational interpreters to share information about a student, though only with teachers and supervisors directly responsible for the student. It encourages interpreters to explain as well as translate lectures and to tutor under a subject teacher's direction.

The Professional Development Endorsement System for Educational Interpreters (PDESEI; National Interpreter Education Project [NIEP], 1996) contains an instructional module that covers some of the noninterpreting tasks that interpreters might encounter in the classroom. These tasks include "reinforcement of class material, vocabulary review, study skills, materials preparation, providing an introduction to the Deaf Community, informal instruction of sign language, and supervisory (lunch, bus, hall, etc.)" (NIEP, 1996, p. 1).

Asking interpreters to take on tasks for which they may not be prepared may force them to violate the principle that they should not accept assignments beyond their capabilities. Are they prepared to be advocates, tutors, and all-around experts on deafness? Few, if any, are. Lawyers who specialize in corporate law do not normally render opinions about criminal law. The otologist does not advise persons with skin disorders. It seems ironic that educational administrators would ask anyone to teach who lacks teaching credentials; yet that is the case for those interpreters who must also tutor. It unwittingly implies that the school administration has less respect for deaf than for nondeaf students.

Establishing expanded roles for interpreters is a decision for the stakeholders of a deaf child's education to make. In making that decision, they need to consider its broader implications. For their part, interpreters may want to tip the balance in favor of maintaining their professional stance as interpreters and nothing else.

Left out from most discussions about the interpreter's role in schools is the question about what an interpreter is to do during down time—that period of time when the deaf student is engaged in seatwork and there is no classroom dialogue to be interpreted. Seal (1998) observed that "To sit idle or to engage in some form of self-stimulation is a common dilemma for educational interpreters who find themselves with a lot of down time" (p. 132). While it might be argued that down time is not a "role" issue, the fact remains that what an interpreter does during this time may affect other people's perceptions of an interpreter's role. What happens, for example, when an interpreter requests to do photocopying for a teacher when the deaf student is doing seatwork (Seal, 1988)? Will the teacher come to expect future interpreters to do the same thing? Will students, deaf and hearing, begin to think of educational interpreters as individuals who double as paraprofessional aides? However down time is occupied, the emphasis should be on the interpreter remaining alert to any communication needs that may arise. Things can be said at any time, and the deaf student has the right to that information.

Position in a School's Hierarchy

Teachers naturally tend to concur with their administrators' regard for interpreters. If administrators see interpreters as aides rather than professionals,
so will the teachers. This places them in conflict with interpreter organizations, which promote interpreters as professionals, and with directors of interpreter education programs, who perceive "a strong need for clarification
of the role of the educational interpreter" (Gustason, 1985, p. 266).

An inherent danger of designating interpreters as teacher aides is that
teacher aides are at the bottom of the educational hierarchy, a fact that weighs
heavily in determining working conditions and wages. In line with such discussions is the question of whether interpreters should join school labor unions.
If they do join, will the unions represent them as teacher aides, with low status
and poor pay, or as professionals, deserving compensation and benefits equivalent to other professionals, like teachers and guidance counselors?

The opinions of deaf students are seldom represented, although students
have a vital interest in decisions bearing on their interpreters' positions in the
school. If the interpreter is an aide, then the quality demands will be corre-
spondingly lower than if the interpreter is a professional. The students' concerns about interpreters' functions are practical. If interpreters are ascribed
responsibilities similar to those of teacher aides, then assigning them tasks like
photocopying and collecting lunch money will be acceptable to the school. But
when interpreters have these additional duties, especially when those duties
take them out of the classroom, the deaf student loses communication—no
small matter to the student.

Ethical Concerns

Ethical concerns are raised when an interpreter passes along to other team
members information gleaned from interactions with the student. Once educational interpreters become members of a team, it is realistic to expect them
to share information they may have about the student with the other team
members. Realistic, yes, but a violation of their profession's ethics. Some interpreters decline to be "members of the team." They argue that, in the long
run, breaching confidentiality teaches students to distrust interpreters, something that interpreters believe is essential to their profession. Alternatively,
Humphrey and Alcorn (1994) suggest that interpreters on educational teams
only provide information pertaining to "the interpreting process, the student's language preference, language skills and the appropriateness of interpreting services within a particular educational setting" (p. 307). At the very
least, if the interpreter is a monitor, should not students be informed that
whatever they say or do may be reported to their teachers?

Similar reasoning may be interposed about the suggestion that interpreters coax students to ask questions or take particular actions in class. By doing so, interpreters not only violate the ethical principles of impartiality and noninterference, but they encourage the very passivity that educators want deaf students to overcome. By such practice, do educational interpreters teach a lesson that will not serve deaf students well when they become adults?

EDUCATIONAL LEVELS

The use of educational interpreters differs as the deaf student progresses from elementary to secondary to postsecondary classes, if only because each level places different linguistic and other demands on the interpreter. In part the alterations have to do with the type of instruction: elementary teachers lecture much less than do secondary or postsecondary teachers. Another factor is the maturity of the students: younger students accept conditions as given, whereas older students tend to question and, occasionally, to resist authority. Students' growing language abilities, too, affect interpreting.

Preprimary and Elementary

Because very young deaf children often interact nonverbally, the need for interpreters by preprimary deaf students may be overlooked. A mother of one five-year-old deaf boy said she was pleased with how well he was doing in a preschool program with no teachers who could sign. Asked if she thought he might be missing anything, she said no. At the other extreme are parents who are adamant about their deaf children having communication support in the lower grades. Their belief in the importance of language development motivates them to insist on appropriate interpreting all the time their deaf children are in school. Luetke-Stahlman (1996) provides an account of one family's struggle to obtain appropriate educational placement for their deaf daughter, including interpreting at the preschool level.

Educators concur that without verbal (signed) prompts accompanying daily activities, many deaf children will lag in language development—something that will be realized in the children's later education. This position is endorsed by the PDESEI, which has a unit devoted solely to providing interpreters with an overview of language acquisition and cognitive development in both deaf and hearing children.

Although having interpreters at the preprimary and elementary levels is essential ensuring that they are qualified is problematic. Interpreting at these levels does not normally pay well, which motivates nationally certified interpreters to seek employment elsewhere. As a result, it is not unusual to find many beginning interpreters working in schools. Some of them may have state-level qualifications, but many do not. They might hope that experience gained by interpreting in schools will help them improve their skills, the reality is that elementary levels of interpreting do not provide adequate practice situations that will help them elevate their skills to national standards.

The Students' Views

Another consideration is that very young students may not regard the interpreter as a person providing them with a service. A director of interpreter services for a large public school system notes that "younger children—kindergarten through second grade—often look to the interpreter as a parent figure." (cited in Zawolkow & DeFiore, 1986, p. 26) For this reason, interpreters should take a different psychological approach to working with a preschool student than with a secondary student. As one textbook states:

> The elementary school interpreter must have excellent interpreting skills plus the common sense and caring heart to be an adult in a child's world and still adhere to the interpreter role. A hug for a kindergartner having a sliver removed by the nurse may be in order at the same time one is voicing, "I don't want it out!" (Frishberg, 1990, pp. 103–104)

Story Reading and Other Linguistic Demands

A psychological adjustment is not the only change that interpreters make when interpreting for younger deaf children. Story reading, for example, occurs frequently in preschool. Mather's (1989) research has shown that expert signers use certain signing techniques to enhance their young audience's comprehension of a story. Interpreted reading at each grade level should be as different as preschoolers' and high school students' linguistic competencies.

While some interpreters and those who employ them in the lower grades may see themselves more as caregivers than interpreters, the communication skills they need are no less demanding than in higher grades. In the opinion of Kluscarits (1994):

> The fact is that the most difficult interpreting, the interpreting that requires the most skill, and the place where the most qualified interpreter is needed is the *primary classroom!* [p. 28, italics in original]. [T]he interpreter is often thrust into the role of primary language model [which] should necessitate that only the most qualified interpreters (preferably native users of ASL), who possess a great deal of knowledge of language development, should interpret in a first grade classroom (p. 32)

Should interpreters fingerspell to young deaf children? The answer, as with most answers to interpreting questions, depends upon the child. Some young children make fingerspelling-like movements in communicating; for them, the interpreter will probably be successful in introducing fingerspelling. In general, teaching fingerspelling independently is not recommended. Still, the repeated use of a name sign and its fingerspelled equivalent can establish the association between the two. Seal (1998) suggests this practice will teach the deaf child that "what I can say, I can also write; what I can write, I can also read; what I can read can be read by others" (p. 67). The interpreter should discuss this philosophy with the teacher, who, after all, has the responsibility for her students' instruction. Together, interpreter and teacher can determine when and how much fingerspelling should be used (Otis-Wilborn, 1992).

Educational interpreters in primary grades find themselves interpreting for a variety of group and individual activities, like seatwork, reading aloud, and field trips. Learning to manage all of these conditions argues for practicum experiences in interpreter education, a practice that more and more interpreter educators are adopting.

Secondary

In secondary classes, instruction is largely spoken, placing greater emphasis on the deaf students' need for educational interpreters. Deaf secondary students tend to believe that interpreters should have no other responsibilities than interpreting. They feel abandoned when interpreters are absent or otherwise engaged. Fifteen deaf students who attended integrated high schools before coming to the National Technical Institute for the Deaf (NTID) reported having very limited support services; only five said they had interpreters for one or more classes. As expressed by one respondent, "Last year, I paid attention [in high] school because of my interpreter . . . But when she wasn't there, I'd just sit back and do nothing" (Foster, 1988, p. 28). Nearly the same thing was said by a deaf high school student in Canada, who remarked that when her interpreter was not available she went either to the school library or to the washroom.

Although most regarded interpreting as essential, a few who had been able to participate in classes without interpreters became dependent on them once they were provided. Deaf secondary students or their families have been known to hire their own interpreters when the school failed to do so. Fortunately, awareness of deaf students' right to interpreting in educational settings has diminished the number of these instances.

Subject-Matter Demands

Instruction at the secondary level confronts interpreters with subjects in which they may have little or no background—biology, geometry, mechanical drawing. Not only do they stretch the interpreter's vocabularies, they also pose managerial problems, since classes can occur in a laboratory, a shop, or other places than classrooms with fixed seating. At the high school level, subject matter is typically taught using a lecture format. When the topic under discussion is abstract, the lecture format makes it difficult even for nondeaf students to process the information being delivered. For deaf students, this type of teaching is usually inappropriate, and using an interpreter does not offer a suitable solution.

The effects of seating (or standing) arrangements on interpreting are largely unexplored. Moores, Kluwin, and Mertens (1985) examined the positioning of a deaf student and an interpreter in high school programs and delineated three seating arrangements, each of which affected interpreting.

For discussions of the importance to interpreting of positioning and of understanding the content of messages, see Chapters 4 and 7.

Substitutes for Interpreting

When interpreting is not available, deaf students must depend on substitute communication, such as volunteer note-takers or other halfway measures. Even when done very well, notetaking still provides only the highlights of lectures. One teacher we know permitted deaf students to read his lecture notes in lieu of having an interpreter, but they did not find it a satisfactory substitute to being able to participate in the class and follow the lecture as it unfolded. On the whole, deaf secondary students appreciate interpreting, especially in conjunction with the services of a notetaker, as one student noted:

> I found out that I could learn more by just watching the interpreter. I don't take notes because if I take [notes and try to watch] the teacher at the same time, then I FAIL, FAIL, FAIL! I can't understand what's going on. It goes over my head [and] it's too fast. But with the note-taking out of the way, I don't have to worry about the notes. I just watch the interpreter and I get everything that the teacher is saying. Those notes help [me] to remember what the interpreter said, so then I learn more. (Foster, 1988, p. 30)

Perhaps deaf students' appreciation of interpreting services while in school will influence them as adults to take a proactive stance in shaping the role of educational interpreters on behalf of future generations of deaf schoolchildren.

Postsecondary

The subject matter is a major consideration in postsecondary education. Interpreters may be assigned to courses without regard for their backgrounds in these subjects. A deaf doctoral candidate tells about her experiences with some interpreters: "Miscommunication can and does occur between deaf and hearing people when using sign-language interpreters in university classrooms" (Johnson, 1991, p. 1). She videotaped 32 hours of interpreted classes and found numerous instances of miscommunication:

> These instances of confusion occurred with the greatest frequency when interpreters were unfamiliar with the subject they were interpreting and/or were required to interpret diagrams or verbal descriptions. The data also showed that the deaf students experienced difficulty looking at the board and at the interpreter simultaneously. (p. 27)

Johnson's study should not be construed as placing sole responsibility for communication on interpreters because it depends upon all of the participants. For instance, talking about diagrams is a complex activity that involves much intellectual involvement on the part of the speaker and the person receiving the message, let alone on the interpreter. Researchers investigating the occurrences of miscommunication should be aware of the many factors that impinge on comprehension.

At the postsecondary as well as the secondary level, it may not be feasible to cover every subject with an interpreter who is knowledgeable about that subject. The Washington Area Consortium of Universities, which includes Gallaudet University, found interpreting a major stumbling block to successfully integrating deaf students into its college classes. The consortium concluded that "work must continue on addressing the difficulties associated with obtaining appropriate interpreters at the various class times" (Kerstetter & Fritz, 1982, p. 19).

One promising solution to this ongoing problem is for postsecondary institutions to maintain, over a long period of time, a group of interpreters who can then acquire knowledge and special skills that will help them interpret scientific and technical courses. At one university, two interpreters were employed to interpret for a deaf student in a four-year veterinary program—a difficult program to interpret because of the heavy reliance on technical and medical terms and because of the logistics of interpreting in laboratories and around animals. The two interpreters and the deaf student developed strategies to solve these problems. Their strategy for handling new terminology was for one of the interpreters to write the unfamiliar words on a pad and pass it on to the student while the other interpreter continued to sign.

The solution most commonly employed to overcome the challenge of subject matter is to give interpreters preparation time. Even in relatively familiar subjects, such as English literature, interpreters improve their performances greatly by having time to review the material to be discussed. When they first read *Hamlet*, for instance, they were probably not thinking about how to sign "To be, or not to be." Some instructors make their lecture notes and course outlines available to interpreters, a courtesy that most interpreters welcome, especially when they are given released time to peruse the materials.

Social Interactions

Deaf postsecondary students may also need interpreters in their social interactions at school. This, however, raises the question of whether or not interpreters should be available to overcome students' anxieties about socializing. One deaf student described his difficulty communicating with nondeaf peers, even with the aid of an interpreter:

> Often I had trouble communicating with hearing people—hard to understand hearing people—makes me very nervous. Every day I'd go in the lab. [I'd] get really nervous if there's a tutor in the class with the hearing and I'm the only one deaf. Even with an interpreter, I'm still shaky . . . It was hard. (Foster, 1988, p. 29)

The concern about interpreting in social situations is partly stimulated by research at the National Technical Institute for the Deaf. It found that, although interpreting facilitated academic integration, it had little effect on socialization between deaf and nondeaf students. Despite the wide availability of interpreters, researchers concluded that "full integration did not occur" (Brown & Foster, 1991, p. 26).

Interpreters who are sensitive to deaf–nondeaf social interactions may need to remind themselves that their primary obligation is to communication. They need not be therapists, counselors, or social workers. They should resist being seen as conduits for social integration. If invited to do so, however, interpreters often can give educators ideas about how to improve deaf–nondeaf social interactions when the focus is on communication.

COMMUNICATION DECISIONS

Educational interpreting forces interpreters to make a host of decisions, most of which must be made on the spot. With experience, interpreters may recognize problems similar to ones they have already encountered and resolved, thus enabling them to fall back on earlier decisions. Then again, they may find themselves facing new problems for which they have no prior experience on which to rely. By presenting some of these difficult situations, we hope to prepare interpreters and participants to the problems and to some solutions that may or may not apply in a given instance.

What to Interpret

Educational interpreters face the same concern about what to interpret as do other interpreters. They must decide when interpreting is unnecessary, intrusive, or excessive. Should the interpreter convert all sounds to signs, even street noises and other nonverbal events? Consider the following account about an integrated classroom:

> After the film, the teacher asks the students to work together in small groups to discuss assigned topics. Immediately, the hearing students call out to each other and rush to sit with their friends. The teacher tells one group to crack their circle of desks and let the deaf student edge in. As the instructor moves to another part of the classroom, the students lean together and start discussing girls, guys, dates, parties, and inside gossip. Through the interpreter, the deaf student 'listens' eagerly, hungry for crumbs of information about social goings-on, even though he knows he is outside it all, neither a subject of conversation nor a participant in it. (Wixtrom, 1988, p. 14)

Profile: Dennis Berrigan

Dennis Berrigan is currently the ASL Training and Evaluation Coordinator at the Kendall Demonstration Elementary School and Model Secondary School for the Deaf, both of which are on the campus of Gallaudet University. His education and experiences well prepared him for this position. He has Deaf parents, attended St. Mary's School for the Deaf, graduated from Gallaudet University, and obtained a master of education degree from Western Maryland College. Inspired to teach by the example of Deaf teachers at Gallaudet University, he took a job at the American School for the Deaf, where he taught physical education and coached various sports.

Dennis refers to himself as a Deaf ASL proponent and is concerned about how mainstreaming programs deprive many deaf children of Deaf role models and exposure to ASL. Ironically, it was at an inservice in a mainstreamed school that he had his first awakening about ASL. At the school, he attended an inservice presentation by two nationally certified interpreters, Dennis Cokely (at that time a researcher in Gallaudet's now defunct Linguistic Research Laboratory) and Ken Rust. During this workshop, Dennis realized for the first time that the language he used at home was ASL. This encouraged him to learn more about ASL, and for a number of years he taught students about ASL

Continued

Profile: Dennis Berrigan *Continued*

structure in the Sign Language Studies Program at Madonna University in Michigan. Here he expresses his thoughts about the qualifications of educational interpreters:

> It is generally conceded that language and culture are inter-twined: ASL is the language of the Deaf people; it is a part of Deaf culture. Another important part of our culture is the Deaf school. For almost 200 years, Deaf schools have flourished and nourished our language and culture to bring them to their present form. Where we educate deaf children is important and today, as in the past, deaf education is strongly associated with language and culture.
>
> It is sad that more than ever deaf students attend main-streaming programs near where they live. Most mainstreamed programs do not have Deaf role models for deaf children. Deaf role models are usually concentrated in Deaf schools. Main-streaming means that interpreters for deaf students and the hearing students and teachers are in great demand.
>
> The Registry of Interpreters for the Deaf does provide pro-fessional interpreting certification. However, the demand for educational interpreters is so great that the education system, either by law or ignorance, is allowing people without certifi-cation to "insufficiently interpret" for deaf students in educa-tional settings. In reality, oftentimes *interpreting* does not occur and the message conveyed to students might be intrusive if not downright dysfunctional. This situation is analogous to having hearing teachers with minimal spoken English skills teach hear-ing children. The result is that many deaf students suffer in their cognitive and literacy development, in their self-identity, and in their self-esteem.
>
> This situation needs serious attention. Making the matter worse is the fact that more schools are hiring people who only possess Quality Assurance (QA) state-level certification. But the purpose of QA certification is to assess a candidate's skill level. Strengths and weaknesses are pointed out so that the candidate can improve weak skills in order to prepare for RID certification. However, the process is being reversed; it is becoming a final goal in itself rather than being used only as an assessment tool.
>
> There are now too many interpreters who are ineffective in sensitive situations and cannot reverse-interpret for students. I cannot picture interpreters with just a QA interpreting for my

Profile: Dennis Berrigan *Continued*

Deaf children or for me. I think part of the problem is that many state boards of education do not value interpreting as a profession and encourage minimal interpreting skills in educational settings that provide *minimal* learning experiences for deaf children in school.

The school boards are fulfilling a demand for educational interpreters rather than seeking to upgrade the overall quality of interpretations. The more I learn about QAs, the more I appreciate the value of RID certification. The QA programs presently used to assess educational interpreters should reflect diagnostic feedback and should not give endorsement to interpreters who are not qualified for interpreting in a school setting.

Deaf adults, interpreters, and others must work together to improve the education programs serving deaf and hard-of-hearing students in this country. Through my experience working in residential, mainstreamed, and university settings, I believe we will be able to provide in-class coaching to help teachers sign better and provide the assistance and support necessary to help interpreters improve their ASL interpreting skills. This is an urgent task because the education of deaf children cannot wait.

In this situation, the interpreter gives access to spoken communication regardless of its instructional context. The interpreter does not pass judgment on the merit of the message before interpreting it. Rather the interpreter signs what is being spoken, allowing the deaf student to determine its value.

The RID code insists that interpreters provide a full account of all auditory events, spoken or otherwise. Though stated without exception, this practice can be difficult to follow in some situations. Students in a classroom do not always speak in turn, extraneous noises often contribute nothing substantive, and some brief remarks might confuse the deaf student when interpolated during a lecture. What to do? The interpreter's judgment prevails, but that judgment will be aided, in the future, by studies and debates that seek to refine the underlying principle of determining what is essential communication in a classroom.

Audiences with Varying Language Levels/Preferences

As in any other interpreting setting, educational interpreters must cogitate about their own philosophical approaches to the concept of equivalence in meaning. Some interpreters edit the complexity out of what is spoken in an attempt to make the message comprehensible to the student. Others follow those translators who endeavor to create "a language structure which would evoke the same reaction in a target-language reader as the original had in its readers" (Kelly, 1979, p. 2). That is an ideal for text translators, who do not have audiences of one and who do have ample time to consider and reconsider the material they are translating, but impracticable for simultaneous interpreters.

To Simplify or Not

If interpreters simplify a message, have they violated deaf students' rights of access to the original message, or does simplifying promote access? How much smoothing of convoluted communication is permissible? These are troubling questions for educational interpreters. On the one hand, deaf students must be linguistically ready for learning in their classes. If the teacher's instructions are constantly modified to clarify them, the deaf student's education may suffer. On the other hand, no instruction has occurred unless the student understands what is said. The dilemma will remain until educators, interpreters, deaf students and their parents come together to resolve it. Their decisions will likely vary from circumstance to circumstance, for the determining factors are numerous and important.

Choices of Signs

Few issues can raise the hackles of professionals and nonprofessionals alike as much as the question of whether ASL or a form of English signing should be used. The arguments invariably touch upon *who* makes the decision. Educators sometimes assume that all deaf students automatically know ASL. (The same educators may expect that all blind students know Braille, but such assumptions defy reality.) Young deaf children, however, may have no knowledge of signs when they come to school, so the interpreter becomes, in effect, the child's sign teacher, opening the next question: Which signs to teach?

The types of signs taught are beyond the scope of this book. But we will point out that complications can ensue when a school's administration adopts a general policy favoring one or another method of signing. The deaf students may not be amenable to the policy, preferring a different option. Or the method of signing may be suitable for some of the students but not others. What is the educational interpreter to do?

As a part of a deaf student's educational team, interpreters may convey a student's preferences to the team but typically lack the authority to override an administrative fiat. Students may complain about too much fingerspelling, as it is fatiguing to watch great amounts of rapid finger movements, but their teachers, insistent on teaching precise English, may demand that many words be spelled rather than signed (see Johnson, 1991, esp. pp. 136–140). Other students may complain that the interpreter is using Signed English when they would prefer ASL, or that ASL confuses them because they have not had enough experience with it. Again, the interpreter can present the problem to the administration, which may or may not comprehend what the argument is about.

Oral examinations and test instructions are of particular interest to interpreters. Testing occurs at all levels of school and consist of informal, teacher generated tests such as spelling and formal, standardized tests such as the Stanford Achievement Test. It seems obvious that the interpreter should simply provide an accurate interpretation of the source message, whether they are questions or instructions. But it is not a simple matter because interpreters are not immune to the stress associated with testing. We are aware of interpreters who have been fired because they provided students with answers. Others have been chastised by deaf students, especially at the high school level, for not assisting them on tests. These situations can only compound the anxiety that interpreters experience as they struggle with their choices of signs for an optimal interpretation. One promising development in the area of interpreting tests is that some test developers have anticipated the difficulties the examination process poses for deaf students and have recommended ways that it should be managed (Educational Testing Services, 1994).

Interpreters have another option: more than one interpreter has said, "When I am interpreting, *I decide* what is best for the student. Who will know the difference?" A dangerous position for the interpreter, perhaps, but one that attempts to assess the problem and resolve it in favor of the student. Is this ethically correct? Would it be better for interpreters and students if the school accepted the interpreters as professionals and left such decisions to them?

WORKING CONDITIONS

Administrative decisions affect interpreting in many ways besides the choice of signs. Working conditions can create morale problems for all concerned, not just the interpreters, and policy decisions about compensation, supervision, and the manner in which interpreters perform can raise ethical dilemmas for the interpreters.

The School Atmosphere

Interpreting in a public school that invites all students and teachers to learn sign makes for a pleasant environment; it enhances interpreters' effectiveness and provides deaf students with more peers with whom to communicate. One Canadian school offered a sign class to its nondeaf students, and over 30 enrolled in a class planned for 17. In a suburban community, parents of young deaf children reported that "everybody wanted to learn to sign. More than 200 students enrolled, when the school offered sign classes" (Schein, 1992, p. 14). In another school, the teacher required that any child who was reciting or answering a question must stand and face the deaf student, to enable him to speechread. Interpreters thrive in schools that demonstrate a sophistication about, and willingness to accommodate, the deaf students' communication needs.

Supervision

Who supervises the educational interpreter? The most frequent answer is, "No one." Why not have the classroom teacher supervise the interpreter? As one teacher said, poignantly, "I wish I knew what [the interpreter] is doing." Beyond checking interpreter attendance, teacher supervision contributes little or nothing, unless the teacher knows sign language and has studied interpreting.

Some parents think they should oversee their children's interpreters, but that arrangement would conflict with most schools' policies. Furthermore, few parents are both fluent in sign *and* knowledgeable about principles of interpreting. An exception might be the deaf parents of a deaf student in an integrated class.

Schools can hire outside evaluators for the sole purpose of assessing interpreter performance. It is not a common procedure. More likely, schools will rely on Quality Assurance (QA) testing. QA is available in some states through the state department of education or other agency responsible for deafness-related issues. Another option is the Sign Communication Proficiency Interview (SCPI), which evaluates signing skills (Newell, Caccamise, Boardman, & Holcomb, 1983). The SCPI has trained evaluators in several states and Canadian provinces. Though not a test of interpreting ability, it does provide a reliable assessment of fluency in signing.

In a few schools, deaf students have been asked to provide confidential ratings of their interpreters. That tactic will be difficult to implement where there is only one student and one interpreter, but where several students and interpreters are in the same school, the students' evaluations contribute a valuable adjunct to the supervisory function. At the very least, they demonstrate the school's respect for the students' opinions, something that students appreciate.

Another possibility is not to supervise educational interpreters. Like other professionals, they should be evaluated, but not told how to practice. Insisting on having someone look over the interpreter's shoulder may betray administrators' lack of confidence. If they accept an interpreter as *profession-ally* qualified, they could rely for assurance against malpractice on that inter-preter's professional organization.

Professional Isolation

Classroom conditions will affect the performance of interpreters. A major de-terminer is whether the school has only one or two deaf students or is a cen-ter for the education of deaf students. In the former, the interpreter will likely be the only one hired; in the latter, there will be several interpreters. Having professional colleagues helps to reduce burnout and contributes to continued development of skills. Workshops and organizational meetings can reduce professional isolation, but daily contact with other interpreters in the same school is preferable.

Joining a professional organization provides more than political clout; it also affords interpreters with support from their peers—something that all professionals need at one time or another (Siple, 1991). Being able to share emotional experiences, discuss problems, and gain advice from other inter-preters can keep an interpreter on an even keel in sailing through difficult ex-periences while interpreting.

The physical demands of interpreting are reduced when one interpreter can share responsibilities with another. As noted in Chapter 4, interpreters are at risk for repetitive-motion injuries if they are required to perform with-out adequate rest periods. If there is only one interpreter in the school, the deaf student must suffer periodic communication blackouts when the lone in-terpreter takes an appropriate break.

Collegial Relations

Administrators' and teachers' opinions of interpreters play roles in educa-tional interpreting. Having an administrator who is knowledgeable about deaf people—or is willing to abide by the recommendations of qualified consultants—is important to the success of an integrated program. It is easy to fault local school administrators and teachers for making arrangements that appear foolish to experts on deafness. These educators usually operate with the best of intentions and set up communication programs that are rea-sonable from their points of view. Yet neither they nor their school boards are apt to have backgrounds in special education, let alone in the education of deaf students.

One school administrator insisted that interpreters only sign *part* of each lesson. Asked why, he replied, "[Deaf students] cannot expect to have interpreters for the rest of their lives; they have to learn to do without them, and school is the right place to practice it." Interviews with some school ad-ministrators found none who was dissatisfied with the communication arrangements in their schools. But few knew anything about sign language, interpreting, or Deaf culture. Why, then, were they satisfied? A typical response to that question was "I don't hear any complaints, so things must be going well" (Schein, Mallory, & Greaves, 1991, p. 17)

It seems that many educators choose not to look closely at interpreting. If they employ someone who serves in that capacity, then they accept that the job is done. One research group proposed calling unprofessional interpreters *communication aides* rather than *interpreters* (Schein et al., 1991). The latter title implies an earned status, one that requires a specific education and relevant experience, and people tend to accept what the name implies. To call anyone who signs in a classroom an *interpreter* confuses the public, disadvantages deaf students, and damages the interpreting profession.

Consider the following example from a U.S. school district, one that tells a great deal about the lack of appreciation of what communication for deaf students means:

> In the same district, two other hearing impaired students were placed in a science class with the assistance of an aide, who was to interpret for the students. Unfortunately, with a moderate to severe hearing loss, the aide had great difficulty understanding what was being said in class. Consequently, the aide interpreted little of what was said, and the two students did not participate in any meaningful way in the life of the class. While unsure how much the two students understood, the teacher of the class believed that the students did not need any additional help from her because they had the aide, who worked individually with the students. (Higgins, 1990, p. 24)

Educators cannot be satisfied that they have met deaf students' needs simply because they have hired someone to sign. Much more must be built into any system that expects to educate deaf students. One example of successful inclusion is the University of New Mexico–Albuquerque Public Schools program that provides college-level interpreters to deaf students. The inclusion effort melds a four-year program of interpreter preparation with educating students in interpreter use, continuous upgrading of interpreters, and a highly flexible language policy. Among its virtues, supporters point to its favorable cost–benefit ratio (Wilcox, Schroeder, & Martinez, 1990).

Student and Parent Relations

Most students at the elementary level have all of their classes with one teacher. If that teacher and student are incompatible, a serious problem arises, often resolved by shifting the student to a different class or even a different school. Does the same apply to interpreter–student incompatibilities? What are the student's and the interpreter's rights? Shifting interpreters among students can be administratively difficult. What matters, however, is that principles applying to these situations be spelled out before problems arise. Such guidance can prevent problems by advising both parties of what they have a right to expect when and if dissatisfactions arise.

Given the low incidence of deafness, in many schools a student may have the same interpreter not only for a year but for many years. Even if the interpreter communicates well with the student and both enjoy each other's company, is such a long-term relationship psychologically salutary? Typically, students must adjust annually to a new teacher. This process of adjustment by itself can be a valuable learning experience. Is having the same interpreter year after year depriving deaf students of valuable learning? At the very least parents and educators should question the arrangement.

In interviews with deaf students and their parents, Schein, Mallory, and Greaves (1991) elicited attitudes not apt to surprise persons familiar with educational interpreting. Overall, the 38 parents and 27 present and former deaf students responded sympathetically to interpreters and somewhat disdainfully to school administrations. Parents commented on the poor pay for interpreters, their onerous list of duties, and the requirement that they interpret for 60 minutes without a rest. Parents acknowledged the shortage of qualified interpreters but felt schools did not do enough to improve conditions. If their comments appear harsh, it should be said that they assume best examples are commonplace and any deviation from them is an assault on their children's education. A positive aspect the survey uncovered was parents' desire to participate more fully in their deaf children's schooling.

Most of the deaf students appreciated their interpreters' support and, as noted, felt lost in classes without interpreters. A few deaf teenagers resented interpreters because interpreting separated them from nondeaf students and because it stigmatized them—or so they thought. These students, a distinct minority, usually had residual hearing and superior speechreading ability that enabled them to function academically without interpreters.

By contrast, some deaf students blossom when interpreting becomes available. Goulet (1989) gives a poignant account of his educational experiences after becoming hard of hearing at age five. He contrasts those early years with his discovery of signing as a teenager. He describes his metamorphosis from a "slow learner" to a college graduate—a change he attributes to interpreted communication.

A highly successful deaf educator, now a dean at NTID, recounts how interpreters contributed to his education. He makes clear why deaf students regard interpreting so highly and why some educators are worried about inclusion:

> As I reflect over my 23 years as a mainstreamed student, it is frightening for me to realize the full implications of Public Law 94-142 as

it impacts on many hearing-impaired students who may need more assistance than just support services in regular classrooms. My experiences clearly point out the struggle that even a highly motivated, self-disciplined and academically well prepared deaf person faces in a mainstreamed situation . . . . Some deaf students may have the capacity to succeed in mainstreaming; others will require continuous cultivation to become successfully mainstreamed students. Still many others may benefit more from alternative schooling experiences in special education classes or in residential schools for the deaf. (Hurwitz, 1991a, pp. 73–74)

Deaf people generally feel that they should be involved in planning for and selecting interpreters. After all, they are knowledgeable. There is a need to keep them informed about school policies and regulations. Yet some educational administrators who regard input from outsiders as intrusive are likely to hide behind the law, claiming that they are complying with state regulations. School districts stand to gain much by taking advantage of input from deaf adults and students.

Acknowledging the value of interpreters for deaf students raises the issue of who teaches deaf students how to use interpreters. Moreover, who will teach the students' parents and their classmates and teachers. We cannot assume that knowledge of signs predisposes a person toward a favorable relationship with an interpreter or that others will acquiesce to the situation. Seal (1998) suggests:

that the teacher of the deaf, hearing-impaired specialist, or responsible administrator in the school system set up orientation meetings or inservice meetings for the class (or grade or school) . . . . that a deaf adult, who has worked with educational interpreters, conduct the meetings. Within this training, I would suggest covering the basic courtesies, functional pragmatics, and potential ethical concerns that could spoil or solidify the working relationship as it becomes established. (p. 107)

SUPPLY AND DEMAND

The chronic shortage of interpreters, extensively covered in Chapter 8, is exacerbated by the specialized nature of educational interpreting. Further discussion is unnecessary here, except to add that the lack of qualified interpreters severely affects the education of deaf students. From his long-term observation of one school, Higgins (1990) writes, "While the [integrated] program that I intensely observed has recently added several skilled interpreters, the program has often experienced a shortage. The lack of interpreters at the elementary program made it difficult to mainstream deaf students. At the secondary level , . . . teachers of the deaf youth tried to mainstream them in groups of two or more so that interpreters would be available . . . . Lack of interpreters constrained teachers and others as they placed deaf students" (pp. 72–73).

Steps to correct the supply–demand imbalance cannot be taken too soon for those concerned with deaf students' welfare.

LEGAL ASPECTS

Laws are in place to provide interpreting services to deaf students in public schools, and most school districts make arrangements to accommodate them. Nonetheless, deaf students occasionally confront school officials who deny them interpreting services. The U.S. Supreme Court ruled against Amy Rowley in her bid to obtain an interpreter for her mainstream classes. Ruling in favor of the school board, the U.S. Supreme Court said, "P.L. 94-142 imposes no clear obligation on recipient states beyond the requirement that handicapped children receive some form of specialized education" (cited in Moores, 1992, p. 24; see also Anthony, 1982). The Court ruled that, although Amy, who is profoundly deaf, might have achieved more academically with an interpreter, she was performing adequately, and therefore the school board was justified in not providing her with an interpreter.

Similarly, the Elmira, New York, school board assigned Jennifer Miranda, a bright deaf student in the fifth grade, a person to act as her interpreter who had no interpreter training and who had taken only two sign language classes at a community college. Jennifer's parents complained that such an arrangement was inadequate and sued the school board. Commenting on the decision against Jennifer's petition, the news account reported:

> Jennifer's supporters were hindered by the fact that the State of New York has no regulations for sign language interpreters . . . . "I feel [the decision] was a slap in the face to all deaf students across New York State," said [Jennifer's mother] Carol Miranda. (*Empire State News*, 1990, Vol. 52, No. 2, p. 7)

In another case involving educational interpreting, Jim Zobrest, a deaf student, demanded that his local school district pay the Catholic high school he was attending for his interpreter. The public school district refused on the grounds that the separation of church and state relieves their obligation to reimburse the $8,500 per year the parents claimed they must spend. In June 1993 the U.S. Supreme Court, ruling in favor of Zobrest, required the state to obey the Americans with Disabilities Act and provide interpreting services. With this ruling, the Court advanced the status of interpreting by recognizing it as essential to deaf students in classrooms in which instructors do not sign. The case is also important in that it marked the first time that "the Court has permitted a public employee to become part of the educational team in the parochial school classroom" (Siegel, 1995, p. 387).

In a review of the Zobrest's case, one author contended that the Court's arguments were flawed because it misinterpreted the role of interpreters. The Court ruled in favor of the Zobrest in part because he likened "the functioning of a sign language interpreter to that of a hearing aid, or a pair of eyeglasses" (Siegel, 1995, p. 389). The Court was not alone in that interpretation and was simply accepting the mechanistic (interpreter as a conduit) view of interpreting.

Siegel (1995) points out that the benefit of using interpreters extends beyond the message that gets interpreted:

> Because the sign language interpreter's clients are both hearing and deaf, she must take affirmative steps to undo the natural power imbalance. These actions may be obvious but they are nonetheless significant. The interpreter may, in some situations, feel obliged to send a message to the deaf client that the hearing client(s) did not actually send. For example, she may explain in ASL that "the reason everyone is not paying attention now is that a downpouring of rain just started and they are distracted by the loud sound of the rain on the roof." (p. 393)

If the judge had assumed the Interactive Model of Interpreting or another nonmechanical perspective, then in all likelihood he would have denied the Zobrests' request, because interpreters, barring any restrictions imposed by the school administration, have flexibility in their choice of signs and in what they choose to interpret.

The legal aspects of educational interpreting can be confusing. Parents, deaf students, school personnel, and interpreters should take advantage of the many resources available to them—resources with knowledge of laws and regulations specific to educational interpreting. They can contact the following for information about legal aspects of educational interpreting in the United States: the National Center on Law and the Deaf, the Convention of American Instructors of the Deaf, RID, and the National Association of the Deaf. In Canada they can contact AVLIC, the Canadian Association of the Deaf, and the Canadian Association of Educators for Deaf and Hard of Hearing.

THE RESEARCH BASIS

There is no shortage of guidelines for educational interpreting, as many school districts and especially those with a substantial enrollment of deaf students have laid out their own principles and procedures for interpreting. But they have done so without the benefits of knowing systematically how interpreters actually perform in the classroom. Research support for the formulation of guidelines is sparse, as Stewart and Kluwin (1996) report: "What the field lacks is research into the theoretical underpinnings of the process of interpretation, both at the laboratory and the field level" (p. 37). They show that what is relied on has sometimes been extrapolated from research in nonschool settings—for example, studies of processing time, which is not a problem for educational interpreters alone. Studies of general educational practices and comprehension of signed lectures have some relevance to educational interpreting, although they would be more cogent if they involved deaf students.

The paucity of research likely has an adverse impact on educational interpreters: "Public school systems in general have been at a significant disadvantage in finding models and guidelines to inform their Boards of Education and leadership administration about the specialized nature of *educational* interpreting" (McGee, 1990, p. 206, emphasis in the original). Lack of scientific evidence often places interpreters on the defensive because there is almost no research on educational interpreters that has "linked their characteristics, assignments, or attitudes with student outcomes" (Mertens, 1991, p. 49). Evidence of an exciting and welcome change in interpreters' views of educational interpreting can be found in a recent issue of the RID newsletter (*RID Views*, Vol. 11, No. 2, 1994), which is almost entirely devoted to questions about educational interpreting. As interpreters have become a fixture in the education of deaf children in regular education classrooms, pertinent research will increase.

Ethnographic studies have emerged to highlight significant factors in school settings. One study showed that educational interpreters are more inclined to call for the use of conceptually appropriate signed English than interpreters outside of school settings. The latter tend to advocate for the greater use of American Sign Language (Kluwin, 1995). Such findings provoke research that discerns deaf students' comprehension of various types of signing under different classroom situations.

Guidelines for educational interpreting developed by government and organizations are now becoming available (Stuckless et al., 1989; AVLIC, 1992). The Province of Alberta has not only prepared guidelines but has also contracted for an independent review of them (Premier's Council on the Status of Persons with Disabilities, 1994, and the review of it by Anderson, 1996).* The review noted that large schools followed the guidelines but that small schools often were unaware of their existence. The review documented parents' feelings that the guidelines "forced ASL as the only choice" while ignoring their

---

*Both documents are available without charge from the Premier's Council on the Status of Persons with Disabilities, Suite 250, 11044 - 82 Avenue, Edmonton, Alberta T6G-0T2.

wishes. Even when such reviews produce discouraging results, they eventually benefit service delivery by illuminating flaws in initial efforts. Follow-up studies, when well done, pay handsome dividends.

A study of NTID students found that they correctly recognized spoken–signed communication significantly more often than interpreted (Caccamise & Blasdell, 1977). Although that study involved almost 300 deaf students, it left many questions open to further research. For example, only one signer served both the interpreted and spoken–signed situations. Second, the signs were presented on videotape, a two-dimensional medium that may not adequately represent signs. Another limiting factor is that the test material involved discrete sentences, not connected discourse. The study also found that students wearing hearing aids did better under all conditions than those who did not, suggesting that speech sounds were an important contributor, going beyond speechreading alone. Finally, the study's results were somewhat puzzling in that comprehension levels for all forms of communication were low overall (ranging from 58.3% to 74.5% percent correct), suggesting the material might have been too esoteric for all of the students.

Livingston et al. (1994) presented 43 deaf college students at LaGuardia Community College with a lecture and a story, each interpreted in ASL for one group and in Signed English for the other. The results favored ASL, but, more important, the study found that regardless of the condition—narrative or lecture, interpreted or transliterated—the average percentage of correct responses were below 75%. Without a control condition in which speakers sign for themselves, the possibility that students' poor scores might have been due to the interpreted communication cannot be eliminated.

The NTID and LaGuardia studies do not offer the final words on the effectiveness of interpreting. Rather, they highlight the need for further research to explore the relationship between the nature and comprehension of interpreted communication by different groups of participants under a variety of conditions.

Another outcome of research is that interpreters, parents, and deaf students now expect schools to engage only fully qualified interpreters. RID, for example, has established a group called EdITOR, which is working toward this end. Parents and deaf students are joining to challenge the hiring of *signers* or *communication aides* rather than educational interpreters. The combined forces of professional organizations and parents force school districts to examine carefully their policies and practices. Gradually, it is becoming more common to find a school district with a highly proficient cadre of interpreters.

SUMMARY

Any notion that educational interpreting can be taken for granted will be quickly dispelled by questions like the following:

- What is the status of interpreters in the school hierarchy?
- What qualifications should educational interpreters have?
- Should an educational interpreter's responsibilities include duties unrelated to communication support for deaf students?
- How do interpreters and teachers relate to one another?
- Who supervises interpreters? Who evaluates their performance?
- Should interpreters discipline students? Interact with them in other ways?
- Do students have a right to select their interpreters and to decide how they should function?
- What are the educational interpreter's rights?

These questions illustrate the complexity of what may have appeared a simple matter to those educators and administrators who saw the use of interpreters as an easy solution to integrating deaf students into regular classrooms. Research will not resolve all of these matters, because many of them are policy decisions. But research and an ongoing dialogue among the participants can delineate the elements of the issues and lead to consistent, informed decisions.

Though obvious, it should be made explicit that educational interpreters represent only one facet of a multifaceted educational enterprise. To succeed, mixing deaf and nondeaf students needs much more than accurate visualization of spoken communication in the classroom. Psychological and social factors enter into the placement of each deaf student. Being able to see or hear everything that happens in the classroom does not assure a student's learning, nor is education solely a matter of transmitting information from teacher to student. Students learn as much from other students as they do from teachers. Therefore, providing for communication between deaf students and teachers does not in itself guarantee the deaf students an equivalent education to that received by their nondeaf classmates.

The beginning of this chapter promised an overview of issues facing educational interpreters and not guidelines. A first step that educators and parents should, and likely will, take in developing appropriate policies is to raise questions. If they stimulate examination of what lies behind the verbal façades of *deafness, interpreting,* and *inclusion,* policy decisions will be optimized. Given the current state of the education of deaf students, no educator can feel complacent about any loss of opportunities to improve it.

At present, it would be prudent for states to establish task forces to revisit the role and status of educational interpreters and to follow up on their implementation. No one disagrees with the idea that educational interpreters are essential to the success of inclusion programs for deaf students. It can be expected that, through training, experience, and professional interactions, future cadres of interpreters will exert an influence in helping to shape their role or roles. Again, in these unfortunate situations the deaf student may be the loser, victimized by consequences of uninformed and improper advice.

11

THE FUTURE

What will sign language interpreting be like in the twenty-first century? Will it continue to grow in importance? Will its use decline, replaced by technological advances or by more general knowledge of sign in the general population? Will the Deaf community develop greater confidence in the abilities of interpreters and in their ethical standards? Will deaf people's respect for interpreters remain the same or deteriorate? What about other professions? Will lawyers, physicians, dentists, and other professionals be more or less accepting of interpreters who accompany deaf clients? And what about the general public? Will it become more or less supportive, more or less willing to bear the costs of interpreting?

Not being fatalists, we do not believe the answers to these questions are "in our stars." Rather, these matters will be determined by the actions and reactions of the parties involved. We have no crystal ball but in this chapter we will point out some trends and express some of our hopes and concerns.

DEMAND

When Rome ruled the world, the dominant language was Latin. At the turn of the twentieth century, German was the scientific language and French the language of diplomacy. Today, scientists and diplomats must know English to function effectively. One hundred years from now that may change again. Indeed, some sociolinguists predict that English will not remain the world's lingua franca into the next century. Language choices refuse to remain constant. However, we feel safe in prognosticating that sign languages will continue to hold a prominent place in Deaf communities throughout the world. Their existence will ensure a demand for interpreters.

Probably the greatest impetus to requests for interpreters comes from the actions of legislators. Laws like the Americans with Disabilities Act mandate interpreters' employment. As discussed earlier, Section 504 of the Rehabilitation Act Amendments of 1973 required that access to facilities using federal funds not be denied people with disabilities—and access for deaf people clearly means having communication in a form they can comprehend. Despite this law has been in place for over two decades, full compliance has yet to be attained. Many issues and concerns need to be addressed if the services rendered because of this law are to achieve their ultimate goals. Providing interpreters does not amount to suitable compliance with the law *unless* the interpreters are qualified for the tasks they are given.

Section 504 is an important marker on the road toward increased use of interpreters. Canada, Sweden, and some other countries have similar laws. With demand supported by legislation, there is little doubt that growth in requests will continue.

The World Federation of the Deaf (WFD) is pledged to work for the availability of interpreters in every country, and interpreters already have a separate WFD section. The Registry of Interpreters for the Deaf (RID) has also cast its eyes abroad. It sponsored the first international conference on sign language interpreting, in Washington, D.C., in August 1975. There are sister interpreter organizations in Australia, Canada, Denmark, England, Finland, Norway, Scotland, Sweden, and, no doubt, other countries, though none, as yet, in Central or South America.

Aiding RID and WFD in their efforts is the expectation that countries will benefit from each other's experiences in developing more effective laws. This expectation assumes that the cost of providing interpreters will not foster an atmosphere of avoidance, a search for less expensive options. Two main forces counter that possibility. First, the disabilities group movement has established itself as a lobby that cannot easily be dismissed. Although setbacks in their efforts can be expected, their overall direction is toward greater benefits for the groups they represent. In conjunction with that movement is the effort of schools to cultivate greater understanding of what different disabilities entail. Second, the growing strength of Deaf communities around the world and the greater sharing of information via electronic networking bode well for the development and preservation of laws mandating services for deaf people.

Another impetus toward increased demand for interpreters comes from improved transportation, which makes intermingling people from distant nations a common occurrence. For reasons of commerce and curiosity, more people than ever before cross their national boundaries to visit lands with languages and customs that differ from their own. As a result, interpreters are finding themselves parts of tours and cruises, many designed specifically to attract deaf travelers.

The movement to include deaf students in classes with nondeaf students has led to a boom in the demand for interpreters. Having become accustomed to interpretation in school, deaf adults will most likely continue to request interpreters after they leave school.

All of these—and other factors broached in earlier chapters—augur well for the likelihood that interpreters will have ample assignments to fill in the coming years. There are few indications of things that will diminish that demand.

REMOTE INTERPRETING

The Kentucky Commission on the Deaf and Hard of Hearing (KCDHH) recently completed research on the use of telecommunication equipment to provide interpreting services (Scoggins, 1997). Like most states, Kentucky suffers from a shortage and maldistribution of interpreters. Videoconferencing is one way to overcome these communication barriers because it removes the need for an interpreter to be physically present. As long as the other participants can be seen and heard clearly via video signals transmitted over telephone lines, then the interpreter can proceed to interpret from a remote location. KCDHH tried three lines over which to deliver video signals: T-1, ISDN, and POTS "plain old telephone service"). These lines coupled various equipment and software. The results of six month trials indicate that T-1 and ISDN lines deliver acceptable signals, with the T-1 performance being preferred. With the latter operating at 768 Kps (786,000 bytes per second), signs appear lifelike and are easily read. The slower the transmission rate, the less intelligible the signing. POTS gave unacceptable signals for interpreting. The report concludes, "[Videoconferencing] enables interpreting services to be utilized more effectively by service providers, because it eliminates the need to pay portal-to-portal expenses of the interpreter . . . [and] it allows more flexibility for scheduling, because travel time is minimized and interpreters can be hired from anywhere in the United States" (Scoggins, 1997, p. 15).

Should interpreters be concerned about this development? Scoggins (1997) thinks not:

> Interpreters currently working in the field will not be threatened by this technology because it supplements live, on-site interpreting and is not an equivalent substitute . . . . [B]ased on the feedback received, a live interpreter on site will always be the first preference; but, when that is not physically possible, remote interpreting is an acceptable substitute in some situations depending on the technical system (T-1, ISDN or POTS) deployed. (p. 15)

Interpreters equipped with laptop computers, videocameras, and newly written software that improves POTS transmission will be able to provide their services from their homes, their cars, or any place that has a telephone. Standardizing and/or linking videoconferencing facilities that now employ different technology will further expand the availability of interpreters to even the remotest areas. As with all emerging technology, remote interpreting has problems—problems that will be resolved as the service grows and matures.

Nevertheless, there are some issues that bear consideration. Some deaf people express concerns about privacy, not knowing who might be watching; these doubts arise especially in mental health counseling. Interpreters, as well as viewers, need adaptation time. In most cases, by their second exposure to the system they find it more satisfactory. Equipment costs are steep at the present time, but cost should decline as the technology improves and as the demand increases. This action should make remote interpreting even more affordable. Despite present difficulties, imperfections, and inconveniences, remote interpreting appears to be an addition to service delivery that will increase in the near future. Even in its present state, it offers so many advantages to interpreters and to those who use their services that its acceptance appears to be assured.

ALTERNATIVES TO SIGN LANGUAGE INTERPRETING

One potential competitor to sign language interpreters is machine translation in its various forms. What will be the impact of speech-to-text and text-to-speech translating machines? Software to accomplish this is already available, although its cost and that of the accompanying hardware are inhibiting factors. The most difficult challenge facing developers in this area is the recognition of vocal input from different speakers and covering a large vocabulary prior to converting it to text. Speed is also a factor. As fast as computers are today, they are not yet capable of recognizing humans speaking at a normal rate.

More readily accomplished is the voicing and signing of typed input. Such a feature is now in place in a CD ROM program called the Personal Communicator that is being used to facilitate the social interactions of deaf children in public schools (Stewart, Heeter, & Dickson, 1996). Problems of portability, costs, and maintenance have not yet been solved, but these will be among the determining points in the future of this technology, the feasibility of which has already been demonstrated.

When such hardware in the form of pocket-sized translators becomes available, will it displace interpreters and drastically lower the demands for their services? We think it will not do so in the foreseeable future. Interpreting involves more than finding a word in one language that is the equivalent in another language, and this is especially true when converting sign language to speech. As long as deaf people prefer to use sign language as their primary language, interpreters will be needed to mediate their communication for those who do not know sign.

Researchers are also working on the computer recognition of signs and nonmanual linguistic signals (Weng & Stewart, 1997). Their hope is one day to develop a program that will convert all signs to text and speech. They face tremendous obstacles, however, as the software also will have to be able to translate ASL grammar in order for the sign-recognition component to have practical application outside of the laboratory. Therefore, the widespread availability of this technology is still far in the future, but we are confident in predicting that one day it will be a reality that will offer an alternative to the use of sign language interpreters in a few, highly controlled circumstances.

Moreover, technological alternatives to interpreters do not take into account the human factor in the interpreted interaction, which may be of irreplaceable value. Communicating via an electronic or mechanical device can be forbidding. No machine has yet been devised that can replace human flexibility and understanding. (See the box titled "Muddling the Machines.") Nonetheless, the option of carrying a personal translator that will obviate the

---

Muddling the Machines

Machines do not think; they do not judge. They must be programmed.

A speaker announced, "Kodak has developed a *new disc* camera." Imagine his surprise at what his company's engineers had wrought when the speech-to-print translator informed the audience, "Kodak has developed a *nudist* camera!"

How does one instruct an electronic device to distinguish between the pronunciation of *patio* and *ratio* ? There are English criteria governing many such instances. For native speakers, it is a matter of experience, knowing when it "sounds right," that makes it difficult for the machine's programmers.

And what if the speaker says *no*, should the machine print *know*? If not, what are the rules by which it will choose? When the machine confronts *bare*, should it print *bear* or *bair*, even though the latter is a nonword? Can a general rule be written for words that sound alike but are spelled differently and have different meanings? After all, English has numerous homonyms—*eye* and *I* , *hi* and *high*, *sigh* and *scythe*, *wait* and *weight*, and many more.

need for interpreters in some situations does have its appeal for deaf people who are fluent in English.

In an earlier review of mediated communication by electronic systems, the following observation was offered:

> Many media differences have been identified, though not as many as might be expected from a reading of the nonverbal communication literature. However, a unitary theoretical explanation for these differences has yet to emerge. A difficulty in the practical application of these results is that one can only be sure that the transfer of a type of face-to-face meeting to a telecommunications medium has no disadvantages *if one is sure that there are no psychological differences in communicating over these two media.* (Williams, 1977, p. 974, emphasis added)

In the two decades that have followed this observation, North American homes have been inundated with an array of powerful computers, facsimile machines, and CD-ROMs. Communication via the Internet or on-line conversations are becoming the norm in many people's lives. Communities are becoming accustomed to impersonal transactions via telecommunication devices. Nevertheless, some deaf people do not read English well, and there is no printed form of ASL, so equipment that requires typed English input and whose output is printed English remains unattractive to a large segment of the deaf population. Moreover, the nurturing influences of Deaf culture on the interchange of messages would seem to need much more than machines can accomplish—at this time and at any time in the near future.

Having said this, we would be less than candid if we denied that the advent of machine translation, no matter how imperfect, will influence the practice of interpreting. This is not an ill omen for interpreters. Interpreters always will be able to offer something that machines cannot. They will be able to compete successfully, if they are empathetic, broadly educated, and skillful at applying their knowledge. Those are the directions in which interpreter education is currently moving: toward better and better prepared interpreters.

SUPPLY

There has been a dramatic increase in the number of institutions of higher education providing interpreter education. They give no signs of having difficulty attracting applicants. From the standpoint of producing new interpreters, the supply side appears bright. In many countries, however, such as Canada, not enough interpreters are graduating to replace those who leave the field annually (Schein, Mallory, & Carver, 1990). Comparable figures have not emerged for the United States, but we suspect the situation may not differ greatly—that interpreter graduates are not keeping pace with the growing demand.

What is more, attrition among interpreters is substantial. Natural losses due to age, marriage, childbearing, sickness, injury, and death are exacerbated by discouragement due to poor working conditions and low pay. Improvements in the latter two areas does not appear to have kept pace with the greater expectations for professionalism among interpreters. As we said at the outset of this chapter, conditions can change rapidly. Indeed, we hope that employment conditions for interpreters will improve as more businesses and agencies try to fulfill their obligations to accommodate deaf people.

RESEARCH

The Interactive Model of Interpreting will, we hope, generate questions amenable to research. Answers to questions promoted by a model have an advantage of being additive. Here are some samples of the kinds of research that can be expected in the near future:

- What is the optimal range of time between message initiation and message transmission? What factors affect this time?
- How do expert interpreters manage problems commonly arising in interpreting situations? Such problems include keeping up with a very rapid speaker or signer, conveying clear interpretations to an audience of varied communication abilities and preferences, and managing a speech with many interior clauses and interpolated remarks. Observing how interpreters manage such stresses successfully can lead to techniques that can be passed along to less experienced, less proficient interpreters.
- How much of what we learn about effective interpreting can be taught?
- To the extent that interpreting is in part a physical activity, what is the extent to which any interpreter's physical endowment can be improved?
- For years, the largest pool from which interpreters have been drawn has been made up of hearing children of deaf parents. Do the advantages of early acquisition of sign language balance any disadvantages they may have as a result of early experiences? How can this balance be tipped in favor of improved interpreting?
- What factors determine the preference for consecutive interpretation as opposed to transliteration? Does the answer vary with the participants, the interpreted material (poetry or science), and setting?
- How can linguistic analyses contribute to educating interpreters? Proponents of some theories might be inclined to overlook such studies, while linguists might insist they are critical. Can research resolve this issue?

We expect change in the average characteristics of interpreters, though in what direction and to what extent should intrigue researchers. Rudser (1986), for example, asked two interpreters to sign the same material they signed twelve years earlier. Contrasting videotapes of the signs they made before with those made recently, he found their current signing had more ASL features. Admittedly, his sample was minute, but this finding deserves follow-up.

Public attitudes toward interpreting will continue to affect the amount of research conducted, as scientific efforts tend to follow funding. Most research cannot be conducted without some financial backing, and government and foundation grants are ultimately affected by how these agencies judge the importance of the proposed studies. Similarly, many university-based researchers do research that enhances their prospects for promotion, as well as contributing to scientific knowledge. They tend to investigate matters that attract popular interest. In short, interpreting research is likely to be stimulated in proportion to the status interpreting holds in the community.

We expect the interpreting profession to improve continually over time, but the profession itself faces a barrier to making these changes. Very few interpreters become actively engaged in directing research on interpreting, largely as a result of the small size of the profession and the emphasis on development of skills. Additionally, an involvement in research is not as well grounded as it is in professions that have a historical precedent for their members to pursue graduate studies and, for some, to develop research skills. The inside knowledge that interpreters possess is invaluable and needs to be tapped. Although there are a few researchers already doing this, more are needed.

TRENDS IN EDUCATIONAL INTERPRETING

In the coming years, more and more educational administrators will realize the significance of employing interpreters and the importance of incorporating knowledge about using interpreters in the curriculum for deaf children. We expect school districts to demonstrate their commitment to improved interpreting services by developing guidelines for interpreters. The success of any guidelines rests on the manner of their derivation, with the best prospects for success arising from consensus among all major stakeholders. In addition to educators, those deciding the issues should include deaf students, their parents, interpreters, and the general public.

The research suggested here and in Chapter 10 will certainly influence the course of educational interpreting. But many critical issues are not researchable; they are policies, choices among options. Among factors potentially influencing school administrations will be the opinions of the Deaf community, the development of machine translators, cost-effectiveness, and the evolution of sign languages.

INTERPRETER DEMOGRAPHICS

What will the average interpreter be like in the year 2020? If changes in working conditions occur as hoped, the typical interpreter will be older, because interpreting will become more attractive as a career, and those who enter the profession will be more inclined to stay in it. The gender discrepancy (now about 4 females to 1 male) will become smaller, although the positive female bias will probably remain—a prediction based on female superiority in language-dependent activities.

We must be cautious, however, because detecting these trends depends on establishing some baselines. For the United States, benchmark demographic studies of interpreters have not been reported. Such research needs to be done in order for the profession to track its own development.

PARTICIPANT CHARACTERISTICS

In time, the attitudes of participants can be expected to change. Deaf participants will be more sophisticated about interpreting, particularly if the schools they come from include interpreting as a subject in their curricula. We have argued that it is important for deaf students to study how to be effective participants in interpreted settings. Educators should not take for granted that, somehow, deaf participants will know their rights, will recognize conditions that impede interpreting, and will firmly but politely intervene to correct such conditions when they arise. These are matters that should be taught rather than left to chance that they will be learned later.

Another change will come from deaf participants, who will move from seeing interpreting as a sometime kindness and relatively low-level service to a right and a complex, professional service. Far from a dependent attitude, deaf people over the next few decades are more apt to regard interpreters in the way that interpreters prefer to be regarded—as professionals delivering a valuable service, impartially and competently.

Recently, concern has been expressed about the possibility of cochlear implants diminishing the requirements for sign language interpreting. We do not foresee this happening for two main reasons. First, late-deafened adults are prime candidates for cochlear implants. These people have always used speech for communication and will continue to do so, with or without an implant, because they are accustomed to using speech and because learning to sign later in life is difficult for adults in general. The second reason stems from the observation that a cochlear implant does not restore hearing to a normal level. Implanted children wear assistive hearing devices, and some of them do not perceive any benefits from the implant while others are able to function as severely hard-of-hearing persons. In the latter case, they will more likely find understanding a sign language interpreter to be much easier than comprehending speech through audition and speechreading.

We expect that many nondeaf participants in professional fields will be encountered who have had experience with interpreted communication. After a session or two, teachers will become accustomed to having their classes interpreted; judges will become familiar with interpreters in their courtrooms; physicians will become cooperative with interpreters in their quarters; and so on. Interpreters can make repeated visits even smoother by explaining to nondeaf participants, at some point, how they can contribute to better communication.

The general public has increasing opportunities to observe interpreting on television, as well as to meet an interpreter in other settings. These exposures help to reduce their anxiety when they are participants. However, they will participate even more effectively if they receive specific instructions in how to cooperate with interpreters.

ETHICS

When interpreters stray from the ethically correct path, they usually do so for one of two reasons: failure to know what is right or the pressure of circumstances. A more experienced profession, with a greater number of certified interpreters and with longer interpreter preparation, will strengthen the profession ethically. We foresee fewer interpreters susceptible to violations. In making this prediction, we rely on our observation that many ethical breaches arise from ignorance of the code, not from malice or greed.

Text translators lay bare their work for all to critique, not once but over and over again. Right or wrong, the printed version of their work testifies for all to see, including critics who were not present when the translator creates the translation. Unlike text translators, interpreters efforts usually lack documentation. That untrustworthy companion of the human psyche, *memory*, forms the basis for marking their score sheets. If they are judged improperly by a participant, they usually have no direct recourse to other experts. Videotaping provides a tangible alternative to the mental recall of a performance. Some courts have insisted on having such a record of what was signed, along with the court reporter's transcript of what was said.

Ethics can be expected to evolve as the profession grows, consumers become more sophisticated, and circumstances change. Interpreters must realize that what they do today may become outmoded and even unethical in a decade or two because many questions about interpreting have not been answered and some not even addressed fully. In the meantime, interpreters need to embrace an aura of professional evaluation in all they do, in order to maintain a high level of professional integrity. To this end, an ongoing dialogue about ethics—as with many other issues in the profession—that includes all of the stakeholders will promote the swift, sure growth of sign language interpreting to its ultimate level of professional competence and to the fullest benefit of deaf and nondeaf participants.

THE COMING CONSENSUS

Throughout this book, we have urged stakeholders to come together and achieve consensus on the major aspects of interpreting in sign. It is with delight, therefore, that we conclude by noting that a giant step has been taken toward that goal. The National Association of the Deaf and RID have established a joint task force to provide a forum for discussing interpreting issues and a vehicle for achieving their resolution and implementation. We unhesitatingly predict that this move will be of benefit to all concerned.

We fervently hope that this cooperative beginning portends additional efforts to bring together other major stakeholders. Perhaps the NAD–RID Task Force can meet next with representatives of relevant government agencies at the federal level: Department of Justice, Department of Health and Human Services, and Department of Education. Later meetings can be with commissions on deafness in those states that have established them and with ad hoc groups in those states that do not yet have such organizations, in order to extend the deliberations and action plans to the state and local levels.

These expanded meetings should welcome input from nongovernmental agencies that are concerned with services to people who are deaf. From time to time, the deliberations might also include representatives of other professional organizations, like teaching, legal, and medical associations, so that they can be alerted to the problems and can have their points of view considered.

Is such a grand consensus only a fantasy? We think not. Rather, for the continued growth and future success of interpreting and for the welfare of deaf people and all of those who work with them, we believe that obtaining such joint understandings and actions from a broad sampling of stakeholders is *essential*.

A

INTERPRETER AND TRANSLITERATOR CERTIFICATIONS

The following list of certifications is provided by the Registry of Interpreters for the Deaf. The information provided is taken verbatim with some minor changes with respect to dates from an RID information package. Further information and current listings of certifications can be obtained from:

> The Registry of Interpreters for the Deaf, Inc.
> 8630 Fenton Street, Suite 324
> Silver Spring, MD 20910
> (301) 608-0050 (v/tty)
> (301) 608-0508 (fax)

1. CI (Certificate of Interpretation)

Holders of this certificate are recognized as fully certified in Interpretation and have demonstrated the ability to interpret between American Sign Language (ASL) and spoken English in both sign-to-voice and voice-to-sign. The interpreter's ability to transliterate is not considered in this certification. Holders of the CI are recommended for a broad range of interpretation assignments.

2. CT (Certificate of Transliteration)

Holders of this certificate are recognized as fully certified in Transliteration and have demonstrated the ability to transliterate between English-based sign language and spoken English in both sign-to-voice and voice-to sign. The transliterator's ability to interpret is not considered in this certification.

Holders of the CT are recommended for a broad range of transliteration assignments.

3. CI and CT (Certificate of Interpretation and Certificate of Transliteration)

Holders of both full certificates (as listed above) have demonstrated competence in both interpretation and transliteration and have the same flexibility of job acceptance as holders of the CSC listed on the following page. Holders of the CI and CT are recommended for a broad range of interpretation and transliteration assignments.

4. CLIP (Conditional Legal Interpreting Permit)

Holders of this conditional permit have completed an RID recognized training program designed for interpreters and transliterators who work in legal settings. Generalist certification (CI and CT, or CSC) is required prior to enrollment in the training program. This permit is valid for a limited period of time. CLIP holders must take and pass the new legal certification examination in order to maintain certification in the specialty area of interpreting in legal settings. Holders of this conditional permit are recommended for a broad range of assignments in the legal setting.

5. Prov. SC:L (Provisional Specialist Certificate: Legal)

Holders of this provisional certificate hold generalist certification and have completed RID approved training required prior to sitting for the SC:L exam. This provisional certification is valid for a limited period of time. Prov. SC:L holders must take and pass the new SC:L exam in order to obtain certification in the specialty area of interpreting in legal settings. Holders of this certificate are recommended for assignments in the legal setting.

6. SC:PA (Specialist Certificate: Performing Arts)

Holders of this certificate were required to hold RID generalist certification (CSC) prior to sitting for this examination and have demonstrated specialized knowledge in performing arts interpretation. Holders of this certificate are recommended for a broad range of assignments in the performing arts. The SC:PA is no longer offered.

7. OIC (Oral Interpreting Certificate)

Holders of this generalist certificate demonstrated ability to transliterate a spoken message from a person who hears to a person who is deaf or hard-of-hearing and the ability to understand and repeat the message and intent of the speech and mouth movements of the person who is deaf or hard-of-hearing.

8. OIC:C (Oral Interpreting Certificate: Comprehensive)

Holders of this generalist certificate demonstrated the ability to transliterate a spoken message from a person who hears to a person who is deaf or hard-of-hearing and the ability to understand and repeat the message and intent of the speech and mouth movements of the person who is deaf or hard-of-hearing. This certification is no longer offered. Individuals wishing oral certification will take OIC exam noted in item 7.

9. OIC:S/V (Oral Interpreting Certificate: Spoken to Visible)

Holders of this partial certificate demonstrated the ability to transliterate a spoken message from a person who hears to a person who is deaf or hard-of-hearing. This individual received scores on the OIC:C examination which prevented the awarding of full OIC:C certification. The OIC:S/V is no longer offered.

10. OIC:V/S (Oral Interpreting Certificate: Visible to Spoken)

Holders of this partial certificate demonstrated ability to understand the speech and silent mouth movements of a person who is deaf or hard-of-hearing and to repeat the message for a hearing person. This individual received scores on the OIC:C examination which prevented the awarding of full OIC:C certification. The OIC:V/S is no longer offered.

11. IC/TC (Interpretation/Transliteration Certificate)

Holders of this partial certificate demonstrated ability to transliterate between English and a signed code for English and the ability to interpret between American Sign Language and spoken English. This individual received scores on the CSC examination which prevented the awarding of full CSC certification. The IC/TC is no longer offered.

12. IC (Interpretation Certificate)

Holders of this partial certificate demonstrated ability to interpret between American Sign Language and spoken English. This individual received scores on the CSC examination which prevented the awarding of full CSC certification or partial IC/TC certification. The IC is no longer offered.

13. TC (Transliteration Certificate)

Holders of this partial certificate demonstrated the ability to transliterate between spoken English and a signed code for English. This individual received scores on the CSC examination which prevented the awarding of full CSC certification or IC/TC certification. The TC is no longer offered.

14. CLIP-R (Conditional Legal Interpreting Permit—Relay)

Holders of this conditional permit have completed an RID recognized training program designed for interpreters and transliterators who work in legal settings and who are also deaf or hard-of-hearing. Generalist certification for interpreters/transliterators who are deaf or hard-of-hearing (RSC or CDI-P) is required prior to enrollment in the training program. This permit is valid for a limited period of time. CLIP-R holders must take and pass the new legal certification examination in order to maintain certification in the specialized area of interpreting in legal settings. Holders of this conditional permit are recommended for a broad range of assignments in the legal setting.

15. CDI-P (Certified Deaf Interpreter—Provisional)

Holders of this provisional certification are interpreters who are deaf or hard-of-hearing and who have demonstrated a minimum of one year experience working as an interpreter, completion of at least 8 hours of training on the RID Code of Ethics, and 8 hours of training in general interpretation as it relates to the interpreter who is deaf or hard-of-hearing. Provisional certification is valid for a limited period of time after the Certified Deaf Interpreter (CDI) examination is made available. Provisional certificate holders must take and pass the CDI examination in order to remain certified as a Deaf Interpreter. Holders of this provisional certificate are recommended for a broad range of assignments where an interpreter who is deaf or hard-of-hearing would be beneficial.

16. CDI (Certified Deaf Interpreter)

Holders of this certification are interpreters who are deaf or hard-of-hearing and who have demonstrated a minimum of one year experience as an interpreter, completion of at least 8 hours of training on the RID Code of Ethics, and 8 hours of training in general interpretation as it relates to the interpreter who is deaf or hard-of-hearing. Holders of this certificate are recommended for a broad range of assignments where an interpreter who is deaf or hard-of-hearing would be beneficial.

17. CSC (Comprehensive Skills Certificate)

Holders of this full certificate have demonstrated the ability to interpret between American Sign Language and spoken English and to transliterate between spoken English and a English-based sign language. The CSC examination was offered until 1987. Holders of this certificate are recommended for a broad range of interpreting and transliterating assignments.

18. MCSC (Master Comprehensive Skills Certificate)

The MCSC examination was designed with the intent of testing for a higher standard of performance than the CSC. Holders of this certificate were required to hold the CSC prior to taking this exam. Holders of this certificate are recommended for a broad range of interpreting and transliterating assignments.

19. RSC (Reverse Skills Certificate)

Holders of this full certificate demonstrated the ability to interpret between American Sign Language and English-based sign language or transliterate between spoken English and a signed code for English. Holders of this certificate are deaf or hard-of-hearing and interpretation/transliteration is rendered in American Sign Language, spoken English, a signed code for English or written English. Holders of the RSC are recommended for a broad range of interpreting assignments where the use of an interpreter who is deaf or hard-of-hearing would be beneficial.

20. SC:L (Specialist Certificate: Legal)

Holders of this specialist certificate have demonstrated specialized knowledge of legal settings and greater familiarity with language used in the legal system. Generalist certification and documented training and experience is required prior to sitting for this exam. Holders of the SC:L are recommended for a broad range of assignments in the legal setting.

B

ETHICALLY CHALLENGING SCENARIOS

Interpreters do not think of themselves as unscrupulous, but they may in fact be functioning in an unethical manner for a variety of reasons, such as lack of awareness and lack of preparation. Complicating the matter, the interpreter often is the only person in the room who can communicate with a deaf person. Because of this, someone's needs for communication assistance can, at times, overrun an interpreter's desire to comply with the Registry of Interpreter's for the Deaf Code of Ethics. The Code of Ethics provides guidance for an interpreter who feels there is a conflict in an assignment or is uncomfortable about a situation. Still, confusion does arise as to which kinds of behavior is ethically correct and which ones are not. Following are 40 scenarios that may challenge an interpreter's adherence to the Code of Ethics. The scenarios are designed to facilitate discussion of how an interpreter should act and to encourage investigation of the type of psychological and social forces that influence an interpreter's decision.

1. During an interpreting assignment you see some people behind the deaf participant making fun of him. You notice that they have set up a trap for the deaf person to try to startle him; however, there is really no chance of anyone getting physically hurt.
2. You are the secretary/interpreter for a large agency. There are several deaf staff persons, including your immediate supervisor. You are aware that he is currently applying for a job elsewhere. You have interpreted a few of his phone calls. The director of the agency, your supervisor's boss, approaches you to verify that, in fact, the supervisor is applying elsewhere.

3. You are hired to interpret for a deaf person in traffic court. After completing his remarks, the judge dismisses the charges and instructs you to take the deaf person outside the court and tell him to drive more carefully in the future.

4. You are approached outside your home by a deaf man who wants you to interpret a surprise shower for his daughter and prospective son-in-law. However, because you are the daughter's best friend, you know that they are busy with other plans on the evening he has requested. He also asks you if you would contribute your time interpreting in place of a gift for his daughter.

5. You are called to interpret in court for a deaf person who has witnessed a murder. She has minimum language competency. Although you have never interpreted in a court before, you feel that you should interpret for her because you know her well and can understand her signing.

6. You are a freelance interpreter interpreting in a Vocational Rehabilitation (VR) office. After the deaf person leaves, the VR counselor asks you, "Do you think [the deaf person] can do the work she wants?"

7. A few interpreters seem to go to every workshop and spend a great deal of time ruining the workshop for others by complaining and gossiping to you about the inadequacy of the interpreters at each workshop.

8. One day, you are approached by a representative of a local charismatic healer. He offers you a substantial sum to interpret a healing ceremony. You personally view faith healers as frauds; you once lost a close friend to cancer because he trusted one rather than seeking conventional medical care.

9. You are a student interpreter and you have learned that a deaf man who works on the Ford assembly line and has a family of nine to support is in need of an interpreter for a visit to his doctor's office. The man is concerned because he knows the doctor will not provide an interpreter, and he has had trouble in the past communicating with him. The man cannot afford to pay for an interpreter but asks if he can negotiate with you.

10. A nondeaf professor lecturing to a class of 150, including about a dozen deaf students, uses a phrase that can be construed in a sexually suggestive manner because of the sound of the words. The nondeaf students all laugh, but not the deaf students. After the laughter dies down, the professor continues his lecture without further comment, but the deaf students are still curious.

11. You are asked to interpret for a deaf couple who are shopping for a new car. You agree and meet them at a dealership. After looking around they decide to go to another dealership. This dealership is the one from which you bought your car, which now spends considerable time in the shop being repaired. The couple decides to purchase a car they like. The

salesman assures the couple that it is very rare that cars sold in this lot have maintenance problems because all cars are inspected by two mechanics. When he steps out of the office, the couple asks for your opinion.

12. You interpret for a deaf woman who was a witness to a robbery and must appear in court to testify. On your way to your car, following your assignment, a news reporter recognizes you and wants a "human interest" story to educate the public more about deaf people. The reporter asks you what the deaf person signed to you in court. When you hesitate, he assures you that anything communicated in a court-room is "public domain."

13. You have always interpreted for a deaf couple at no charge because they are friends of yours. They also don't have the finances to pay for an interpreter. Your colleagues feel differently. They think that if other people in the Deaf community find out, then they also will want the services of an interpreter at no charge.

14. You are interpreting for a psychotherapist and you have had an extremely rough day. He is unfamiliar with the Code of Ethics, and with interpreting in general and bawled you out for interpreting his disparaging remarks about his client during a therapy session. Another deaf person refused to let you interpret for him and belittled your signing abilities. Your frustration level has peaked and when you return home your husband, also an interpreter, asks you if you would like talk about your day's experience.

15. You are an interpreter in an elementary school. You have worked with a student for several months. As the school days pass, you begin to notice that the child you interpret for is becoming more withdrawn than usual and cries very easily. One day you notice several bruises on the child's cheek and leg.

16. You are looking forward to relaxing 'on a long plane trip. You have worked for a long time without a break and feel a strong need to get away from working as an interpreter for awhile. As the final passengers board the plane, you notice a woman signing to the stewardess. It's obvious she's upset, and the stewardess is pushing her along so that the remaining passengers can board. No one has asked you for help because no one knows that you understand sign language. You are debating whether or not you should offer to help.

17. You interpret for a woman in a doctor's office who is told that she needs major surgery. You learn that she doesn't want her husband to know about the surgery. At night, her husband calls you and demands to know why his wife is so upset.

18. A deaf person contacts you to interpret for him in court regarding a car accident. He tells you about the accident and says that he was not at fault. Prior to this call, another passenger who was in the deaf person's car at

the time of the accident has told you an entirely different account of the accident.

19. You interpret in a class where a deaf student is habitually late and tends to fall asleep. One day when the student is nodding off, the instructor says to the class that he isn't impressed with deaf students if this one deaf student is any example.

20. You are sent out on an assignment to interpret at an Alcoholics Anonymous (AA) meeting by a local agency. A week later, one of your fellow staff interpreters at the agency is curious about the assignment. He asks you how AA meetings are run, what the other people at AA are like, and what types of things are said at meetings. He remarks, "Oh, I know you can't tell me about the deaf person. I'm just curious about what it's like, you know, in general."

21. An interpreter is called to interpret for three deaf adults for a training program. Two of the participants arrive on time. One of the deaf participants calls to say that he is having car problems and will be late because he must take the bus. Thirty minutes later, the third deaf participant arrives. While interpreting, the instructor asks the interpreter to "go and greet the deaf person and bring him to this room while I retrieve a third training manual for him."

22. An interpreter finished an assignment interpreting at a co-worker's wedding. After the assignment, she sent the appropriate bill to the co-worker, but heard nothing and was not paid. After several months, the co-worker finally told the interpreter she thought the interpreting had been done for free because they were friends.

23. You have been asked to find a second interpreter for an assignment you have accepted. You call an interpreter whom you have not seen for a long time, and she accepts the assignment. When she arrives, just 15 minutes before you are to begin, you are shocked to see that she has dyed her hair green and acquired a nose ring. She has maintained her RID membership and feels qualified for the job, though she tells you she has not interpreted for two years.

24. You go to a meeting as an observer where you meet many deaf people with whom you are on good terms. During the meeting, several deaf people approach you and ask if you would take over the interpreting, as they are having a hard time understanding the interpreter.

25. You are a practicum student working alongside an educational interpreter in a high school biology class. The interpreter asks you if you would like to interpret, and you accept. As the class begins, the interpreter signs, "I'll be right back," and leaves you interpreting the class.

26. You are interpreting for a girl at a doctor's office, when the doctor tells her that she has AIDS. She becomes very upset and says that she got it

from some man and now they will "all" pay. Afterwards, you see her at a function socializing with some friends of yours. One of your male friends comes up to you and says he would like to date her and asks you what she is like.

27. You interpret all of the classes for a deaf student in junior high school including his homeroom period. During homeroom class, the deaf student buys some M&Ms from another boy for $2.00. You interpret the cost and what organization the money is going to. You think that is an unrealistic price, but you say nothing. During the boy's lunch period, the principal calls you to the office along with the homeroom teacher. They start asking you questions about the M&Ms. They tell you that they think the students are selling marijuana in the form of a joint in the box of M&Ms. They ask you what you think about the price.

28. During an interpreter workshop, a discussion arises in which different interpreters share unique interpreting experiences and situations. Someone who is sharing is interrupted by another interpreter who says, "Hey! The same thing happened to me, and with someone I think may be the same deaf person. Can you describe the deaf person to me, please?"

29. You are interpreting for a deaf student taking a test. During the test the teacher walks out, and one student starts calling the deaf student names and using vulgar language. The deaf student has not looked up at you and doesn't realize what is happening.

30. You are driving and witness an awful car accident. You stop and get out to help the people in the vehicles. The police and ambulance arrive. The ambulance takes the people in one car away. The police talk to you because you witnessed the accident. You tell them exactly what you saw. The police now approach the deaf couple who were in the other car to hear their account of the accident. The deaf people ask you to interpret for them.

31. You are asked to interpret a church service for a deaf woman who uses signs from a manually coded English system. You explain that your signs are primarily ASL but the deaf woman says that she understands both systems. Five minutes after the service begins, another deaf woman slips into the pew. She watches you sign with a puzzled expression on her face. She begins to sign to the first woman that she can't understand you. Each time she looks at you she gives you a puzzled look.

32. A friend whose deaf child will begin school soon has asked you to interpret his child's classes. He feels his son will be more comfortable and learn better with a familiar person around. Although you already work in the school district where the deaf boy attends school, you are not responsible for the assignment of interpreters.

33. You are interpreting in a poetry class. In order not to offend or embarrass anyone, you substitute signs that are still conceptually correct but are not as explicit in their meaning as the words in a poem suggest. You do this

to deter the other students from making fun of some of the more graphic signs. The rhyme and the content remain intact.

34. You have been interpreting a long-term counseling assignment but must cancel one week. You have found another interpreter, but, because of the sensitive nature of the treatment and slow progress due to communication misunderstandings, it is important that he be aware of the situation. You explain the details of the deaf woman's background, what has transpired in the sessions so far, and the treatment plan the doctor has been encouraging.

35. You are asked to interpret with another interpreter at a nursing home for a lecture series on senior nutrition. All of the staff involved have been asked to come dressed as something representing one of the major food groups. You and your partner have been asked to dress as an apple and a banana.

36. You are a female interpreter in a high school. One of the deaf students is a handsome young man. He is a senior who has just transferred to the school this year. He is involved in some extracurricular activities for which you interpret. Late one Friday afternoon, he makes a romantic advance toward you. You explain that this wouldn't be proper, but he is persistent.

37. You interpret at a church on a regular basis. It is the church's procedure to have people from the congregation read the scripture lessons on an assigned basis. A few of the readers become very nervous when reading in public. When it is their turn, they do not speak directly into the microphone, they read quickly, and their speech is a mumbled monotone.

38. You and another interpreter are doing an assignment together. The information that is being presented is very important and you notice that the other interpreter is missing a lot of the information that is being presented, which the deaf participant needs to know.

39. During a course, a professor gives precise instructions for an assignment. The deaf student receives an "F," which leads to her failing the course. She makes an appointment with the professor and asks you to interpret at the meeting. During the meeting, she tells the professor that she did not get a good grade because you did not accurately relay all of the instructions for doing the assignment.

40. You are interpreting at the home of a deaf person for a meeting with his counselor. The meeting is interrupted by a phone call, which the deaf person answers on the TTY. Noticing it is a voice call, you are asked to interpret it and find out it is for the counselor, who takes the call and is on the phone for nearly five minutes. During this time you interpret the only side of the conversation that can be heard. After the call, the counselor apologizes to the deaf person for the interruption and then, turning to you smiles, lowers his voice, and says, "For future reference, my calls are no one's business but my own!"

C

ENCOUNTERS WITH REALITY: A COLLECTION OF SIGN LANGUAGE INTERPRETER STORIES

Sign language interpreters face many unpredictable situations during the course of their careers. These situations shed light on the nature of the human psyche and the foibles of communication. Talking about them help interpreters to prepare themselves mentally for the unexpected. But unusual incidents, pleasant or otherwise, have a nasty habit of sometimes detracting from the immediate task of interpreting communications. While we can't offer a magic potion for making interpreters superhuman, we do have some thought-provoking stories told to us by interpreters. They remind us that problems do arise in the course of day-to-day interpreting, and even with the best of preparation they cannot always be avoided. Not all of the stories show appropriate ethical behavior—but then, how would you react if you were in the same situation? And that's the point of the stories—they offer an opportunity for reflection and discussion on the part of interpreters and other participants. We have listed them here by the setting in which they occurred.

EDUCATION

1. An interpreter was interpreting a remedial math class. One day two girls drew knives and began fighting while the teacher was not in the room. The interpreter physically separated the two girls and sent for help.
2. An interpreter was interpreting at a school event for several deaf students who were making a presentation. The students' classroom teacher con-

tinually interfered when the interpreter used a sign with which she did not agree. Eventually she started interpreting alongside the interpreter.

3. An interpreter was interpreting a high school history class for a student who seldom paid attention to her. When asked a question to which he did not know the answer, the student responded, "My interpreter isn't signing the information to me that I need to answer your question."

4. An interpreter realized that a deaf student in an automotive class was lighting his torch using the wrong tank and an excessively hot torch. The interpreter took the torch away, which embarrassed the student. The instructor explained that if he had lit the torch, the whole building would have exploded.

5. Near the last day of school, the students had a party for their parents. A student brought in her parents and proudly introduced them to the interpreter. The parents asked the interpreter, "When will she [their daughter] stop acting like she is deaf and talk like a normal person?"

6. A substitute interpreter was told to leave by the teacher after the first few minutes of class because that was what the regular interpreter did. The interpreter said that she would interpret for the child the whole day, which seemed to make the teacher uncomfortable.

LEGAL

1. An interpreter, interpreting for a man accused of murdering his father, was asked by the judge if she thought the deaf man understood the questions. She interpreted the judge's questions but did not respond. The judge was persistent, and she finally said in signs and speech, "Yes, I think so."

2. In court, a deaf woman nodded her head while the interpreter voiced "no." The judge stopped the interpreter and asked if she was qualified to handle this case. The interpreter explained that the deaf woman's answer was "no" but that she was nodding to indicate that she understood the question.

3. An interpreter arrived at a police station and was told to leave because the deaf man was able to read lips. The interpreter silently spoke to the police officer, whose face went blank. The interpreter then said aloud, "I asked you for 15 cents." She was allowed to continue interpreting.

PERFORMING ARTS/PLATFORM

1. An interpreter had rehearsed with a comedian and knew all of his jokes, but once on stage the comedian got stage-fright and was not funny. The interpreter changed the timing of her interpretations so that the jokes were not funny for the deaf audience as well.

2. An interpreter was interpreting at a political rally for the President of the United States. She was searched by the Secret Service and warned not to move from the spot where she was interpreting. It was cold and windy, and she was very uncomfortable. But she valued her life and remained firmly in place.

RELIGIOUS

1. An interpreter was not told that her assignment was for a predominantly Spanish-speaking congregation. When mass began, she signed that she didn't understand Spanish. A deaf woman then sent her daughter to translate the sermon to English and whisper everything to the interpreter.
2. A minister was delivering a sermon with the "fire of God." The interpreter unexpectedly started choking back a nervous laughter. After the service, members of the congregation hugged and thanked him for his emotional involvement in the sermon. Fortunately, they thought he had been crying.
3. A woman was playing a flute solo at church, and the interpreter decided to sign the words of the song. After the service, a deaf girl asked the flutist, "Does that play words?" The girl had thought that, because the interpreter had signed, the flute must be saying words.
4. A certified interpreter was interpreting at a state conference attended by the governor and 1,000 people. While interpreting the invocation, she blanked on the sign for God. She had to keep fingerspelling G-O-D. For that short period of time, she simply couldn't remember the sign.

MINIMAL LANGUAGE COMPETENCY

1. A deaf man was undergoing a psychiatric review in court for an armed robbery. The deaf man answered "yes" to every question the psychiatrist asked. Finally, the psychiatrist asked, "Can you read lips?" The man once again answered, "Yes." The interpreter was dismissed, and the deaf man was subsequently institutionalized.
2. A deaf man in a group home was getting bawled out. He became upset and tried to attack the interpreter physically. The interpreter stepped out of role and explained, "It's not me talking, it's her." The deaf man finally calmed down, but still obviously believed the interpreter was bawling him out.

MENTAL HEALTH

1. A female interpreter was interpreting for a deaf person in a sexuality class for men at an addictions treatment program. During one group session, she overheard a man whisper, "Watch how she interprets this!" The deaf person was very embarrassed, and couldn't bear to watch half of the time.
2. An interpreter was interpreting a therapy session where a deaf girl, who had been raped, explained to her parents what had happened to her. Her parents had not previously understood the extent of the violation, and they began to cry.
3. A deaf family was in a counseling session with their rebellious hearing child. The child criticized the skills of the interpreter, corrected her signing, and insisted that she was misrepresenting his parents' signs.
4. A substitute interpreter told the regular interpreter about a deaf person being HIV-infected. The deaf person met a friend who now knew about his condition. He became furious and confronted the director of the interpreter referral agency, who questioned both the substitute and the regular interpreter about leaking sensitive information.

MEDICAL

1. A doctor was using electrocautery to remove a cyst from a deaf woman. The doctor, thinking that he was being funny, told the woman that she was burning. The woman said nothing but had a worried look. So the interpreter voiced, "That scares me," and so the doctor explained what he meant.
2. A deaf woman was calling a doctor obscene names, saying that he didn't know what he was talking about, and using foul language. The interpreter voiced everything she said, and later the doctor told the interpreter that he was appalled that she would talk to him like that in front of the patient.
3. Unable to communicate with a doctor whom they had encountered while out of state, a deaf couple gave the doctor a business card from an interpreter in their hometown. He needed the pregnant woman's medical history, so he called the interpreter, who gave the doctor the name of the hospital where she interpreted for the woman.
4. An interpreter was interpreting in the delivery room for a woman's deaf husband. In the middle of the delivery, claiming that the interpreter was in the way, the doctor ordered the interpreter to leave and decided the nondeaf mother-to-be could interpret for her husband instead.

5. A deaf man's lover had been hospitalized for what they thought was cancer. They had never used an interpreter during their visits to the doctor relying instead on written notes. When they finally did use an interpreter, they realized that "acquired immune deficiency syndrome" meant AIDS and not cancer as they thought.
6. A young deaf child had traumatic head injury. The doctor was asking questions like "Who is the president of the United States?" to which the child could not respond. The interpreter suggested to the doctor that the child might know where the local deaf club was, and this proved to be correct.

FREELANCE

1. In prison, a fast-talking officer was angry while talking to a deaf prisoner. When he was finished, the prisoner stated that he didn't understand because the interpreter was having to sign so fast. The officer turned to the interpreter, declared her incompetent, and had the guard remove her.

REFERENCES AND BIBLIOGRAPHY

Alberta Education Response Centre. (1988). *The use of an interpreter in an educational setting: Guidelines and standards.* Edmonton, Alberta: Author.

Alberta Education Response Centre. (1991). *Education of deaf and hard of hearing students in Alberta: 1989–1990.* Edmonton, Alberta: Author.

Alexander, R. N. (1986). The law and reasonable accommodation of the handicapped in federal government: Focus on deafness. *Journal of Rehabilitation of the Deaf, 20*(2), 24–26.

Altshuler, K., & Abdullah, S. (1981). Mental health and the deaf adult. In L. K. Stein, E. D. Mindel, & T. Jabaley (Eds.), *Deafness and mental health.* New York: Grune & Stratton.

Anderson, D. E. (1996). *Interpreting standards in educational settings: Implementation review.* Edmonton, Alberta: Premier's Council on the Status of Persons with Disabilities.

Anderson, G. (1995–1996). Enhancing interpreting service delivery within the state/federal rehabilitation system. *JADARA, 29,* 25–30.

Anderson, G. B., & Rosten, E. (1985). Towards evaluating process variables in counseling deaf people: A cross-cultural perspective. In G. B. Anderson & D. Watson (Eds.), *Counseling deaf people: Research and practice.* Little Rock: University of Arkansas, Rehabilitation Research and Training Center on Deafness and Hearing Impairment.

Anderson, G. B., Rosten, E., & Stauffer, L. K. (1991). Identifying standards for the training of interpreters for deaf people. *Journal of the American Deafness and Rehabilitation Association, 25*(3), 35–46.

Anderson, G. B., & Thornton, M. (1993). Unresolved issues in the provision of mental health services to people who are deaf. In O. Welsh (Ed.), *Research and practice in deafness.* Springfield, IL: Charles C Thomas.

Anthony, P. (1982). The Rowley case. *Journal of Educational Finance, 8*(1), 106–115.

Association of Visual Language Interpreters of the Deaf (AVLIC). (1992, June). *Interpreters in the educational setting: A resource document.* Calgary, Alberta: Author.

Bailey, J. L., & Straub, S. A. (1992, June–July). Interpreting services. *Asha, 34*, 51–53.

Baker, A. (1995). Conflicts between the ethical confidentiality requirement and legal obligations to disclose. *Proceedings of the Thirteenth National Convention of the Registry of Interpreters for the Deaf*, 21–39.

Baker, C., & Cokely, D. (1980). ASL: A teacher's resource text on grammar and culture. Silver Spring, MD: National Association of the Deaf.

Baker-Shenk, C. (Ed.). (1990). *A model curriculum for teachers of American Sign Language and teachers of ASL/English interpreting*. Silver Spring, MD: RID Publications.

Bartlett, S. J. (1991). Postcompulsory education and training for hearing impaired students in New Zealand. In E. G. Wolf-Schein & J. D. Schein (Eds.), *Postsecondary education for deaf students* (pp. 66–71). Edmonton: University of Alberta.

Battison, R. (1978). *Lexical Borrowing in American Sign Language*. Silver Spring, MD: Linstok Press.

Bayley, J. (1993, November). One life, one writing. *The New York Review of Books, 4*, 31–32.

Bellugi, U., & Klima, E. (1980). *The signs of language*. Cambridge, MA: Harvard University Press.

Bess, L. P. (1977). Who is a signer? Who is an interpreter? *Reporting for Deaf Virginians* (quarterly newsletter of the Virginia Council for the Deaf), 4(3).

Bess, L. P. (1978). Guidelines for interpreters; If you need an interpreter and are deaf; If you need an interpreter and are a service provider. *Reporting for Deaf Virginians* (quarterly newsletter of the Virginia Council for the Deaf), 5(4).

Bornstein, H., Saulnier, K., & Hamilton, L. (1983). *The comprehensive Signed English dictionary*. Washington, DC: Gallaudet University.

Bornstein, H., Woodward, J., & Tully, N. (1976). Language and communication. In B. Bolton (Ed.), *Psychology of deafness for rehabilitation counselors*. Baltimore, MD: University Park Press.

Boros, A. (1983). Alcoholism and deaf people. *Gallaudet Today, 13*, 9–11.

Bowen-Bailey, D. (1996, March). The challenges of educational interpreting. *Views, 13*(3), 16–17.

Boyd, S. J. (1988). Full integration—full support: An interim report. *The ACEHI Journal, 14*, 33–40.

Bragg, B. (1990). Communication and the Deaf community: Where do we go from here? In M. Garretson (Ed.), *Communication issues among Deaf people: A Deaf American monograph* (pp. 9–14). Silver Spring, MD: National Association of the Deaf.

Brain, J. (1990). Potential impact of World Games for the Deaf on the deaf community in New Zealand. *Palaestra, 6*(2), 44, 46–47.

Brauer, B. (1990). Caught in the middle: Does interpreting work in a mental health setting? *Gallaudet Today, 20*(3), 46–49.

Brewer, K. (1995, December). Convention interpreting. *Views, 12*(11), 1, 26.

Brill, R. G. (1978). *Mainstreaming the prelingually deaf child.* Washington, DC: Gallaudet College Press.

Brown, P. M., & Foster, S. B. (1991). Integrating hearing and deaf students on a college campus. *American Annals of the Deaf, 136*, 21–27.

Brown, P., & Fraser, C. (1979). Speech as a marker of situation. In K. R. Scherer & H. Giles (Eds.), *Social markers in speech.* London: Cambridge University Press.

Bruce, R. V. (1973). *Bell: Alexander Graham Bell and the conquest of silence.* Boston: Little, Brown.

Caccamise, F., & Blasdell, R. (1977, November). Interpreted and simultaneous reception of sentences by hearing impaired persons. *The Deaf American,* 5–7.

Caccamise, F., Dirst, R., DeVries, R., Heil, J., Kirchner, C., Kirchner, S., Rinaldi, A., & Stangarone, J. (Eds.). (1980). *Introduction to interpreting.* Silver Spring, MD: Registry of Interpreters of the Deaf.

Canary, D. J. (1993). At the crossroads: Some points where psychology, communication, and linguistics intersect. *Contemporary Psychology, 38,* 531–535.

Cannon, C. B. (1983). Using an interpreter in cross-cultural counseling. *School Counselor, 31,* 11–16.

Cerney, B. (1996, February). Interpreter working conditions: Sharing the vision. *Views, 13*(2), 1, 32.

Chatoff, M. (1976). Legal interpreting: Some issues. *Journal of Rehabilitation of the Deaf, 9*(3), 22–24.

Ching, J. G. (1985). Educational program offered to hearing-impaired students. In *The International Congress on the Education of the Deaf, 1985.* Manchester, England: University of Manchester.

Chukovsky, K. I. (1984). *The art of translation: Kornei Chukovsky's "A high art"* (L. G. Leighton, Trans.). Knoxville: University of Tennessee.

Cohen, H., & Jones, E. G. (1990). Interpreting for cross-cultural research: Changing written English to American Sign Language. *Journal of the American Deafness and Rehabilitation Association, 24*(2), 41–48.

Cohn, L., Lowry, R. M., & Hart, S. (1990). Overuse syndromes of the upper extremity in interpreters for the deaf. *Orthopedics, 3*(2), 207–209.

Cokely, D. (1981). Sign language interpreters: A demographic study. *Sign Language Studies, 32,* 261–286.

Cokely, D. (1983). When is a pidgin not a pidgin? An alternate analysis of the ASL–English contact situation. *Sign Language Studies, 38,* 1–24.

Cokely, D. (1986). The effects of lag time on interpreter errors. *Sign Language Studies, 53,* 341–376.

Cokely, D. (1990). The effectiveness of three means of communication in the college classroom. *Sign Language Studies, 69*, 415–442.

Cokely, D. (1992). *Interpretation: A sociolinguistic model.* Burtonsville, MD: Linstok.

Collett, L. T. (1985). Educating profoundly deaf children in ordinary schools. In *The International Congress on the Education of the Deaf, 1985.* Manchester, England: University of Manchester.

Colonomos, B. (1992). *Processes in interpreting and transliterating: Making them work for you.* (video). Available from Front Range Community College, 3645 West 112th Avenue, Westminister, CO 80030.

Commission on Education of the Deaf. (1988). *Toward equality: Education of the deaf.* Washington, DC: U.S. Government Printing Office.

Conway, L. C. (1990). Issues relating to classroom management. In M. Ross (Ed.), *Hearing-impaired children in the mainstream.* Parkton, MD: York.

Coppock, P. J. (1992). Interpreting discourse—signs for the future? In *Expanding horizons: Proceedings of the Twelfth National Convention of the Registry of Interpreters for the Deaf, August 6–11, 1991.* Silver Spring, MD: RID Publications.

Cornett, C. O. (1967). Cued Speech. *American Annals of the Deaf, 112,* 3–13.

Cornett, C. O. (1971). *Cued Speech: What and why?* Unpublished manuscript.

Council of State Administrators of Vocational Rehabilitation. (1971). *VR agency practices regarding payment for interpreter services in postsecondary education: Results of a questionnaire survey.* Washington, DC: Author.

Crammatte, A. B. (1987). *Meeting the challenge.* Washington, DC: Gallaudet University.

Cundy, L. H. (1988, December–January). Mother knows best. *The NAD Broadcaster,* 25.

Dahl, C., & Wilcox, S. (1990). Preparing the educational interpreter: A survey of sign language interpreter training programs. *American Annals of the Deaf, 135,* 275–279.

Davis, J. (1989). Distinguishing language contact phenomena in ASL interpretation. In C. Lucas (Ed.), *The sociolinguistics of the Deaf community* (pp. 85–102). New York: Academic Press.

Davis, J. (1990). Linguistic transference and interference: Interpreting between English and ASL. In C. Lucas (Ed.), *Sign language research: Theoretical issues* (pp. 308–321). Washington, DC: Gallaudet University.

"D.C. trial spotlights challenge." (1992, June 22). *Washington Post,* p. B1.

DeCaro, J. J., Feuerstein, M., & Hurwitz, T. A. (1992). Cumulative trauma disorders among educational interpreters. *American Annals of the Deaf, 137,* 288–292.

DeFrancis, J. (1989). *Visible speech: The diverse oneness of writing systems.* Honolulu: University of Hawaii Press.

Dickert, J. (1988). Examination of bias in mental health evaluation of deaf patients. *Social Work, 33*(3), 273–274.

DiPietro, L. J. (Ed.). (1978). *Guidelines on interpreting for deaf–blind persons.* Washington, DC: Gallaudet College Press.

Dorrance, P. K. (1986). Mainstreaming from a residential setting. *American Annals of the Deaf, 131,* 48–50.

Doull, E. (1979). A study of the need of interpreters for the deaf by hearing impaired persons. In M. Rodda & G. Buranyi (Ed.), *Proceeding of the Fourth Conference of the Association of Canadian Educators of the Hearing Impaired* (Vol. 2). Edmonton: University of Alberta.

Drasgow, E. (1993). Bilingual/bicultural deaf education: An overview. *Sign Language Studies, 80,* 243–266.

DuBow, S. (1979). Federal actions on interpreters and telecommunications. *American Annals of the Deaf, 124,* 93–96.

DuBow, S., & Geer, S. (1981, May). Eliminating communications barriers for hearing-impaired clients. *Clearinghouse Review,* 36–38.

DuBow, S., & Goldberg, L. (1981). Legal strategies to improve mental health care for deaf people. In L. K. Stein, E. D. Mindel, & T. Jabaley (Eds.), *Deafness and mental health* (pp. 195–210). New York: Grune & Stratton.

Ebbinghaus, H., & Hessmann, J. (1986). Sign language interpreting in a diglossic context (Berlin-Foschung). *Sign Language Studies, 53,* 377–380.

Editorial. (1978). How to communicate with hearing impaired patients. *Behavioral Medicine, 5*(9), 45–51.

ETS Committee for People with Disabilities. (1994). *Recommendations and guidelines for the use of interpreters in ETS test administrations with deaf and hard-of-hearing candidates.* Princeton, NJ: Educational Testing Services.

Elkins, E. F. (1995). Emergency services: A new era. *Proceedings of the Thirteenth National Convention of the Registry of Interpreters for the Deaf,* 40–47. Silver Spring, MD: RID Publications.

Elliott, H., & Lee, M. (1987). The process: An overview. In H. Elliott, L. Glass, & J. W. Evans (Eds.) *Mental health assessment of deaf clients* (pp. 23–34). Boston: Little, Brown.

Elliott, R. N., & Powers, A. R. (1995). Preparing interpreters to serve in educational settings. *The ACEHI Journal, 21,* 132–140.

Ellis, D. G. (1992). *From language to communication.* Hillsdale, NJ: Lawrence Erlbaum.

Erting, C. (1987). Cultural conflict in a school for deaf children. In P. C. Higgins & J. E. Nash (Eds.), *Understanding deafness socially* (pp. 123–150). Springfield, IL: Charles C Thomas.

Farrugia, D. (1989) Practical steps for access and delivery of mental health services to clients who are deaf. *Journal of Applied Rehabilitation Counseling, 20*(1), 33–35.

Feuerstein, M., & Fitzgerald, T. E. (1992, March). Biomechanical factors affecting upper extremity cumulative trauma disorders in sign language interpreters. *Journal of Occupational Medicine*, 1–8.

Fink, B. (1982). Being ignored can be bliss. *The Deaf American, 34*(6), 5–9.

Finnegan, M. H. (1986). *Interpreter effectiveness in sign-to-voice interpreting for deaf children*. Ph.D. dissertation, Temple University, Philadelphia.

Fischer, S., & Siple, P. (Eds.). (1990). *Theoretical issues in sign language research*. Chicago: University of Chicago.

Fischer, T. J. (1995). *Establishing a freelance interpretation business: Professional guidance for sign language interpreters*. Hillsboro, OR: Butte.

Fleetwood, E., & Metzger, M. (1990). *Cued Speech transliteration: Theory and application*. Silver Spring, MD: Calliope.

Foster, S. (1988). Life in the mainstream: Deaf college freshmen and their experiences in the mainstreamed high school. *Journal of the American Deafness and Rehabilitation Association, 22*(2), 27–35.

Foster, S., Barefoot, S. M., & DeCaro, P. M. (1989). The meaning of communication to a group of deaf college students: A multidimensional perspective. *Journal of Speech and Hearing Disorders, 54*, 558–569.

Foster, S., & DeCaro, P. M. (1990). Mainstreaming hearing-impaired students within a postsecondary educational setting: An ecological model of social integration. *Bridge, 9*(2), 3–4.

Franklin, E., & Varady, K. (1988). Computer software for scheduling interpreters. In K. B. Jursik (Ed.), *Third Regional Conference on Postsecondary Education for Hearing-Impaired Persons..* Knoxville: University of Tennessee.

Freeman, R. D., Carbin, C. F., & Boese, R. J. (1981). *Can't your child hear?* Baltimore, MD: University Park Press.

Freeman, S. T. (1989). Cultural and linguistic bias in mental health evaluations of deaf people. *Rehabilitation Psychology, 34*(1), 51–63.

Friedenreich, K. M. (1996, February). Report on the National Testing System. *Views, 13*(2), 24.

Friend, M., & Bursuck, W. (1996). *Including students with special needs: A practical guide for classroom teachers*. Boston: Allyn and Bacon.

Frishberg, N. (1975). Arbitrariness and iconicity: Historical change in American Sign Language. *Language, 51*, 696–719.

Frishberg, N. (1986). *Interpreting: An Introduction*. Silver Spring, MD: Registry of Interpreters for the Deaf.

Frishberg, N. (1990). *Interpreting: An introduction* (revised). Silver Spring, MD: Registry of Interpreters for the Deaf.

Gallaudet encyclopedia of deaf people and deafness. (1987). New York: McGraw-Hill.

Gardner, E. (1983, March). Legal implications of professional sign language interpreting. *NCLD Newsletter*, 2–5.

Gardner, E. (1987). On guard! *Gallaudet Today, 17*(4), 31–38.

Gerber, B. M. (1980). Interpreting for hearing-impaired patients in mental health settings. *American Journal of Orthopsychiatry, 50*(4), 722–724.

Gerber, B. M. (1983). A communication minority: Deaf people and mental health care. Special issue: The psychiatric care of minority groups. *American Journal of Social Psychiatry, 3*(2), 50–57.

Gibbins, S. (1989). The provision of school psychological assessment services for the hearing impaired: A national survey. *The Volta Review,* 91 95–103.

Gish, S., Russell, D., & Whalen, H. (1989). *Ontario Interpreter Services Review.* Toronto, ON: Canadian Hearing Society.

Goldsmith, L., & Schloss, P. J. (1986). Diagnostic overshadowing among school psychologists working with hearing-impaired learners. *American Annals of the Deaf, 131*(4), 288–293.

Gorman, P. (1991). *My use of oral interpreters (silent speakers).* Presentation to the Interpreter Training Program, Grant MacEwan Community College, Edmonton, Alberta.

Goulet, W. (1989). My past personal experience. *Canadian Journal of the Deaf, 3*(3), 101–104.

Green, K. (1981). The nursing center and interpreter training program—a joint venture. *Journal of Rehabilitation of the Deaf, 15*(3), 20–24.

Gustason, G. (1985). Interpreters entering public school employment. *American Annals of the Deaf, 130,* 265–266.

Gustason, G., Pfetzing, D., & Zawolkow, E. (1980). *Signing Exact English.* Rossmoor, CA: Modern Signs.

Hanson, J. H., & Corthell, D. (1980). *Interpreter services for deaf clients: Guidelines for rehabilitation personnel.* Menomonie, WI: Stout Vocational Rehabilitation Institute.

Hanson, M. (1987). Programs for special populations: A cost analysis for the hearing impaired. *Journal of Rehabilitation of the Deaf, 20*(3), 15–21.

Hardman, M., Drew, C., & Egan, M. W. (1996). *Human exceptionality: Society, school, and family* (5th ed.). Boston: Allyn and Bacon.

Harvey, M. A. (1982). The influence and utilization of an interpreter for deaf persons in family therapy. *American Annals of the Deaf, 127,* 821–827.

Harvey, M. A. (1986). The magnifying mirror: Family therapy for deaf persons. *Family Systems Medicine, 4*(4), 408–420.

Heller, B. (1987). Mental health assessment of deaf persons. A brief history. In H. Elliott, L. Glass, & J. W. Evans (Eds.), *Mental health assessment of deaf clients* pp. 9–20. Boston: Little, Brown.

Higgins, P. C. (1990). *The challenge of educating together deaf and hearing youth: Making mainstreaming work.* Springfield, IL: Charles C Thomas.

Hughes, V., Wilkie, F., & Murphy, H. J. (1974). The use of interpreters in an integrated liberal arts setting. *Journal of Rehabilitation of the Deaf, 7*(3), 17–19.

Humphrey, J. H., & Alcorn, B. J. (1994). *So you want to be an interpreter: An introduction to sign language interpreting.* Salem, OR: Sign Enhancers.

Hurwitz, T. A. (1980). *Interpreters' effectiveness in reverse interpreting: Pidgin Signed English and American Sign Language.* Ph.D. dissertation, University of Rochester, Rochester, NY.

Hurwitz, T. A. (1986). Two factors related to effective voice interpreting. *American Annals of the Deaf, 132,* 248–252.

Hurwitz, T. A. (1991a). Notes on my education. *Deaf American Monograph, 41*(1,2), 71–74.

Hurwitz, T. A. (1991b). Quality of communication services for deaf and hard-of-hearing clients: Current issues and future directions. *Journal of the American Deafness and Rehabilitation Association, 25*(1), 1–7.

Hurwitz, T. A., & Witter, A. (1979). Principles of interpreting in an education environment. In M. Bishop (Ed.), *Mainstreaming: Practical ideas for educating hearing-impaired students.* Washington, DC: Volta Bureau.

Ingram, R. M. (1974). A communication model of the interpreting process. *Journal of Rehabilitation of the Deaf, 7*(3), 3–9.

Ingram, R. M. (1985). Simultaneous interpretation of sign languages: Semiotic and psycholinguistic perspectives. *Multilingual, 4*(2), 91–102.

Ingram, R. M. (1988). Interpreters' recognition of structure and meaning. *Sign Language Studies, 58,* 21–36.

Intervention. Special pull-out section. (1994). *Talking Sense, 39*(4), 11–21.

Jacobs, L. R. (1976). *The efficiency of sign language interpreting to convey lecture information to deaf students.* Ph.D. dissertation, University of Arizona, Tucson.

Janofsky, J. C. (1993, March 15). Whoever wrote ADA regs never ran a business. *The Wall Street Journal,* p. A12.

Janzen, T. (1988). The Canadian evaluation system. In *Papers from the 1988 Conference of the Association of Visual Language Interpreters of Canada, 30 June–4 July 1988.* Toronto, Ontario: AVLIC.

Johnson, K. (1991). Miscommunication in interpreted classroom communication. *Sign Language Studies, 70,* 1–34.

Johnson, R. E., & Erting, C. (1989). Ethnicity and socialization in a classroom for deaf and hard-of-hearing children. In C. Lucas (Ed.), *The sociolinguistics of the deaf community* (pp. 41–83). New York: Academic Press.

Joint Committee of American Speech–Language–Hearing Association and the Council on Education of the Deaf. (1995). Technical Report: Service provision under the Individuals with Disabilities Education Act—part H, as amended (IDEA—Part H) for children who are deaf and hard-of-hearing, ages birth to 36 months. *American Annals of the Deaf, 140,* 65–70.

Jones, Y. E. (1985). The double whammy. *Emotional first aid: a journal of crisis intervention, 2*(4), 39–41.

Joyce, E., & Mathay, G. (1986). A study of closed cases: Implications for the administration of deafness rehabilitation services. *Journal of Rehabilitation of the Deaf, 20,* 5–13.

"Judge orders deaf man to pay for interpreting." (1993, November). *Tulsa World,* August 14. Cited in Silent News, p. 3.

Kahn, E. J., Jr. (1981, August 31). A reporter at large: The indigenists. *The New Yorker,* pp. 60–77.

Kanda, J., & Colonomos, B. (1990). Issues in interpreter education. In C. Baker-Shenk (Ed.), *A model curriculum for American Sign Language and teachers of interpreting* (pp. 175–192). Silver Spring, MD: RID Publications.

Kanda, J. H. (1987). Interpreting. In *Gallaudet encyclopedia of deaf people and deafness* (Vol. 2 pp. 89–98).

Kannapell, B. (1982). Inside the Deaf community. *Deaf American, 34,* 23–26.

Kates, L., & Schein, J. D. (1980). *A complete guide to communication with deaf–blind persons.* Silver Spring, MD: National Association of the Deaf.

Kelly, L. G. (1979). *The true interpreter: A history of translation theory and practice in the West.* New York: St. Martin's Press.

Kerstetter, P. P., & Fritz, G. S. (1982). Undergraduate hearing impaired students in the collegiate mainstream: The Washington Area Consortium of Universities. *Journal of Rehabilitation of the Deaf, 15*(3), 17–19.

Khan, F. J. (1987). Educating deaf adults: The LaGuardia Community College model. *Community Services Catalyst* (p. 87). Columbus, Ohio: National Council on Community Services and Continuing Education.

Kincaid, J. M. (1995). *Legal issues specific to serving students who are deaf or hard-of-hearing in institutions of higher learning.* Columbus, OH: AHEAD Publications.

Klima, E., & Bellugi, U. (1979). The signs of language. Cambridge, MA: Harvard University Press.

Kluscarits, P. T. (1994, February). Toward the certification of educational interpreters: Some basic questions we must first ask. *RID Views, 11*(2), 2, 28, 32.

Kluscarits, P. T. (1995). The professionally involved interpreter. *Proceedings of the Thirteenth National Convention of the Registry of Interpreters for the Deaf,* 48–54.

Kluwin, T. N. (1985). The acquisition of content from a signed lecture. *Sign Language Studies, 48,* 269–286.

Kluwin, T. N. (1995). Interpreting services for youngsters who are deaf in local public school programs. *JADARA, 28,* 21–29.

Kluwin, T. N., Moores, D. F., & Gaustad, M. G. (Eds.). (1992). *Toward effective public school programs for deaf students.* New York: Teachers College, Columbia University.

Kluwin, T. N., & Stinson, M. S. (1993). *Deaf students in local public high schools: Backgrounds, experiences, and outcomes.* Springfield, IL: Charles C Thomas.

Koran, N. K. (1989). Hurdling the barriers to the legal system. *Shhh, 10*(5), 6–10.

Kuntze, M. (1990). ASL: Unity and power. In M. Garretson (Ed.), *Communication issues among Deaf people: A Deaf American monograph* (pp. 75–78). Silver Spring, MD: National Association of the Deaf.

Lawler, D. M. (1986). Mental health service planning for deaf persons: A beginning. *Journal of Rehabilitation of the Deaf, 19*(3–4), 1–4.

Leighton, L. G. (1991). *Two worlds, one art: Literary translation in Russia and America.* DeKalb: Northern Illinois University.

Levine, E. S. (1974). Psychological tests and practices with the deaf: A survey of the state of the art. *Volta Review, 76,* 298–319.

Liddell, S. (1978). Nonmanual signals and relative clauses in American Sign Language. In P. Siple (Ed.), *Understanding language through sign language research* (pp. 59–90). New York: Academic.

Liddell, S. (1980). *American Sign Language syntax.* The Hague: Mouton.

Livingston, S., Singer, B., & Abrahamson, T. (1994). Effectiveness compared: ASL interpretation vs. transliteration. *Sign Language Studies, 82,* 1–54.

Llewellyn-Jones, P. (1981). Simultaneously interpreting. In B. Woll, J. Kyle, & M. Deuchar (Eds.), *Perspectives on British Sign Language and deafness.* London: Croom Helm.

Lloyd, G. T. (Ed.). (1971). *Guidelines for effective participation of deaf persons in professional meetings.* Knoxville: University of Tennessee.

Lloyd, G. T. (Ed.). (1976). Use of interpreters in vocational rehabilitation. *Journal of Rehabilitation of the Deaf, 9*(4), 11–15.

Loera, P. A. (1994). The use and application of cognitive-behavioral psychotherapy with deaf persons. In R. C. Nowell & L. E. Marshak (Eds.), *Understanding deafness and the rehabilitation process.* Boston: Allyn and Bacon.

Lucas, C. (Ed.). (1990). *Sign language research: Theoretical issues.* Washington, DC: Gallaudet University.

Lucas, C., & Valli, C. (1989). Language contact in the American Deaf community. In C. Lucas (Ed.), *The sociolinguistics of the Deaf community* (pp. 11–40). New York: Academic.

Lucas, C., & Valli, C. (Eds.). (1992). *Language contact in the American Deaf community.* New York: Academic.

Luckner, J. L. (1991). Mainstreaming hearing-impaired students: Perceptions of regular educators. *Language, Speech, and Hearing Services in Schools, 22,* 302–307.

Ludders, B. B. (1987). Communication between health care professionals and deaf patients. *Health and Social Work, 12*(4), 303–310.

Luetke-Stahlman, B. (1992). Sign interpretation in preschool. *Perspectives in Education and Deafness, 10,* 12–15.

Luetke-Stahlman, B. (1996). *One mother's story: Raising deaf children: An educator becomes a parent.* Los Alamitos, CA: Modern Signs.

Lutes, J. (1988). More oral interpreters needed. *Vibrations,* December, 7–8.

MacKenzie, A. (1964). The Deaf Welfare Examination Board. In J. M. Smith (Ed.), *Workshop on interpreting for the deaf.* Muncie, IN: Ball State Teachers College.

Maher, P., & Waters, J. E. (1984). The use of interpreters with deaf clients in therapy. *Journal of Rehabilitation of the Deaf, 17*(4), 11–16.

Malkowski, G. (1991). *Intervenors and sign language interpreters* . Legislative Assembly of Ontario.

Marcos, L. R. (1979). Effects of interpreters on the evaluation of psychopathology in non-English-speaking patients. *American Journal of Psychiatry, 136*(2), 171–174.

Marschark, M., & Shroyer, E. H. (1993). Hearing status and language fluency as predictors of automatic word and sign recognition. *American Annals of the Deaf, 138,* 370–375.

Marvin, C., & Kasal, K. R. (1996). A semantic analysis of signed communication in an activity-based classroom for preschool children who are deaf. *Language, Speech, and Hearing Services in Schools, 27,* 57–67.

Masear, V. R., Hayes, J. M., & Hayes, A. G. (1986). An industrial cause of carpal tunnel syndrome. *Journal of Hand Surgery, 11,* 222–227.

Mather, S. A. (1989). Visually oriented teaching strategies with deaf preschool children. In C. Lucas, (Ed.), *The sociolinguistics of the deaf community* (pp. 165–187). New York: Longman.

Maxwell, L. (1983). Concerned interpreter speaks out. *The Deaf Texan, 67*(1), 11–12.

Maxwell, M. M., & Boster, S. (1982). Interpreting hymns for deaf worshippers. *Sign Language Studies, 36,* 217–231.

Mayer, P., & Lowenbraun, S. (1990). Total communication use among elementary teachers of hearing-impaired children. *American Annals of the Deaf, 135,* 257–263.

McClure, W. J. (1964). Introduction. In J. M. Smith (Ed.), *Workshop on interpreting for the deaf.* Muncie, IN: Ball State Teachers College.

McCrone, W. P., & Payette, B. A. (1989). A statutory remedy for negligent hiring in deafness rehabilitation. *Journal of the American Deafness and Rehabilitation Association, 23*(1), 1–6.

McGee, D. (1990). Recognizing heterogeneity: Increasing educational opportunities through mainstreaming. In M. Ross (Ed.), *Hearing impaired children in the mainstream.* Parkton, MD: York.

McKee, M. K. (1993). Accessibility of mental health services and crisis intervention to the deaf. *American Annals of the Deaf, 138,* 26–30.

McIntire, M. L. (Ed.). (1986). *Interpreting: The art of cross cultural mediation.* Proceedings of the Ninth National Convention of the Registry of Interpreters for the Deaf. Silver Spring, MD: RID Publications.

McIntire, M. L., & Sanderson, G. (1995). *Bye-bye! Bi-bi!: Questions of empowerment and role.* Proceedings of the Thirteenth National Convention of the Registry of Interpreters for the Deaf, 94–118. Silver Spring, MD: RID Publications.

McNeil, E. E. (1984). *Physician's attitudes toward deaf persons and the communication methods used with their deaf patients.* Ph.D. dissertation, Oregon State University.

Meadow, K. (1980). *Deafness and child development.* Berkeley: University of California Press.

Mendelsohn, M., & Rozek, F. (1983). Denying disability: The case of deafness. *Family Systems Medicine, 1,* 37–47.

Mertens, D. M. (1991). Teachers working with interpreters: The deaf student's educational experience. *American Annals of the Deaf, 136*(1), 48–52.

Mills, J. (1996, March). Educational interpreting at the elementary level. *Views, 13*(3), 1, 38.

Mindel, E. D., & Vernon, M. (1971). *They grow in silence.* Silver Spring, MD: National Association of the Deaf.

Minnesota Registry of Interpreters for the Deaf. (1996, March). New tool for educational interpreters in the works. *Views, 13*(3), 18.

Mintz, D. (1993, December). Correcting interpretation errors. *RID Views, 10*(11), 1, 10.

Moores, D. F. (1992). An historical perspective on school placement. In T. N. Kluwin, D. F. Moores, & M. G. Gaustad (Eds.), *Toward effective public school programs for deaf students* (pp. 7–29). New York: Teachers College Press.

Moores, D. F., Cerney, B., & Garcia, M. (1990). School placement and least restrictive environment. In D. F. Moores & K. P. Meadow-Orlans (Eds.), *Educational and developmental aspects of deafness.* Washington, DC: Gallaudet University.

Moores, D. F., & Kluwin, T. N. (1986). Issues in school placement. In A. Schildroth & M. Karchmer (Eds.), *Deaf children in America* (pp. 105–123). San Diego, CA: College-Hill.

Moores, D. F., Kluwin, T. N., & Mertens, D. (1985). *High school program for deaf students in metropolitan areas.* Gallaudet Research Monograph No. 3. Washington, DC: Gallaudet University.

Moores, D. F., & Meadow-Orlans, K. P. (Eds.). (1990). *Educational and developmental aspects of deafness.* Washington, DC: Gallaudet University.

Moxham, T. (1996). *How to use a sign language interpreter: A guide for businesses.* Hillsboro, OR: Butte.

Myers, L. J. (1969). *How to write a model law for interpreters for the deaf.* Chicago: Author.

Myers, L. J. (1971a). *How does the interpreter get paid in a court case involving a deaf person?* Chicago: Author.

Myers, L. J. (1971b). *How to get a new state law for court interpreters for the deaf.* Chicago: Author.

Myers, P. C., & Danek, M. M. (1989). Deafness mental health needs assessment: A model. *Journal of the American Deafness and Rehabilitation Association, 22*(4), 72–78.

Naeve, S. L., Siegel, G. M., & Clay, J. L. (1992). Modifications in sign under conditions of impeded visibility. *Journal of Speech and Hearing Research, 35,* 1272–1280.

National Association of the Deaf (NAD). (1988). 198–88 national study of deaf adults' satisfaction with interpreters. *The NAD Broadcaster, 6,* 21.

National Center for Education Statistics, U.S. Department of Education. (1994). *Deaf and hard of hearing students in postsecondary education.* NCES 94–394. Washington, DC: U.S. Government Printing Office.

National Interpreter Education Project. (1996). *Professional development endorsement system: A curriculum for training interpreters for the deaf in educational and rehabilitation settings.* Winsted: Northwestern Connecticut Community–Technical College.

National Technical Institute for the Deaf. (1979). *Interpreting television for hearing impaired viewers: A guidebook for producers and interpreters.* Rochester, NY: Author.

Newell, W., Caccamise, F., Boardman, K., & Holcomb, B. (1983). Adaptation of the Language Proficiency Interview (LIP) for assessing sign communicative competence. *Sign Language Studies, 41,* 311–352.

New Jersey State Department of Labor Division of the Deaf. (1987). *Deafness and interpreting.* Trenton, NJ: Author.

Northcutt, W. H. (1979). Guidelines for the preparation of oral interpreters: Support specialists for hearing-impaired individuals. *The Volta Review, 81,* 135–138.

Northcutt, W. H. (1983). The professional oral Interpreter. *Hearing Rehabilitation Quarterly, 8*(3), 8–13.

Northcutt, W. H. (Ed.) (1984). *Oral interpreting: Principles and practices.* Baltimore, MD: University Park Press.

Orr, F. C., DeMatteo, A., Heller, B., Lee, M., & Nguyen, M. (1987). Psychological assessment. In H. Elliott, L. Glass, & J. W. Evans (Eds.), *Mental health assessment of deaf clients* (pp. 93–106). Boston: Little, Brown.

Otis-Wilborn, A. (1992). Developing oral communication in students with hearing impairment: Whose responsibility? *Language, Speech, and Hearing Services in Schools, 23,* 71–77.

Owens, P. (1989). *Handbook for interpreters in the mental health setting.* Olathe, KS: Johnson County Community College.

Padden, C., & Humphries, T. (1988). *Deaf in America: Voices from a culture.* Cambridge, MA: Harvard University Press.

Palmer, J. U., & others. (1982). *Developing a statewide community/junior college consortium to enrich interpreting for the deaf—networking, July 1, 1981–June 30, 1982.* Eastfield College.

Paul, P., & Quigley, S. (1990). *Education and deafness.* New York: Longman.

Petronio, K. (1988). Interpreting for deaf–blind students: Factors to consider. *American Annals of the Deaf, 133,* 226–229.

Phalen, G. S. (1972). The carpal tunnel syndrome: Clinical evaluation of 598 hands. *Clinical Orthopaedics, 83,* 29–40.

Plant-Moeller, J. (1992). *Expanding horizons.* Silver Spring, MD: Registry of Interpreters for the Deaf.

Premier's Council on the Status of Persons with Disabilities. (1994). *Standards for interpreting in educational settings: Early childhood services to grade 12.* Edmonton, Alberta: Premier's Council on the Status of Persons with Disabilities.

President's Committee on Employment of People with Disabilities. (1994). *Operation People First: Toward a National Disability Policy.* Washington, DC: Author.

Price, J. (1975). Foreign language interpreting in psychiatric practice. *Australian and New Zealand Journal of Psychiatry, 9,* 263–267.

Prickett, H. T., & Prickett, J. G. (1992). Vision problems among students in schools and programs for deaf children. *American Annals of the Deaf, 137,* 56–60.

Proetz, V. (1971). *The astonishment of words.* Austin: University of Texas Press.

Quigley, S. P., & Youngs, J. P. (1965). *Interpreting for deaf people, a report of a workshop on interpreting* . Washington, DC: U.S. Government Printing Office.

Rainer, J. D., Altshuler, K. Z., Kallman, F. J., & Demming, W. E. (1963). *Family and mental health problems in a deaf population.* New York: New York State Psychiatric Institute.

Registry of Interpreters for the Deaf (RID). (1995). *RID Membership Directory.* Silver Spring, MD: Author.

Reisman, G., Scanlan, J., & Kemp, K. (1977). Medical interpreting for hearing-impaired patients. *Journal of the American Medical Association, 237,* 2397–2398.

Ries, P. (1994). Prevalence and characteristics of persons with hearing trouble: United States, 1990–91. *Vital and Health Statistics,* Series 10, No. 188.

Riester, A. E. (1992). Partnering to run a community-based program for deaf-blind young adults. *American Annals of the Deaf, 137,* 411–415.

Riley, K. (1996, February). FTC sues over rules regulating interpreters. *Views, 13*(2), 14–15.

Rittenhouse, R. K. (1987a). Analysis of educational interpreter services for hearing-impaired students. *Journal of Rehabilitation of the Deaf, 20*(4), 1–6.

Rittenhouse, R. K. (1987b). The attitudes of teachers toward mainstreaming of hearing-impaired high schoolers. *Journal of Rehabilitation of the Deaf, 20*(3), 11–14.

Rittenhouse, R. K., Rahn, C. H., & Morreau, L. E. (1989). Educational interpreting services for hearing impaired students: Provider and consumer disagreements. *Journal of the American Deafness and Rehabilitation Association*, 22(3), 57–63.

Robinson, D. (1991). *The translator's turn*. Baltimore, MD: Johns Hopkins University Press.

Roe, D. L., & Roe, C. E. (1991). The third party: Using interpreters for the deaf in counseling situations. *Journal of Mental Health Counseling*, 13(1), 91–105.

Rosen, R. G. (1981). *Recommendations on educational placement and special services for hearing-impaired children by four types of administrators*. Ph.D. dissertation, Catholic University.

Rosen, R. (1992, June–July). The president signs on. *The NAD Broadcaster*, 3.

Rosen, R. (1993, May). The president signs on. *The NAD Broadcaster*, 3.

Ross, M. (1990). (Ed.). *Hearing impaired children in the mainstream*. Parkton, MD: York.

Rowley v. Hendrick Hudson Board of Education and the Commissioner of Education of the State of New York, 1979.

Roy, C. B. (1992). A sociolinguistic analysis of the interpreter's role in simultaneous talk in face-to-face interpreted dialogue. *Sign Language Studies*, 74, 21–61.

Rudser, S. (1986). Linguistic analysis of changes in interpreting: 1973–1985. *Sign Language Studies*, 53, 332–340.

Rudser, S., & Strong, M. (1986). An examination of some personal characteristics and abilities of sign language interpreters. *Sign Language Studies*, 53, 315–331.

Russell, D., & Malcolm, K. (1992). Interpreting in Canada. In *Expanding horizons*. Silver Spring, MD: RID Publications.

Salem, J. M., & Fell, B. P. (1988). The impact of P.L. 94-142 on residential schools for the deaf. *American Annals of the Deaf*, 133, 68–75.

Salend, S. J., & Longo, M. (1994). The roles of the educational interpreter in mainstreaming. *Teaching Exceptional Children*, 26, 22–28.

Sanderson, R. G. (1964). Interpreting as the deaf see it. In J. M. Smith (Ed.), *Workshop on interpreting for the deaf*. Muncie, IN: Ball State Teachers College.

Sandler, W. (1989). *Phonological representation of the sign: Linearity and nonlinearity in American Sign Language*. Providence, RI: Foris.

Sandler, W. (1990). Temporal aspects and ASL phonology. In S. Fischer & P. Siple, (Eds.), *Theoretical issues in sign language research* (Vol. 1, pp. 7–35). Chicago: University of Chicago Press.

Saur, R. E., Layne, C. A., Hurley, E. A., & Opton, K. (1986). Dimensions of mainstreaming. *American Annals of the Deaf*, 131, 325–330.

Schein, J. D. (1972). Principles of interpreting for deaf people. *Journal of Rehabilitation of the Deaf*, 6(2), 190–193.

Schein, J. D. (1974). Personality characteristics associated with interpreter proficiency. *Journal of Rehabilitation of the Deaf*, 7, 33–43.

Schein, J. D. (1980a). How well can you see me? *Teaching Exceptional Children,* 12(2), 55–58.

Schein, J. D. (1980b). *Model state plan for rehabilitation of deaf clients. Second revision* (3rd ed.). Silver Spring, MD: National Association of the Deaf.

Schein, J. D. (1981). Educating hearing-impaired children to become emotionally well-adjusted adults. *Journal of the Canadian Educators of the Hearing Impaired,* 7(2), 3–9.

Schein, J. D. (1982). Group techniques applied to deaf and hearing-impaired persons. In M. Seligman (Ed.), *Group psychotherapy and counseling with special populations.* Baltimore: University Park.

Schein, J. D. (1984). *Speaking the language of sign.* New York: Doubleday.

Schein, J. D. (1986). The eyes have it. *Soundbarrier, 5,* 10–11.

Schein, J. D. (1989a). *At home among strangers* . Washington, DC: Gallaudet University.

Schein, J. D. (1989b). A national study of interpreting. *AVLIC News,* 7(2), 7.

Schein, J. D. (1990). *Facilitating communication for postsecondary students with impaired hearing.* Edmonton: Western Canadian Centre of Studies in Deafness, University of Alberta.

Schein, J. D. (1991). *Canadians with impaired hearing.* Ottawa: Statistics Canada.

Schein, J. D. (1992). *Communication support for deaf elementary and secondary students: Perspectives of deaf students and their parents.* Edmonton: Western Canadian Centre of Studies in Deafness, University of Alberta.

Schein, J. D., & Delk, M. T. (1974). *The deaf population of the United States.* Silver Spring, MD: National Association of the Deaf.

Schein, J. D., Greaves, S., & Wolf-Schein, E. G. (1990). Visual language interpreters in Alberta. In J. D. Schein (Ed.), *Facilitating communication for postsecondary students with impaired hearing* (p. 62). Edmonton: Western Canadian Centre of Studies in Deafness, University of Alberta.

Schein, J. D., Mallory, B., & Carver, R. (1990). Preparing interpreters for deaf Canadians. *Canadian Journal of Rehabilitation,* 3(2), 71–75.

Schein, J. D., Mallory, B. L., & Greaves, S. (1991). *Communication for deaf students in mainstream classrooms.* Western Canadian Centre for Studies in Deafness Monograph No. 2. Edmonton: University of Alberta.

Schein, J. D., & Stewart, D. A. (1995). *Language in motion: Exploring the nature of sign.* Washington, DC: Gallaudet University.

Schein, J. D., & Yarwood, S. (1990). The status of interpreters for deaf Canadians. *The ACEHI Journal,* 16(2–3), 127–141.

Schildroth, A. N., & Hotto, S. A. (1994). Inclusion or exclusion? Deaf students and the inclusion movement. *American Annals of the Deaf, 139,* 239–243.

Schildroth, A. N., & Hotto, S. A. (1996). Changes in student and program characteristics, 1984–85 and 1994–95. *American Annals of the Deaf, 141,* 68–71.

Schildroth, A. N., & Karchmer, M. A. (Eds.). (1986). *Deaf children in America.* San Diego, CA: College-Hill.

Schlesinger, H. S., & Meadow, K. P. (1972). *Sound and sign: Childhood deafness and mental health.* Berkeley: University of California Press.

Schmitz, K. (1990, Winter–Spring). Signs of the times: A pioneer program takes a new direction. *NTID Focus,* pp. 20–21.

Schreiber, F. C. (1964). Recruitment of interpreters by and for the deaf. In J. M. Smith (Ed.), *Workshop on interpreting for the deaf* (pp. 35–36). Muncie, IN: Ball State Teachers College.

Schreiber, F. C. (1981). Recruitment of interpreters by and for the deaf. In J. D. Schein (Ed.), *A rose for tomorrow* (pp. 50–53). Silver Spring, MD: National Association for the Deaf.

Schwartz, M. (1994). How about a relay service for interpreters? *GA-SK Newsletter, 25*(4), 10.

Scoggins, B. B. (1997). *Deaf TeleLink demonstration.* Project Final Report. Frankfort: Kentucky Commission on the Deaf and Hard of Hearing.

Seal, B. C. (1998). *Best practices in educational interpreting.* Boston, MA: Allyn and Bacon.

Seleskovitch, D. (1978). *Interpreting for international conferences.* Washington, DC: Pen & Booth.

Seleskovitch, D. (1992). Fundamentals of the interpretive theory of translation. In Plant-Moeller (Ed.), *Expanding horizons.* Silver Spring, MD: Registry of Interpreters for the Deaf.

Sergent, M. T., et al. (1988). *Services offered to disabled students in higher education: A five-year national review.* College Park, MD: Counseling Center, University of Maryland.

Shaw, R. (1987). Determining register in sign-to-English interpreting. *Sign Language Studies, 57,* 295–322.

Sherrill, C. (1993). *Adapted physical activity, recreation, and sport: Crossdisciplinary and lifespan.* Madison, WI: WCB Brown & Benchmark.

Shroyer, E. H., & Compton, M. V. (1994). Educational interpreting and teacher preparation: An interdisciplinary model. *American Annals of the Deaf, 139,* 472–479.

Siegel, G. M., Clay, J. L., & Naeve, S. L. (1992). The effects of auditory and visual interference on speech and sign. *Journal of Speech and Hearing Research, 35,* 1358–1362.

Siegel, P. (1995). What they didn't know may have helped us: How the Supreme Court misinterpreted the role of sign language interpreters. *American Annals of the Deaf, 140,* 386–395.

Simon, S. C. (1980, April). Oral interpreting. *The Florida School Herald,* 1–2.

Siple, L. (1991). The functions of mentoring. *RID Views, 8,* 28–29.

Siple, L. (1993). Interpreters' use of pausing in voice to sign transliteration. *Sign Language Studies, 79,* 147–180.

Sloman, L., Perry, A., & Frankenburg, F. (1987). Family therapy with deaf member families. *American Journal of Family Therapy, 15*(3), 242–252.

Smith, J. M. (1964). *Workshop on Interpreting for the Deaf.* Muncie, IN: Ball State Teachers College.

Smith, S. B., & Rittenhouse, R. K. (1990, November–December). Real-time graphic display: Technology for mainstreaming. *Perspectives in Education and Deafness, 9*(2), 2–5.

Smith, T. (1992). *Deaf-blind: Communication and community* (videotape). Burtonsville, MD: Sign Media.

Solow, S. (1981). *Sign language interpreting: A basic resource book.* Silver Spring, MD: National Association of the Deaf.

Spear, J. (1986). A second look. *Voice, 2*(4), 10.

Spragins, A. B., Karchmer, M. B., & Schildroth, A. N. (1981). Profile of psychological service providers to hearing-impaired students. *American Annals of the Deaf, 126,* 94–105.

Stangarone, J. (1979). The role of interpreters for the deaf. *The Volta Review, 81,* 138–145.

Stansfield, M. (1981). Psychological issues in mental health interpreting. *Professional Interpreting, 1*(1), 18–31.

Stansfield, M., & Veltri, D. (1981). Assessment from the perspective of the sign language interpreter. In H. Elliott, L. Glass, & J. W. Evans (Eds.), *Mental health assessment of deaf clients* (pp. 153–164). Boston: Little, Brown.

Stedt, J. D. (1989). Carpal tunnel syndrome: The risk to educational interpreters. *American Annals of the Deaf, 134,* 223–226.

Stedt, J. D. (1992a). Interpreter's wrist: Repetitive stress injury and carpal tunnel syndrome in sign language interpreters. *American Annals of the Deaf, 137,* 40–43.

Stedt, J. D. (1992b). Issues of educational interpreting. In T. N. Kluwin, D. F. Moores, & M. G. Gaustad (Eds.), *Toward effective public school programs for deaf students* (pp. 83–99). New York: Teachers College, Columbia University.

Steinberg, A. (1991). Issues in providing mental health services to hearing-impaired persons. *Hospital and Community Psychiatry, 42*(4), 380–389.

Sternberg, M. L. A., Tipton, C., & Schein, J. D. (1973). *Interpreter training: A curriculum guide.* New York: Deafness Research and Training Center, New York University.

Stewart, D. A. (1988). Educational interpreting for the hearing impaired. *B.C. Journal of Special Education, 12*(3), 273–279.

Stewart, D. A. (1990, Winter). Directions in bilingual education for deaf children. *Teaching English to Deaf and Second-Language Students, 8,* 4–9.

Stewart, D. A. (1991). *Deaf sport: The impact of sports within the Deaf community.* Washington, DC: Gallaudet University.

Stewart, D. A., Heeter, C., & Dickson, P. (1996, January–February). Enhancing communication with CD-ROM technology. *Perspectives in Education and Deafness, 14*(3), 11, 16–17.

Stewart, D. A., & Kluwin, T. N. (1996). The gap between guidelines, practice, and knowledge in interpreting services for deaf students. *Journal of Deaf Studies and Deaf Education, 1,* 29–39.

Stewart, D. A., & Lindsey, J. D. (1990). Code of ethics: Implications for interpreters for the deaf. *European Journal of Special Needs Education, 5,* 211–219.

Stewart, L. G. (1981). Counseling the deaf client. In L. K. Stein, E. D. Mindel, & T. Jabaley (Eds.), *Deafness and mental health* (pp. 133–160). New York: Grune & Stratton.

Stewart, L. G., & Schein, J. D. (1971). *Tarrytown Conference on Current Priorities in the Rehabilitation of Deaf People.* New York: Deafness Research and Training Center, New York University.

Stinson, M., Meath-Lang, B., & McLeod, J. (1981). *Recall of different segments of an interpreted lecture by deaf students.* Paper Series No. 41. Rochester, NY: National Technical Institute for the Deaf.

Stokoe, W. C. (1978). *Sign language structure* (rev. ed.). Silver Spring, MD: Linstok Press.

Stokoe. W. C., & Battison, R. M. (1981). Sign language, mental health and satisfactory intervention. In L. K. Stein, E. D. Mindel, & T. Jabaley (Eds.), *Deafness and mental health* (pp. 179–194). New York: Grune & Stratton.

Stone, H. E., & Hurwitz, T. A. (1994). Accessibility to the hearing world: Assistive devices and specialized support. In R. C. Nowell, & L. E. Marshak (Eds.), *Understanding deafness and the rehabilitation process.* New York: Allyn and Bacon.

Straub, E. F. (1976). Interpreting for the deaf in a psychiatric setting. *Journal of Rehabilitation of the Deaf, 10*(2), 15–21.

Strong, M., & Rudser, S. F. (1985). An assessment instrument for sign language interpreters. *Sign Language Studies, 49,* 343–362.

Strong, M., & Rudser, S. F. (1986a). An assessment instrument for sign language interpreters. *Sign Language Studies, 49,* 343–362. Ratings of videotaped samples.

Strong, M., & Rudser, S. F. (1986b). The subjective assessment of sign language interpreters. *Sign Language Studies, 53,* 299–314.

Stuckless, E. R., Avery, J. C., & Hurwitz, T. A. (1989). *Educational interpreting for deaf students: Report of the National Task Force on Educational Interpreting.* Rochester, NY: Rochester Institute of Technology.

Sutherland, E. (1985). Music to their eyes: Song-to-sign interpreting at the Hudson Clearwater Festival. *Sign Language Studies, 49,* 363–373.

Taff-Watson, M. (1983). Sign language interpretation in the mental health setting. In D. Watson & B. Heller (Eds.), *Mental health and deafness: Strategic perspectives.* Silver Spring, MD: American Deafness and Rehabilitation Association.

Taylor, C., & Elliott, R. (1994). Competencies needed for educational interpreters: Interpreter and teacher perceptions. *Sign Language Studies, 83,* 179–190.

Taylor, M. (1988). Sign language interpreter education in Canada. In *Papers from the 1988 Conference of the Association of Visual Language Interpreters of Canada, 30 June–4 July 1988.* Toronto, Ontario: AVLIC.

Texas State Technical Institute Waco. (1981). *Continued development of curriculum for interpreter training programs in vocational education.* Texas Education Agency, Austin.

Tipton, C. (1974). Interpreting ethics. *Journal of Rehabilitation of the Deaf, 7*(3), 10–16.

Tipton, C. (1988). *Development of an instrument to measure proficiency in American Sign Language.* Ph.D. dissertation, New York University.

Trott, L. A. (1984). Providing school psychological services to hearing-impaired students in New Jersey. *American Annals of the Deaf, 129,* 319–323.

Twain, D. (1975). Developing and implementing a research strategy. In E. L. Struening & M. Guttentag (Eds.), *Handbook on evaluation research* (pp. 27–52). Beverly Hills, CA: Sage Publications.

Vallandingham, D. (1991). Short term memory abilities of skilled signers. *Journal of the American Deafness and Rehabilitation Association, 24*(3, 4), 68–71.

Vernon, M. (1980). Perspectives on deafness and mental health. *Journal of Rehabilitation of the Deaf, 13*(4), 8–14.

Vernon, M., & Andrews, J. F. (1990). *The psychology of deafness.* New York: Longman.

Vidrine, J. A. (1979). *Historical study of the neo-professional organization: Registry of Interpreters for the Deaf, Inc.* Ph.D. dissertation, Walden University.

Waldron, M. B., & Diebold, T. J. (1985). The use of visual aids by interpreters: A cognitive model for mainstreamed education. In David S. Martin (Ed.), *Cognition, education, and deafness.* Washington, DC: Gallaudet University.

Wallin, C. (1994). The study of sign language in society. In C. J. Erting, R. C. Johnson, D. L. Smith, & B. D. Snider (Eds.), *The Deaf way* (pp. 318–330). Washington DC: Gallaudet University.

Walworth, M., Moores, D. F., & O'Rourke, T. J. (Eds.). (1992). *A free hand.* Silver Springs, MD: TJ Publishers.

Warner, H. C. (1986). The marketing of interpreter services for the deaf. *American Annals of the Deaf, 131,* 365–366.

Washington Governor's Committee on Disability Issues and Employment. (1986). *Unrealized promises: Ensuring the educational rights of deaf/hard of hearing youth.* Olympia, WA: Author.

Weng, J. J., & Stewart, D. A. (1997). *Recognizing multi-object hand signs.* Unpublished manuscript.

Wentzer, C., & Dhir, A. (1986). An outline for working with the hearing impaired in an inpatient substance abuse treatment program. *Journal of Rehabilitation of the Deaf, 20*(2), 11–16.

West, L. (1979). *Breaking the sound barrier: Working with hearing-impaired adults in an educational setting* . Beverly, MA: North Shore Community College.

Wilbur, R. B. (1979). *American Sign Language and sign systems.* Baltimore, MD: University Park.

Wilbur, R. B. (1987). *American Sign Language: Linguistic and applied dimensions* (2nd ed.). Boston: Little, Brown.

Wilcox, P., Schroeder, F., & Martinez, T. (1990). A commitment to professionalism: Educational interpreting within a large public school system. *Sign Language Studies, 68,* 277–286.

Wilcox, S. (Ed.). (1989). *American Deaf culture: An anthology.* Silver Spring, MD: RID Publications.

Williams, B. R. (1964). Foreword. In J. M. Smith (Ed.), *Workshop on interpreting for the deaf.* Muncie, IN: Ball State Teachers College.

Williams, E. (1977). Experimental comparisons of face-to-face and mediated communication: A review. *Psychological Bulletin, 84,* 963–976.

Winston, E. (1989). Transliteration: What's the message? In C. Lucas (Ed.), *The sociolinguistics of the Deaf community* (pp. 147–164). New York: Academic Press.

Wisowaty, S. (1996, May). Repetitive motion injury (RMI) impacts the workplace. *RID Views, 13*(5), 20–22.

Witter-Merithew, A. (1982). The function of assessing as part of the interpreting process. *RID Interpreting Journal, 1*(2), 8–15.

Witter-Merithew, A., & Dirst, R. (1982). Preparation and use of educational interpreters. In D. G. Sims, G. C. Walter, & R. L. Whitehead (Eds.), *Deafness and communication: Assessment and training* (pp. 395–406). Baltimore, MD: Williams & Wilkins.

Wixtrom, C. (1988, Summer). Alone in the crowd. *The Deaf American 38*(12), 14–15.

Wolf-Schein, E. G., & Schein, J. D. (1990). Postsecondary education of deaf students: An international perspective. *The ACEHI Journal, 16,* 13–19.

Woll, B., Kyle, J., & Deuchar, M. (1981). *Perspectives on British Sign Language and deafness.* London: Croom Helm.

Woodward, J. (1973). Some characteristics of Pidgin Sign English. *Sign Language Studies, 3,* 39–46.

Woodward, J. (1977). Sex is definitely a problem: Interpreters' knowledge of signs for sexual behavior. *Sign Language Studies, 14,* 73–88.

Woodward, J. (1979). *Signs of sexual behavior.* Silver Spring, MD: TJ Publishers.

Woodward, J. (1980). *Signs of drug use.* Silver Spring, MD: TJ Publishers.

Woodward, J. (1982). *How you gonna get to heaven if you can't talk with Jesus: On depathologizing deafness.* Silver Spring, MD: TJ Publishers.

Workshop on Interpreting for the Deaf. (1964). Muncie, IN: Ball State Teachers College.

Wrigley, D. (1996). *The politics of deafness.* Washington DC: Gallaudet University.

Youngs, J., Jr. (1967). Interpreting for deaf clients. *Journal of Rehabilitation of the Deaf, 1,* 49.

Zawolkow, E. G., & DeFiore, S. (1986). Educational interpreting for elementary- and secondary-level hearing-impaired students. *American Annals of the Deaf, 131,* 26–28.

Zemelman, S., Daniels, H., & Hyde, A. (1993). *Best practice: New standards for teaching and learning in America's schools.* Portsmouth, NH: Heinemann Educational Books.

Ziev, J. D. (1989). *Summary of laws on interpreting services for deaf and deaf-blind people in New York State.* New York: New York Society for the Deaf.

INDEX